Burdens of Proof

Burdens of Proof

Cryptographic Culture and Evidence Law in the Age of Electronic Documents

Jean-François Blanchette

The MIT Press
Cambridge, Massachusetts
London, England

© 2012 Massachusetts Institute of Technology

All rights reserved. No part of this book may be reproduced in any form by any electronic or mechanical means (including photocopying, recording, or information storage and retrieval) without permission in writing from the publisher.

MIT Press books may be purchased at special quantity discounts for business or sales promotional use. For information, please email special_sales@mitpress.mit.edu or write to Special Sales Department, The MIT Press, 55 Hayward Street, Cambridge, MA 02142.

This book was set in Stone Sans and Stone Serif by Toppan Best-set Premedia Limited. Printed and bound in the United States of America.

Library of Congress Cataloging-in-Publication Data

Blanchette, Jean-François
Burdens of proof : cryptographic culture and evidence law in the age of electronic documents / Jean-François Blanchette.
  p. cm.
Includes bibliographical references and index.
ISBN 978-0-262-01751-0 (hardcover : alk. paper)
1. Electronic evidence. 2. Data encryption (Computer science)—Law and legislation. I. Title.
K2269.5.B58 2012
347'.064—dc23

2011041185

10 9 8 7 6 5 4 3 2 1

Contents

1 Introduction   1

2 Communication in the Presence of Adversaries   17

3 On the Brink of a Revolution   39

4 The Equivalent of a Written Signature   63

5 Written Proof   93

6 Paper and State   123

7 The Cryptographic Imagination   159

8 Epilogue   187

Acknowledgments   191
Notes   193
Bibliography   233
Index   255

1 Introduction

In the waning days of the summer of 2009, a full-blown media storm erupted over the qualifications of Barack Obama to serve as president of the United States, a controversy hinging on the claim that he had actually been born in Kenya, rather than in Hawaii. More ratings-friendly than health-care reform, the spectacle featured all of the usual elements of American conspiracy theories—lawsuits, websites, counter-websites, bumper stickers, and much cable news coverage of fringe characters. At the center of the controversy, the questioned authenticity of an ordinary bureaucratic artifact—the birth certificate.

To counteract these claims, the Obama campaign distributed a digital scan of a document known as a "short-form" certification of live birth (see figure 1.1). Short-form certificates list only the essential data from the original ("long-form") certificate, as the latter may contain confidential (e.g., epidemiological) information.[1] The strategy backfired, however, as the scan looked nothing like an original record produced at the time of Obama's birth would: in the 1990s, agencies computerized the production of the certificates by transcribing them into databases, cutting down on the time and labor needed to produce official copies. Presented with a printout from a database, "birthers" clamored for the president to exhibit the original, with the assumption that tangible clues—embossed seals, handwritten signatures, yellowed paper—would testify to its (lack of) genuineness, clues utterly missing in computerized documents.

The birthers controversy descended further into farce when pictures of Obama's purported "original" Kenyan birth certificate circulated, later shown to have been crudely manufactured from an online scan of an Australian form. Indeed, the issue continued to agitate political commentators on slow news days until April 2011, when Obama released a scanned

Figure 1.1
President Obama's "short-form" certification of live birth, released by his presidential campaign on June 12, 2008, available at http://www.fightthesmears.com/articles/5/birthcertificate (accessed June 24, 2011). In the public domain.

copy of the long-form certificate of live birth, complete with original signatures of Obama's mother, the attending physician, the hospital registrar, as well as that of the Hawaii State Registrar, certifying the truthfulness of the copy itself (see figure 1.2).

The lingering doubts over President Obama's birth certificate signal the loss of the ways by which official documents convey their authority and authenticity, formally and informally. This loss is a direct consequence of the current society-wide shift in the ways administrative documents are created, communicated, classified, and preserved. Today, almost all are

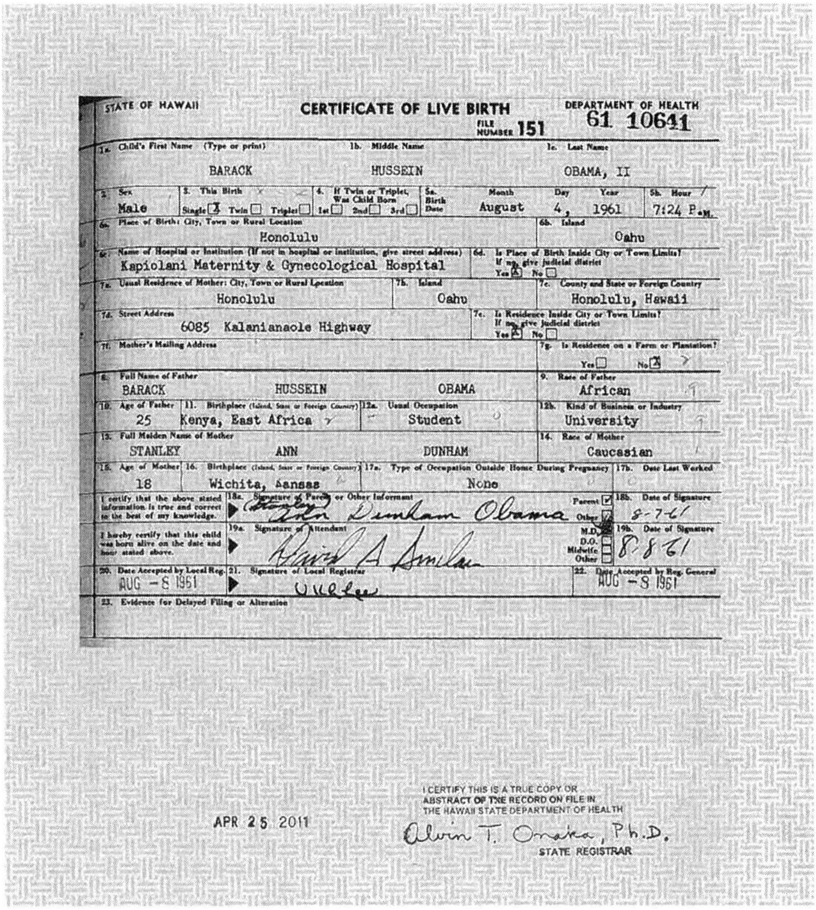

STATE OF HAWAII

CERTIFICATE OF LIVE BIRTH

FILE NUMBER 151

DEPARTMENT OF HEALTH

61 10641

1a. Child's First Name (Type or print): BARACK
1b. Middle Name: HUSSEIN
1c. Last Name: OBAMA, II
2. Sex: Male
3. This Birth: Single [X] Twin [ ] Triplet [ ]
4. If Twin or Triplet, Was Child Born: 1st [ ] 2nd [ ] 3rd [ ]
5a. Birth Date: Month August; Day 4, Year 1961
5b. Hour: 7:24 P.M.
6a. Place of Birth: City, Town or Rural Location: Honolulu
6b. Island: Oahu
6c. Name of Hospital or Institution (If not in hospital or institution, give street address): Kapiolani Maternity & Gynecological Hospital
6d. Is Place of Birth Inside City or Town Limits? If no, give judicial district: Yes [X] No [ ]
7a. Usual Residence of Mother: City, Town or Rural Location: Honolulu
7b. Island: Oahu
7c. County and State or Foreign Country: Honolulu, Hawaii
7d. Street Address: 6085 Kalanianaole Highway
7e. Is Residence Inside City or Town Limits? If no, give judicial district: Yes [X] No [ ]
7f. Mother's Mailing Address:
7g. Is Residence on a Farm or Plantation? Yes [ ] No [X]
8. Full Name of Father: BARACK HUSSEIN OBAMA
9. Race of Father: African
10. Age of Father: 25
11. Birthplace (Island, State or Foreign Country): Kenya, East Africa
12a. Usual Occupation: Student
12b. Kind of Business or Industry: University
13. Full Maiden Name of Mother: STANLEY ANN DUNHAM
14. Race of Mother: Caucasian
15. Age of Mother: 18
16. Birthplace (Island, State or Foreign Country): Wichita, Kansas
17a. Type of Occupation Outside Home During Pregnancy: None
17b. Date Last Worked:
I certify that the above stated information is true and correct to the best of my knowledge.
18a. Signature of Parent or Other Informant: (Stanley) Ann Dunham Obama
Parent [✓] Other [ ]
18b. Date of Signature: 8-7-61
I hereby certify that this child was born alive on the date and hour stated above.
19a. Signature of Attendant: David A Sinclair
M.D. [X] D.O. [ ] Midwife [ ] Other [ ]
19b. Date of Signature: 8-8-61
20. Date Accepted by Local Reg.: AUG - 8 1961
21. Signature of Local Registrar: UKLee
22. Date Accepted by Reg. General: AUG - 8 1961
23. Evidence for Delayed Filing or Alteration:

I CERTIFY THIS IS A TRUE COPY OR ABSTRACT OF THE RECORD ON FILE IN THE HAWAII STATE DEPARTMENT OF HEALTH

APR 25 2011

Alvin T. Onaka, Ph.D.

STATE REGISTRAR

Figure 1.2

President Obama's "long-form" certificate of live birth, released by the White House on April 27, 2011, available at http://www.whitehouse.gov/sites/default/files/rss_vieemphasis wer/birth-certificate-long-form.pdf (accessed June 24, 2011). In the public domain.

computerized at some point of their life cycle, and the integration of computing, imaging, and printing technologies makes it easier than ever to scan, copy, alter, distribute, print, and store high-quality documents. If the moral authority of paper records has correspondingly diminished, the electronic documents replacing them appear to us even more malleable.

Although scholars have examined the shift from print to digital in the context of photography, newspapers, scholarly communication, and technical design, the impact of digitization on the evidentiary characteristics of documents and its consequences for the functioning of bureaucracy has been largely confined to expert discussions in the fields of law, computer science, archives, and records management.[2] Yet, paper records (and paperwork) form the material foundation on which the legitimacy and the day-to-day operation of the nation-state rests—from the constitution itself, to birth certificates, voting ballots, judgments, real estate deeds, and so on. As Bruno Latour has remarked, Western culture typically dismisses the crucial role of these material artifacts: "Common sense ironically makes fun of these 'gratte papiers' and 'paper shufflers,' and often wonders what all this 'red tape' is for; but the same question should be asked of the rest of science and technology. In our cultures 'paper shuffling' is the source of an essential power, that constantly escapes attention since its materiality is ignored."[3] Thus, although artfully disguised as a technocratic debate over banal bureaucratic instruments, the definition of a new evidentiary regime for the digitally powered State has far-reaching implications, as the digitization of these instruments inevitably entails the renegotiation of their power to testify truthfully, to apportion liability, to enforce accountability, to constitute memory.

This book is about a proposed technical foundation for this new evidentiary regime, digital signatures based on the mathematics of public-key cryptography. Invented in 1976 by two Stanford computer scientists, digital signatures offered a method to confirm the origin and the integrity of an electronic document, a method backed by mathematical proof. The concept took the business world by storm in the late 1990s, riding a worldwide movement of evidence law reform that sought to update the often centuries-old rules that govern the admissibility of written evidence in court. Lawmakers, legal scholars, and businessmen unanimously sang the praise of a technology that would provide the secure framework needed for the Information Society to blossom—or so the argument went.

Digital signature technology rode on the coattails of its more famous sibling, encryption. In the mid-1970s, a nascent academic community had begun to challenge the historical subjection of cryptographic research to military and national security needs. Over the course of the next decade, through a series of public confrontations over control of research agendas and freedom of scientific communication, the community advocated for a renewed public role for cryptography in shaping the character of emerging computer networks. The explosion of the Internet propelled cryptography to the forefront of the cyberlibertarian movement, with its promise to protect electronic free speech from the prying ears of governments.

At the same time, and beginning with public-key cryptography itself, the cryptographic research community broadened its research agenda from its historical focus on confidentiality to the design of technologies that could replicate for networked information systems the protocols, procedures, and artifacts that ensure the integrity of information necessary to a functioning democracy—signatures, voting, electronic cash, copyright protection, certified mail, and the like. Driven by an explicit commitment to combat the propensity of electronic networks for fine-grained surveillance, this research agenda not only produced intriguing and innovative mathematical techniques but also attracted the necessary venture capital to translate these techniques into hardware, software, and services and to ready them for a predicted multibillion-dollar market for cryptographic products.

Yet as the fumes of the dot-com crash cleared, much of cryptography's project laid in the rubles. The expected market for public-key infrastructures (PKI), the computing infrastructure necessary for the deployment of cryptographic technologies, utterly failed to materialize. Once valued at £5.5 billion, Baltimore Technologies, the darling of the European PKI industry, sold its core software assets in 2003 for £5 million. The rest of the cryptographic research agenda similarly failed to translate into actual infrastructure, as the business case for anonymous cash, encryption, and digital signatures failed to carry the marketplace. The prophesied cryptographic revolution did not come to be.[4]

This book develops a series of arguments to account for cryptography's failure to perform, focusing on the case of digital signatures.

One line of argumentation questions the adequation of the digital with the immaterial that pervades not only popular literature but also much of the cryptographic and legal conceptual space. In this narrative, the Internet (as cyberspace) offers the conditions for information's long-awaited emancipation from its material shackles (with paper as the arch villain). Indeed, information-age pundits have consistently underlined how an essential element of the Internet's revolutionary power lies in its nature as a frictionless communication network where the ordinarily limitations of physical media cease to apply.[5] John Perry Barlow, for example, claimed that "legal concepts of property, expression, identity, movement, and context" did not apply to the Internet because "they are all based on matter, and there is no matter here."[6] Less lyrical but equally influential, Nicolas Negroponte also structured the argument of *Being Digital* around the liberation of information from matter. Contrasting the costly and laborious movement of physical goods with "the global movement of weightless bits at the speed of light," he concludes that in the digital era, "the medium is no longer the message."[7]

It might be tempting to dismiss Barlow's and Negroponte's manifestos as the expression of an irrational exuberance long since tempered by the crash of the dot-com economy. Yet the conceptualization that on a fundamental level, digital information has escaped the constraints of the material world continues to pervade both popular and specialized discourses. A recent treatise on digital evidence states, for example: "Writings in the digital realm are different. They do not depend on the alteration of matter. Such records are very close to 'pure information,' and exist by virtue of a mere succession of the differentiation of 1s and 0s, distinguished by electricity flowing in machine systems. In writing today, we deal in pure information objects, unfettered by matter. They can be whisked or shaken or rearranged in an instant."[8]

In this logic, because of its immateriality, digital information can only be secured through the similarly immaterial mathematics of cryptography. The authoritative *Handbook of Applied Cryptography* precisely articulates this view: "What is needed then for a society where information is mostly stored and transmitted in electronic form is a means to ensure information security which is independent of the physical medium recording or conveying it and such that the objectives of information security rely solely on digital information itself."[9]

I argue that this characterization has set up multiple challenges for the translation of cryptographic research into actual software and hardware artifacts. The implicit hierarchy that places the combination of digital information and cryptography at the top of the electronic security ladder has translated into disregard for the security affordances of paper. In particular, information security designers have tended to ignore the ways in which these affordances have evolved in concert with work practices, institutional contexts, and broader cultural settings. As Sellen and Harper have argued in *The Myth of the Paperless Office*, technology developers often rely on a "'Velcro' model of success," hoping that whatever new technology is thrown into a given social context will, somehow, somewhere "stick."[10] Instead of this (costly) hit-and-miss approach, Sellen and Harper suggest that designers should start from the premise that "the role of paper in office life needs to be understood as having coevolved with work practices and thus as being hard to disentangle and alter."[11] Indeed, the spread of computational devices into both work and domestic contexts since the mid-1980s has spurred interest in frameworks for systems analysis and design sensitive to the ways in which information is "deeply bound up with the material practices by which people organize their lives together."[12] Yet an immaterial, disembodied view of information technology retains powerful appeal, an appeal that puzzled systems design theorist Claudio Ciborra: "How come researchers privilege the geometry of the line connecting abstract concepts in a model, while they remain blind to the blurred reality that any, even slight, ethnographic study would have revealed?"[13]

In this book, I offer an empirical counterpoint to this fetishism of the "geometry of the line" by following the deployment of electronic signatures within the very professions entrusted with the production and management of documentary evidence. As a member of a task force appointed in 1999 by the French Ministry of Justice to provide guidance on the reform of the rules governing the admissibility of written evidence in French courts, I enjoyed extended access to the bureaucracies and legal professions that produce the documents whose evidential value is crucial to the functioning of the French state—real estate contracts, birth certificates, and land titles. The practical responses of these groups to demands for computerization varied widely, as did their appreciation for the complex entanglement of their professional practices with paper. Yet in the examination of such concrete material and organizational practices lies, I believe, the lessons for a usable framework for electronic evidence, one in which—

beyond mere rhetorical appeal—"technologies have clear value for people in the activities they already carry out."[14]

A second line of argumentation focuses on the mathematization of cryptography, a process that became central to the field with the publication in 1976 of Whitfield Diffie and Martin Hellman's "New Directions in Cryptography."[15] Instead of cryptographers' traditional reliance on trial and error for establishing the effectiveness of cryptosystems, "New Directions" proposed a new compact between mathematics and cryptography, one that would transform an ancient craft into a modern science. Henceforth, the effectiveness of cryptosystems would be modeled within the framework of algorithmics and computational complexity, two branches of mathematics devoted to the quantification of computational processes. With this move, cryptographers would finally achieve the historically elusive goal of "provable security," leaving behind the heuristics, beliefs, and intuitions that had so often failed the field. Correspondingly, the mathematical foundations of digital signatures would also translate into an improved evidentiary paradigm for electronic documents, leaving behind handwriting analysis, document forensics, and other legal practices of questionable scientific credentials.

Yet, the mathematization of cryptography has met with mixed success. Several fundamental types of cryptographic objects, such as hash functions and block ciphers, have resisted mathematical formalization, with important implications for the "provable security" paradigm.[16] Security practitioners have found computational complexity largely irrelevant to their concerns for products that deliver reasonable guarantees of security while maintaining high levels of efficiency. And new and devastating classes of attacks have entirely sidestepped the mathematical defenses of cryptosystems by focusing on their physical embodiment in software and hardware devices.

This resistance of certain phenomena to mathematization matters. The defining computing project of our time, the mass quantification of social processes necessary for Google's project "to organize the world's information," could not succeed without the cultural authority of number, data, and algorithm. Indeed, modernity itself is indissociable from an understanding of the social body as following "statistical laws that looked like brute, irreducible facts," laws "that could only be noticed after social phenomena had been enumerated, tabulated and made public."[17] The business of the modern state—from accounting to policy, economics, and planning—is suffused with this authority, "among the gentlest and yet most pervasive forms of power in modern democracies."[18]

Cryptography's reliance on the authority of proof to justify the superiority of digital signatures as evidence (and the appeal of this authority within the legal community) can thus be viewed as another chapter in the mutually beneficial relationship of state power and mathematics—a relationship somewhat at odds with the self-identification of cryptographers as cyberlibertarians. I will argue that in fact, the yearning for the moral authority provided by "provable security" has marginalized research on phenomena less amenable to mathematical formalization, but with the potential for greater social impact.[19] Thus, for cryptography, the dominance of analytical proof as the most authoritative method of mathematical persuasion also comes with a price, that of a certain irrelevance, as the objects it seeks to realize in the electronic realm—signatures, votes, cash—are irreducibly tied to the fuzzy and inexact worlds of bodily performances, human psychology, and long-standing social institutions.

And last, I will argue that the specific ways in which cryptographers modeled signatures had significant implications for the practical success of the technology. Here, I seek to foreground the role of modeling as a repressed dimension of cryptographic practice.[20] Both algorithmics and computational complexity rely on idealized models of computation that abstract away its physicality—the particular arrangements of processing power, storage, and connectivity that define concrete computational devices. Yet cryptographers have little language to discuss the trade-offs inherent in any representation of real world phenomena and few conceptual tools with which to approach the inescapable gaps that arise between physical computational artifacts and their mathematical models.[21]

These gaps manifested themselves on multiple fronts. As befits the military roots of cryptography, the digital signature threat model posited adversaries with considerable resources and motivation to break strong cryptographic schemes—in short, nation-states with considerable intelligence capabilities. This assumption translated into a one-size-fits-all risk analysis of documentary evidence, conflating together the costs and risks of very different types of transactions—for example, signing a mortgage and paying for groceries with a credit card. Cryptography's much touted superiority—its ability to withstand military-grade computational firepower—required the deployment of complex public-key infrastructures whose cost could be justified for only a small fraction of all transactions.[22]

The superior evidential qualities of digital signatures were also conveyed through the technical concept of "non-repudiation," the claim that the mathematical properties of digital signatures made it impossible for parties to "repudiate" their participation in a contractual exchange. That is, the strength of the evidence provided by digital signatures simply eliminated the need for adjudication of disputes by courts or rather reduced their role to one of passive confirmation. Although now firmly established in the security literature, non-repudiation never fully gained traction as a legal concept, as it seemed to preempt the very process by which the qualities of a given form of evidence are gradually established through the adversarial process.[23] Regardless of the eventual success or failure of digital signatures, as more and more categories of records are produced, exchanged, and stored in digital form, courts are under enormous pressure to establish the coordinates of the new electronic evidentiary paradigm.

Where are such coordinates to found? In recent years, science studies scholars have become increasingly involved in the sometimes acrimonious debates between scientists and the courts over how to best distinguish between "good science" and "junk science." In contrast to TV shows like *CSI* on which forensic experts seek to "let the evidence speak for itself," these scholars approach the issue from the premise that no evidence has independent powers of speech. As Sheila Jasanoff puts it, "Good science is not a commodity that courts can conveniently shop for in some extra-social marketplace of pure knowledge. There is no way for the law to access a domain of facts untouched by values or social interests."[24] In their examination of the development of forensic methods such as fingerprinting, DNA profiling, or document examination, scholars have indeed demonstrated that the eventual stabilization of any form of evidence occurs through a lengthy process of mutual adjustment between scientific and legal norms and practices, a process usually powered by the adversarial dynamics of the courtroom.[25] The definition of the forensic properties of digital signatures took an altogether different path: a series of political, legal, and regulatory bodies—among others, the American Bar Association, the United Nations Commission on International Trade Law, and the European Union—sought to establish the parameters of courts' evaluation of electronic documentary evidence prior to any case law.

Introduction 11

This process took place at the same time the legal community debated Lawrence Lessig's theory of information technology regulation, as articulated in his highly influential *Code and Other Laws of Cyberspace*.[26] In Lessig's theory, computer programming, especially as it pertains to the design of network architectures, is understood as a normative practice with power to influence behavior as great as that of social norms, markets, and even law itself. In such a view, information technology regulation is most effective when these four practices are coordinated within an "optimal mix" in which each subordinates its particular logic to the higher calling of regulation. In this spirit, the evidence law reform that swept the globe at the end of the 1990s thus sought to ensure not only the modernization of evidential requirements, but also optimal competitive conditions for widely anticipated markets for electronic authentication services. Evidence law turned out to be a poor test case for Lessig's theory of information technology regulation, however: law's empire is one wholly built of paper, and the rules that dictate the appreciation of its evidentiary qualities extend far and deep into law's most quotidian activities. In the end, the inner logic of evidence law could not be so easily subordinated to the broader regulatory goals of ensuring societal acceptance of cryptographic technologies.

In articulating these arguments, I bring together fields of practice and inquiry that have remained largely separated by the concepts they seek to share. Cryptographers, legal scholars, archivists, and social scientists bring distinct sensibilities, disciplinary commitments, and professional constraints to the study of electronic evidence. Yet I am distrustful of attempts to heal disciplinary relationships in the name of intellectual tolerance. Like Rosemary Coombe, in her insightful cultural analysis of intellectual property law, I would rather foster a space of "continuous and mutual disruption—the undoing of one term by the other."[27] In the airing out of conceptual dirty laundry lies, I believe, the necessary first steps for the emergence of a more workable evidentiary paradigm for electronic documents.

I am hoping this airing of differences will not be perceived as denunciation, as if the very existence of negotiations over the specific meaning of evidence that obtains in different disciplines would somehow point to their "socially constructed" character and thus their irremediable failure to meet their own professional norms. Such a move would be both trivial and trivializing. Isabelle Stengers has pointed out how the delegitimation of scientists' knowledge claims by sociologists is no less violent than that performed, for example, by scientists when they seek to debunk the supposed irrationality that drives the appreciation of scientific evidence by a court of law.[28] Thus, I do not take the long-standing cryptographic controversy over the meaning of "provable security" to signal some kind of normative lapse, but rather as a symptom that after many years of reliable service, certain disciplinary commitments are in need of attention and revision. The persistent discrepancies between the breadth and depth of cryptography's social ambitions and their actual realization would seem more than ample justification for one such attempt at diagnosis and revision.

Still, a nagging concern remains: after all, the state cannot be expected to function without a stable framework for written evidence. As the birthers controversy has highlighted, the legitimacy of *l'état de droit* fundamentally depends on public faith in the origin and integrity of the documents that signify the rule of law. Is there a point then in lifting the veil on the necessarily messy circumstances of the birth of a new evidentiary paradigm? One answer might be that this project is intellectually aligned with cryptographers' critique of "security through obscurity," an approach they have forcefully decried as ultimately resulting in flawed security design.[29]

Plan of the Book

Chapter 2, "Communication in the Presence of Adversaries," sets the stage by providing a short overview of the history of cryptographic technologies, periodized along successive "information ages."[30] In each of these periods, a dominant information and communication technology—paper, telegraph, radio, electromechanical computing, and networked computers—drives the development of cryptographic techniques and devices. By situating the development of these techniques within their social, institutional, and material context, a picture emerges that highlights some often unarticulated dimensions of the cryptographic experience, with important implications for modern cryptographic design: how the embodiment of cryptographic techniques in physical artifacts provides resources for defeating their security objectives; the logistical issues that have historically plagued the large-scale deployment of cryptographic technologies, in particular, the inherently difficult problem of key distribution; the design trade-offs that seem to perpetually obtain between high-grade security and user-friendliness; and, given the special interest of the state in both listening to and securing important communications, the unique structural forces that have shaped the development of the field.

In chapter 3, "On the Brink of a Revolution," I analyze a turning point in the history of cryptographic innovation, the 1976 publication of Diffie and Hellman's "New Directions in Cryptography." The founding document of cryptography's modern era, "New Directions" argued not only for radically new applications of cryptography for the coming age of computer networks, but also for a new paradigm of provable security based on the certification of cryptosystems through the mathematical frameworks of complexity theory and algorithmics. The invention of public-key cryptography unleashed a creative explosion in the field, the growth of a research community independent of the military and intelligence establishment, and the development of a broad research program aiming at providing all functions necessary to the integrity of electronic information, including the signatures needed to secure e-commerce transactions. In addition to these achievements, by the 1990s cryptography had also emerged as the Internet's first native political movement and cyberlibertarianism's most prominent voice. However, this chapter underlines how cryptography's emerging scientific program supported a broad range of positions on the social purposes of cryptographic research, many of a more conservative bent than crypto's well-publicized image suggested.

In chapter 4, "The Equivalent of a Written Signature," I examine the gradual crystallization of a cryptographic model for an "electronic equivalent to handwritten signatures." The model defines both the function of signatures, that is, the provision of the three security services of identification, integrity, and non-repudiation, as well as the specific threats and adversaries these services must protect against. The market demise of public-key infrastructures provides a concrete and powerful critique of the digital signature model, in addition to a powerful reminder that key distribution remains the Achilles' heel of any large-scale deployment of cryptographic technologies. I argue the considerable difficulties met in translating this model into a commercially successful technology point to cryptographers' problematic relationship with the representational nature of models. In adopting the ideals, methodologies, and epistemological standards of a modern, theory-oriented mathematical discipline, cryptographers found few available concepts from which to engage with the possibilities and constraints of modeling real-world systems. There were thus trade-offs in the mathematization of cryptography, rather than a simple promise of upward mobility for the discipline.

Chapter 5, "Written Proof," traces the path of a parallel definitional process, that of the *legal* model for electronic signatures. In the later part of the 1990s, the model made its way through a series of political, regulatory, and professional bodies, from the American Bar Association to the European Commission and the French government. These institutions struggled to reconcile the often centuries-old rules that govern the admissibility of written evidence in courts with the new electronic regime of contractual proof. As the technological front-runners, digital signatures powerfully informed the discussion of what kind of evidence an electronically signed document might provide and how that evidence might be judged reliable. Yet there was no simple translation of the cryptographic signature model into the legal one. If legislators happily embraced the claim that the mathematics of digital signatures would ground documentary forensics in the scientific process, French courts balked at the idea of relinquishing their power to appreciate evidence based on judges' intimate conviction. I frame this process within the well-known debate between Lessig and Easterbrook over law's proper role in taming the unruliness of information technologies: vehicle for regulatory goals or after-the-fact response to social conflicts?[31]

Chapter 6, "Paper and State," shifts the focus to the real-world trials and tribulations of three bureaucratic organizations as they wrestle with the application of electronic signatures to real estate contracts, birth certificates, and land titles. Because of the fundamental importance of these documents to the operation of state bureaucracy, French law requires that special care be taken of their creation, authentication, and retention. The diverging routes taken by notaries, officers of civil status, and land registry clerks in computerizing these documents demonstrate the need to pay attention to the specific material conditions and institutional contexts that govern the production of written evidence. Indeed, the integration of digital signatures with work practices, institutional settings, legal traditions, and user's cognitive models required significant transformations to the original cryptographic model. In particular, I outline how the technical conditions necessary for the long-term legibility of electronic documents present a significant challenge to the forensic value of cryptographic signature verification.

Chapter 7, "The Cryptographic Imagination," returns to a defining feature of modern cryptography: its ability to provide mathematical certification of the effectiveness of cryptosystems, in contrast to the heuristic methods of yore.[32] The last decade has seen two important challenges to this element of Diffie and Hellman's project: first, a new powerful class of "side-channel attacks" that has required cryptographers to take into account the physical embodiment of mathematical algorithms in computing devices; second, a long-standing controversy over the scope of the mathematical idealizations under which "provable security" obtains. I argue that both issues point to the representational nature of models as the source of inescapable gaps between the mathematics of cryptography and their concrete realization in software and hardware artifacts. I then provide examples of successful integration in cryptographic models of the embodied capabilities of human beings—including memory, perception, and cognition—and of the security properties of familiar material technologies—including books, paper, and envelopes. Such integration, I suggest, may provide a potential avenue toward broader social acceptance of cryptographic design goals.

In the epilogue, I revisit the preceding arguments in light of another major area of cryptographic investigation: voting technologies. Because their design proceeds from assumptions similar to those that informed the cryptographic signature model, I suggest their widespread adoption will likely face similar difficulties. I argue that directly addressing these blind spots will enable cryptographers to more fully account for the *creative* dimension of their design practices and help reinvigorate their sociotechnical agenda.

2 Communication in the Presence of Adversaries

By all accounts, the face of cryptography has changed dramatically in the last twenty-five years. *The Code Book*, Simon Singh's best-selling popular history of the field, describes it as the resolution of the centuries-old battle of wits between codemakers and codebreakers: "It is clear that cryptographers are winning the battle of information. Not only are today's codes, in fact, unbreakable, but the key distribution problem has been solved."[1] *Crypto*, Steven Levy's dramatic account of the birth of public-key cryptography, argues that "code rebels" created the military-grade tools necessary to ensure free and democratic access to electronic privacy in the coming information society. In doing so, they succeeded in wrestling control of the field away from Big Brotherian intelligence agencies and established cryptography as an independent academic discipline.[2]

Insiders have tended to portray the evolution of the field as that of maturation from a craft to a bona-fide mathematical science, spurred by the embrace of mathematical formalism in the second half of the twentieth century. For example, in a historical survey of the discipline, Massey states, "Our reason for calling the period up to 1949 the pre-scientific era of cryptology is that cryptologists generally proceeded by intuition and 'belief,' which they could not buttress by proofs."[3] Similarly, Jacques Stern, a researcher and author of a popular account of the field, *La Science du Secret*, makes the case for a cryptology that would have evolved in three distinct stages:

What is cryptology? Is it an art? A technique? A science? It is perhaps all three—or rather, it has been successively, during three periods of uneven duration, similar to the stages of life or those of the development of the earth. We have chosen to stay with this metaphor and to organize our reflections on history in three periods: the artisanal age, the technical age, and the paradoxical age. The passage from one period to the other happened through a kind of break, of qualitative jump, which enabled cryptologists to break free of the mechanical and conceptual constraints which limited the blossoming of their art.[4]

My purpose in this chapter is to provide a different account of the historical evolution of cryptography—one that challenges an evolutionary narrative that is perhaps a little too clean, perhaps a little too predictable. Most important, this account questions the premise that the digital represents the final stage of a long struggle for information to emancipate itself from the shackles of materiality, from the "mechanical constraints" that had previously limited its potential. It is one argument of this book that the tendency to conceptualize digital information as immaterial has marginalized important dimensions of cryptographic theory and practice. These repressed dimensions have now become recurrent stumbling blocks for the fulfillment of the cryptographic community's scientific and social aspirations.

In fact, cryptography's formal disengagement with the material dimension of information is a contemporary phenomenon. For much of its history, cryptographers had recourses to methods for *hiding information* just as much as they had to ciphers. Such methods involve the creative dissimulation of one signal within another—for example, embedding Morse code in an ordinary document using the dots of the *i*s and *j*s and the dashes of *f*s and *t*s. Rather than direct attack on the technical characteristics of the mechanisms themselves, it is also through such material properties that the effectiveness of many cryptographic schemes is often subverted. In the previous century, for example, as the quantity of encrypted military communications grew, methods of *traffic analysis* extracted considerable intelligence from mere communication patterns, even if the content of those communications remained inaccessible. Whether as marks on papers or radio waves, the physical embodiment of cryptographic mechanisms thus provides both resources and threats for the accomplishment of security goals. As I shall explore in chapter 7, computerization has only exacerbated this state of affairs.

In this chapter, I read the history of cryptography as it unfolds together with the various technologies that have successively dominated (military) communications—namely paper, telegraph, radio, electromechanical devices, and networked digital computers. Given that David Kahn's authoritative survey, *The Codebreakers*, comes in at just under 1200 pages, the goal

Communication in the Presence of Adversaries

is not to provide an exhaustive account.[5] Rather, I aim to situate cryptographic techniques within their material and social context, including medium of transmission, modes of encoding, operating procedures, political and military organization, and the contrary means developed to defeat their security objectives. Such contextualization highlights how the effectiveness of cryptographic systems cannot be reduced to their mere mathematical strength but must necessarily evaluate within the broader environments of their deployment. At the same time, this historical overview provides the opportunity to present basic vocabulary, concepts, and techniques of cryptography so as to build expertise for the arguments developed in the rest of the book.

Paper

Although traces of cryptographic activity have been found in most ancient civilizations from Mesopotamia to the Roman Empire, the systematic development of codes and ciphers awaited the flowering of modern European diplomacy in the sixteenth century. In 1542, for example, the Venetian state employed three "cipher secretaries" assigned to the development of such techniques. Though they enjoyed a relatively high status within Venetian society, betrayal of the cryptological secrets in their possession was deemed worthy of punishment by death.[6] As ciphers increasingly gained in sophistication, so did the methods for solving them: by the eighteenth century, most European nations had established "black chambers," secret organizations specializing in deciphering foreign diplomatic dispatches. By the 1850s, the principles of good cipher construction were fairly well developed, if not widely disseminated and necessarily understood in mathematical terms. Classical ciphers relied on two basic methods, *monoalphabetic* and *polyalphabetic* substitution, often combining the two in *codebooks*.

Monoalphabetic Substitution

For each letter of the alphabet, this technique substitutes another one. For example, the famous Caesar Cipher constructed the *ciphertext* (the enciphered message) by substituting each letter used in the *plaintext* (the original message) with the letter located five places after in the alphabet. If the letters are converted to numbers (A = 1, B = 2, etc.), this corresponds to addition modulo 26; that is, all results are within the 0–25 (A–Z) range. If the plaintext is "philosophy," the process is as follows:

	p (16)	h (8)	i (9)	l (12)	o (15)	s (19)	o (15)	p (16)	h (8)	y (25)
+	(5)	(5)	(5)	(5)	(5)	(5)	(5)	(5)	(5)	(5)
=	u (21)	m (13)	n (14)	q (17)	t (20)	x (24)	t (20)	u (21)	m (13)	d (4)

The resulting ciphertext would read "umnqtxtumd."

Such an *algorithm* provides little security, because the key space is too small, as there are only twenty-five possible keys, corresponding to the twenty-five possible substitutions. To cryptanalyze the resulting ciphertext, the adversary can merely use an *exhaustive key search* (or *brute-force attack*), that is, try each key until a meaningful message emerges, assuming of course he is aware that the message has been enciphered using this technique.

The ciphertext would also easily fall to *statistical analysis*, because monoalphabetic substitution preserves all of the statistical properties of the plaintext's language. These properties include the frequency distribution of individual letters in the English language (*e* occurs about 13% of the time; *v, k, j, x, q,* and *z,* less than 1%) as well as that of pairs and triplets (the most frequent pairs in English are *th* and *er*). Cryptanalysis can thus begin by simply replacing the most frequently occurring symbols of the ciphertext with the most frequent letters of the plaintext language and proceed on the basis of this partial solution.

Polyalphabetic Substitution

Here the substitution is more complex, as identical plaintext letters can correspond to different symbols of the ciphertext. The classic Vigenère cipher is based on the following algorithm: the plaintext is chopped into blocks of *m* letters (say, 5) and a key of length *m* is chosen (say, "plato"). The letters of the plaintext are then added, modulo 26, to the letters of the key:

	p (16)	h (8)	i (9)	l (12)	o (15)	s (19)	o (15)	p (16)	h (8)	y (25)
+	p (16)	l (12)	a (1)	t (20)	o (15)	p (16)	l (12)	a (1)	t (20)	o (15)
=	f (6)	t (20)	j (10)	f (6)	d (4)	g (7)	a (1)	q (17)	b (2)	n (14)

Communication in the Presence of Adversaries

The resulting ciphertext would read "ftjfdgaqbn." Note that each of the two *p*s, *h*s, and *o*s of the plaintext encrypt to distinct symbols in the ciphertext.

Polyalphabetic substitution improves over a simple substitution cipher because the key space is much larger: there are 26^m keywords of length *m* (26 choices for the first letter times 26 choices for the second, and so on), so even for small values of *m*, an exhaustive key search would be quite long, at least by hand (26^5 is greater than 11 million combinations, 26^6 greater than 300 million). In addition, because each alphabetic character of the plaintext can be mapped to one of *m* possible alphabetic characters (if the key contains all distinct letters), cryptanalysis based on letter frequency is more difficult. Still, such a cipher can also be broken through more complex forms of statistical analysis.[7]

Codebooks

Both of the ciphers mentioned in the previous section ignore the semantic units of the messages and view the plaintext as strings of letters, encrypting them either individually or in blocks. Codebooks encrypt whole words at a time by replacing each plaintext word with a numerical or other symbolic equivalent as listed in the codebook, such as [England, 34]. Deciphering proceeds by a corresponding inverted codebook, such as [34, England]. Although such a system might seem rather simplistic, it actually dominated the cryptographic world longer than any other enciphering method: for about 500 years, from the fourteenth century to the nineteenth century, much of the world's diplomatic correspondence was secured through the use of *nomenclators*, a mixed cipher-code system that relied on codebooks to replace certain specific words or sentences together with a simple monoalphabetic cipher to replace the rest of the text.[8]

A major advantage of nomenclators over ciphers was easier (and thus more accurate) encryption and decryption: semantic units such as words and sentences are more readily processed by humans than meaningless blocks of letters of fixed length. Nomenclators also offered substantial security, including a large key space, and good resistance to frequency analysis.[9] However, because specific words are always encoded with the same code words, codebooks are susceptible to cryptanalysis by *known-plaintext attack*, where the cryptanalyst has access to the encrypted version of a message of her own creation. The attack immediately reveals code words for all words in the plaintext—not a total break, but providing a starting point for cryptanalysis. Given access to a sufficiently large number of ciphertexts, a cryptanalyst could also perform *word frequency analysis*. Both of these shortcomings imply a need to frequently *refresh* the key— that is, the codebook itself—which, as Kahn notes, was both costly and inconvenient: "Their initial strengths, which was due to the extent of the lexicon and the many homophones, eventually proved a weakness: the foreign service was reluctant to change a nomenclator that, in the late 1700s, cost £150, or to order separate nomenclators for separate countries. Thus some remained in use for a dozen years or more, and some simultaneously served several embassies."[10] In the end, because codebook-based encryption cannot be easily automated, it fell into disgrace with the rise of modern communications-based warfare and the need for mass enciphering and deciphering of military communications.[11]

This short overview of ciphers and codes has introduced some of the fundamental concepts of contemporary cryptographic theory: encryption algorithms are step-by-step procedures for transforming plaintext messages into ciphertexts. A *key* is a parameter to the procedure known only to the communicating parties. Because schemes become increasingly vulnerable as adversaries intercept ciphertexts on which to base their cryptanalysis, it is necessary to regularly refresh keys, and thus to devise secure procedures for key distribution while the communicating parties are in the field.

Desirable features of cryptographic schemes are their ability to defeat adversaries by, on the one hand, exhibiting a key space sufficiently large to preclude exhaustive key search (or brute-force attacks) while, on the other hand, producing a ciphertext void of the statistical regularities that characterize natural languages and thus defeat frequency analysis. In addition, encryption and decryption procedures should remain as simple as possible, both for efficiency purposes and because operator mistakes in handling complex cryptographic procedures often provide points of entry for cryptanalysts to break the schemes.

In evaluating the security of a cryptographic algorithm, experts make various worst-case assumptions regarding the resources available to the adversary: she may have complete knowledge of the enciphering method, have access to plaintext/ciphertext pairs of her choosing, or neither. A *strong assumption*—for example, that the adversary has no knowledge of the encryption method—provides for a weaker certification of security.

Information Hiding

At the minimum, any encrypted message leaks the information that the content of the message is valuable enough to protect, fueling in turn the desire to break through its protections. Kerckhoffs notes in his 1883 survey of the field that "in the 17th century, the simple fact of having corresponded in secret characters was still considered an aggravating circumstance by English tribunals."[12] Thus, in many cases, it may be easier, more appropriate, or more efficient to hide information than to encrypt it.

For these reasons, methods for *hiding information* (steganography) were often more developed than methods for *scrambling* information (cipher and codes). In the former, the sender leaves the message in the clear, but hides it in a way known only to the recipient and invisible to others. In the latter, a transformation is applied to the linguistic code itself so that it becomes meaningless to whoever does not have the information necessary to invert the transformation (i.e., the key). With steganography, one is confident that the adversary cannot discover that a message has been transmitted at all. With ciphers, one is confident that even though the adversary is able to access a scrambled message, the method is strong enough to withstand attempts to decode it.

Steganographic techniques embed a message within a *cover signal* or *cover text*, taking advantage of their properties to avoid detection. The message may be encoded in the visual, auditory, linguistic, or physical domains using a wide range of techniques, including invisible inks, using only some of the letters of a message, such as the first letter of every word, or the least significant bits of a digital image. Information hiding may also be used for authentication: in the seventeenth and eighteenth centuries, publishers of logarithmic tables deliberately introduced errors in the least significant digits of some entries so that any copy of the tables could be traced back to its legitimate producer. The practice is still relied on today by database and mailing list vendors who insert bogus entries to identify customers who try to resell their product.

Historically, information hiding and cryptography evolved in an intimate relationship, and methods from either approach were traditionally discussed together. Kerckhoffs's 1883 survey begins by noting that "it is under the rubric: *steganography*, *cipher*, or *secret writing* that certain encyclopedic dictionaries provide information which relate to cryptography."[13] It is thus worth remarking that contemporary cryptography textbooks make no mention of information hiding, as its applications do not seem to fit prevalent taxonomies of the field.[14] Yet the relationship between the two has continued to generate new problems and solutions, including unforeseen types of attacks on ciphers, applications in the field of copyright protection, as well as the highly innovative work of David Chaum on transactional anonymity, which will be explored in more detail in chapter 3.

Telegraph

Much like would later happen with the emergence of Internet-based communications, the rise of telegraphic communication services was accompanied by public concerns over the fact that messages circulated in the clear, openly available to view by service providers, operators, or anyone else who cared to tap the wires.[15] Only one year after Morse sent his first message, his lawyer and promotional agent published the first commercial code specifically designed to protect the privacy of telegraphic communications.[16] The security of such codes was relative, because anyone could purchase them, but as Kahn points out, they "afforded sufficient security for most business transactions by simply precluding an at-sight comprehension of the meaning."[17] Perhaps more important, they reduced costs by replacing whole sentences with single words, a practice much frowned upon by the telegraph operators.[18]

The impact of the telegraph on cryptography would be most felt in the theater of the American Civil War as part of a new kind of warfare based on massive modern armies, raised through conscription and coordinated through modern communication and transportation technologies: "The telegraph enabled commanders, for the first time in history, to exert instantaneous and continuous control over great masses of men spread over large areas."[19] Such control could be exerted only if messages were protected from eavesdropping, elevating cryptography to the role of vital instrument of warfare it hasn't lost since. The specific needs of mobile armies spelled the end of the nomenclator, though. Its capture in the field required issuing new codebooks to every military communication outpost, a process much too slow and cumbersome for battle conditions. Ciphers, such as the Vigenère, proved more appropriate as their procedures could be printed and distributed on mere sheets of paper, and keys renewed with relative ease.[20] The strategic importance of ciphers also invigorated attempts to defeat them, and the 1863 break of the Vigenère signaled the onset of the race between cryptographers and cryptanalysts.

Perhaps the most significant theoretical development to emerge from such widespread fielding of cryptographic technologies is Auguste Kerckhoffs's desiderata listed in his 1883 *Cryptographie militaire*. In a paper whose genre oscillates between the survey, the pamphlet, and the textbook, Kerckhoffs lists six desirable design criteria that cryptographic systems designers should bear in mind:

(1) the system must be practically, if not mathematically, unbreakable; (2) its compromise at the hands of the enemy must not be cause of inconvenience; (3) it must be possible to communicate and remember the key without the help of written notes, and to change or modify it depending on the communicating parties; (4) it must be applicable to telegraphic communications; (5) it must be portable, and its operation must not require the help of several people; and (6) it is necessary, given the circumstances which dictate its application, that the system be of easy use, requiring neither tension of the mind nor knowledge of a long series of rules to observe.[21]

As we shall observe throughout this book, Kerckhoffs's desiderata would lose little of their relevance over the years. Principle 1 stems from Kerckhoffs's impatience with claims of mathematically "unbreakable" ciphers, and the importance of submitting proposed systems to sustained cryptanalytic attack by the community.[22] Principle 2 is usually cited as Kerckhoffs's major contribution to cryptographic design: the idea that effective security must depend on confidentiality of the key only, rather than on keeping secret the characteristics of the system itself. The principle articulates what is perhaps the earliest critique of "security through obscurity," an approach routinely decried in modern cryptographic practice. Taken together however, the six principles offer a holistic view of the technical, organizational, and human-factor issues encountered in the large-scale deployment and operation of cryptographic systems, issues with the potential to negatively impact security if not properly addressed by systems designers. Indeed, Kerckhoffs suggests somewhat sarcastically that the task of designing a cryptosystem both "easy and secure" may resemble "the philosophical stone of ancient chemists."[23]

Radio

The radio completed the communications revolution in modern warfare, as well as fostering the growth and systematization of the second leg of cryptology, that is, cryptanalysis. Because it provides military commanders with a copy of every enemy ciphertext, the radio made cryptanalysis even more important than cryptography, a weapon that could be depended upon to continuously provide fresh information relevant to ongoing operations.[24] After World War I, cryptanalysis thus became a permanent and major element of military intelligence and espionage. The significance of radio transmission for intelligence did not however lie solely in the ability to cryptanalyze enemy texts, but also in analyzing patterns in communications themselves. On the Great War's Western Front, for example, French intelligence personnel

> recorded call-signs, volume of traffic, and correspondents for all stations. These soon segregated themselves into four main networks, each of which, the French assumed, belonged to a combat group. The patterns of correspondence defined the headquarters stations and volume soon differentiated the fast-moving and fast-sending cavalry stations from the infantry. Occasional clear-text signatures disclosed the commanders' names. In this way, the French gradually built up a picture of the German forces facing them. . . . Traffic analysis aided in delineating the enemy order of battle, and frequently forewarned of important enemy activities by detecting an increase in message volume.[25]

Increased reliance on cryptographic communication also gave rise to new difficulties. As radio increased the number of messages pouring in and out of army communication centers by an order of magnitude, organizational problems of scale and human factors impeded the efficiency of the ciphering systems. The important resources devoted to cryptanalysis meant the slightest mistake would be immediately exploited by the adversary, while the pressures of military operations provided little of the serene conditions propitious to the performance of complex ciphers. Training had to be provided, as well as observed. Thus, "the great practical lesson of World War I cryptology was the necessity of infusing an iron discipline in the cryptographic personnel," and the head of the French cryptologic section sternly warned his cipher clerks: "Encode well or do not encode at all. In transmitting cleartext, you give only a piece of information to the enemy, and you know what it is; in encoding badly, you permit him to read all your correspondence and that of your friends."[26]

Yet another problem involved authentication of encrypted messages. Encryption between parties relied on a shared secret key. If enciphering material and keys were seized by the enemy, one could be fed false information, in what the Germans called a *funkspiel*. To authenticate encrypted material, and thus prevent funkspiels, two distinct methods were used. The first relied on inserting within the message itself an *authenticator*, a security check agreed upon in advance—for example, an additional x after every tenth letter of plaintext. The absence of an authenticator was meant as a "silent alarm," indicating to the receiving party that something was amiss.[27]

The second method took advantage of the fact that Morse operators could not help but identify themselves in the process of keying information. The radio signal itself embedded biometric information uniquely identifying its human operator—its "fist," or "sending touch," "as distinctive as handwriting."[28] Such biometrics provided another layer of authentication, one much more difficult to defeat: Kahn explains that "Nazi radio spies were trained in a school near Hamburg . . . each agent's 'fist' was recorded to make radiotelegraph forgery by the Allies that much more difficult."[29]

Electromechanical Devices

In the aftermath of the Great War, technological advances made possible the development of ciphers both remarkably powerful and simple to operate—the *Enigma machines* used by Germany during World War II and the *Vernam one-time pad*, used in diplomatic communications. These would spur corresponding advances in both theory and practice of cryptanalysis and eventually pave the way for Alan Turing's foundational work in digital computing and Claude Shannon's mathematical theory of information and communication.

Enigma and Hagelin Machines

In 1918 and 1919, several inventors developed, refined, and commercialized a series of electromechanical devices that provided extremely powerful encryption capabilities: One of these inventors, Swede Boris Hagelin, was to become cryptography's first millionaire; another one, German Arthur Scherbius, commercialized a portable, battery-powered machine called the

Enigma that was to enter history as the Nazi regime's cryptosystem of choice to secure its military communications.

The essential component of these devices was the wired rotor wheel, a mechanism that hardwired a single monoalphabetic substitution of 26 inputs to 26 outputs—for example, *a* to *m*, *p* to *z*, and so on. Two techniques vastly multiplied the power of this simple mechanism: first, wheels were placed alongside and connected to two or more additional rotors wheels, each implementing distinct substitutions, so that the outputs of one rotor fed the inputs of its neighbor; second, after the encryption of each single letter, a stepping mechanism moved the first rotor forward one position, while the second wheel moved forward one position after a complete revolution of the first wheel, and so on with the third wheel—in the manner of a car odometer. This resulted in each letter of the plaintext being encoded with a completely different set of substitutions.[30]

Using a different ciphering alphabet for each plaintext letter was a well-established cryptographic technique, dating back as far as Trithemius's 1516 *Six Books of Polygraphy*. The longer the *period*—the number of different cipher alphabets used before the same sequence of plaintext/ciphertext alphabets is reused—the stronger the cipher and the more involved the ciphering and deciphering process. The automation provided by rotor machines enabled the period to grow to astronomical length (for the Enigma, 26^3 or approximately 17,000) without loss of accuracy. Because most military messages were of a much shorter length, Enigma-encrypted ciphertexts thus rarely exhibited the kind of frequency patterns so crucial to cryptanalysis. Brute force attacks were similarly difficult, as the total key space exceeded 3×10^{114}: 26^3 choices for the initial position of the rotors, 6 further choices for their ordering, and an additional 26! choices from a plugboard that implemented a fixed but easily modified monoalphabetic substitution.

The procedures for key agreement were sophisticated. Each organizational unit (groups of planes, U-boats, etc.) was issued a codebook listing the original position of the rotors and plugboard for each day. After setting up the machine with the codebook parameters, the operator would observe the following procedure: for each new message, randomly select new rotor positions, encrypt these using the codebook settings for the day, and transmit the result as the first part of the message (the *indicator*); continue encryption of the message using the random rotor positions. In order to limit the damage caused by compromise at the hand of the enemy, codebooks usually contained key material for a single month. U-boats' codebooks were printed using water-soluble ink, and if compromise was suspected, operators switched to the following month's keys or followed special procedures known only to officers.

For all its theoretical security, the Enigma was broken even before the start of the war by three mathematicians working for the Polish intelligence service. Not only did they succeed in fully cryptanalyzing the Enigma, they also designed and built *bombes*, special-purpose electromechanical devices that could decrypt Enigma-secured communications in real time. A replica of the Enigma as well as plans for the bombes were eventually transmitted to French and English intelligence services in August 1939, providing the initial impetus for work at Bletchley Park, the British headquarters of the Allied cryptanalytic effort.

Ironically, the machine's user-friendliness proved a liability. Once daily procedures for key agreement were performed, messages could be encrypted and decrypted as fast as they could be typed and read off the "screen"—three rows of letters above the keyboard, backlit by light bulbs. Secret military communications had never been so easy: "Wehrmacht officers found the machines so convenient, so portable, that they could not bring themselves to reserve the machine for only high-grade (secret) traffic. Instead Enigma carried all grades of messages, from New Year's greetings and routine supply reports and requests to virtually all U-boat orders and Herr commands' daily situation reports."[31] Even if the Germans were aware of the importance of limiting the amount of signals sent, "they could not bring themselves to observe it rigorously."[32] Routine signals, in particular, created ideal conditions for cryptanalysis, carrying repetitive information, with repetitive traffic patterns. Stereotyped language, such as forms of salutation, address, and signature also strongly patterned the content of the messages, providing a foothold for Allied cryptanalysis efforts.[33]

But mostly, cryptanalysis thrived on procedural error, both systematic and random. The practice of double encipherment of the indicator at the beginning of each message provided the Poles with their initial break. The operator's "random" choice of rotor positions would often in practice involve adjacent letters on the keyboard, or meaningful initials. As the war dragged on, cryptographic fatigue led clerks to reuse portions of codebooks.

When worries over the efficacy of the Enigma led the Germans to switch to a new four-rotor system in February 1942, Allied cryptanalysts were able to break the enhanced Enigma by taking advantage of simple errors by cipher operators: "Once, in December a U-boat cipher operator had carelessly let [the fourth wheel] move out of this [neutral] position while enciphering a message; Hut 8 had noted the ensuing gibberish, and also spotted the re-transmission of the message on the correct setting. This elementary blunder of repetition, so easy to make while the Germans held complete trust in their machines, had allowed the British analysts to deduce the wiring of the wheel."[34]

Though these cryptanalytic successes meant the Allies enjoyed extensive foreknowledge of German military operations, they were faced with the serious problem of not showing they knew too much—indeed, how could the information be used without giving away the breaking of Enigma? They resorted to performing forms of reverse funkspiel, elaborate disinformation strategies to provide German military commanders with alternative explanations for their losses.

More important, they could count on the German's unfailing faith in the technical merits of their cryptosystems and their corresponding willingness to blame spy networks for the leaks.[35] As Hodges notes, "Bletchley's continued successes depended upon the willingness of German authorities to believe that ciphers were *proved* secure, instead of asking them whether they actually were. It was a military Gödel theorem, in which systematic inertia rendered German leadership incapable of looking at their system from the outside."[36] Indeed, it was only after the British government confirmed the break in 1974 that former German officers came to accept that their communications infrastructure had been compromised.[37]

Perfect Secrecy

In 1917, an American engineer working for AT&T, Gilbert Vernam, stumbled upon the perfect cipher while attempting to devise a system to improve the secrecy of the teleprinter, the printing telegraph.[38] The principle was remarkably simple: to represent characters, the teleprinter used the Baudot code, which assigned to twenty-six alphabetical character and six nonprinting control characters a five-bit binary code made of either marks or spaces (2^5 = 32). Thus, the letter *a* is *mark, mark, space, space, space*; the letter *b* is *space, space, mark, mark, space*, and so on. A teleprinter

Communication in the Presence of Adversaries

message is a sequence of such marks and spaces, which can be represented by the presence or absence of an electrical current. Vernam's idea was to print out a key consisting of a random sequence of such marks and spaces and to add it to the teleprinter message. At the receiving end, the key would be subtracted from the ciphertext. The arithmetic was simple: *mark + mark = space, mark + space = mark, space + mark = mark*, and *space + space = space*. In binary notation, where mark = 1 and space = 0, this gives the exclusive-or (XOR) operator of binary arithmetic:

XOR	mark/1	space/0
mark/1	space/0	mark/1
space/0	mark/1	space/0

The beauty was that the process necessitated little modification to an ordinary teleprinter—only the addition and subtraction logic, and some tape-feeding mechanism to be coordinated at either end: "Messages were enciphered, transmitted, received, and deciphered in a single operation—exactly as fast as a message in plain English. . . . The advantage was the assimilation of encipherment into the overall communication process. Vernam created what came to be called 'on-line encipherment.' He freed a fundamental process in cryptography from the shackles of time and error. He eliminated a human being—the cipher clerk—from the chain of communication."[39]

It suffered however from two important limitations: in order to ensure secrecy, the key tape had to be made extremely long. In fact, even though no formal proof existed, it was believed the tape had to be of a length comparable to the message itself. Furthermore, it appeared the key had to be absolutely random, and any attempt to circumvent these requirements by reusing key material resulted in rapid break of the system. These limitations severely limited the practical use of the cipher, and the device failed commercially: "Cable companies passed it over in favor of the old-fashioned commercial codes, which substantially shortened messages, thereby cutting cable tolls, and which gave a modicum of secrecy as well."[40]

The practical impact of Vernam's cipher was thus limited to certain diplomatic channels, in particular those of Germany that instituted the system between 1921 and 1923. The Germans based it on simple pads of paper containing lists of random numbers to be added to diplomatic codebooks, with each sheet of the pad torn off after use, never to be reused again (thus the name *one-time pad*).

In the later stages of World War II, the Germans combined the Enigma and the Vernam designs into a teleprinter-based cryptographic apparatus, the Lorenz cipher. Each letter of the plaintext was encrypted individually, using a random key generated by a system of stepping wheels similar to the Enigma's rotors. By setting the wheels of the encryption and decryption apparatus to the same initial positions, an identical pseudorandom key sequence could be generated at both ends.[41] The system proved no more resistant to the Allies than the Enigma. Taking advantage of operator blunders, Bletchley Park's codebreakers eventually deduced the design of the wheels and went on to build the famous "Colossus" electromechanical computer to automate cryptanalysis of the intercepts.[42]

It would take Claude Shannon to turn Vernam's original intuition into a full-fledged mathematical theory of cryptography. In his 1945 paper "Communication Theory of Secrecy Systems," Shannon enquired: "How secure is a system against cryptanalysis when the enemy has unlimited time and manpower available for the analysis of the intercepted cryptograms?"[43] He proved the Vernam one-time pad to be, in fact, unbreakable even by such an enemy if the key was indeed as long as the plaintext, genuinely random, and used only once. It was the first mathematical result of its kind in cryptography, the proof of a cryptosystem's efficacy *regardless of the adversary's computational resources*. Shannon distinguished such "theoretical" proofs from those obtaining in the case of "practical secrecy," in which the goal is to build systems "which will require a large amount of work to solve." The distinction was a conceptual milestone, but one that also highlighted the gap between cryptographic theory and practice, between the laboratory and the field, with the one-time pad relegated to niche applications such as the Washington-Moscow hotline.[44]

Shannon's mathematical theory also firmly situated steganography outside of cryptography proper:

There are three general types of secrecy system: (1) concealment systems, including such methods as invisible ink, concealing a message in an innocent text, or in a fake covering cryptogram, or other methods in which the existence of the message is concealed from the enemy; (2) privacy systems, for example speech inversion, in which special equipment is required to recover the message; (3) "true" secrecy systems where the meaning of the message is concealed by cipher, code, etc., although its existence is not hidden, and the enemy is assumed to have any special equipment necessary to intercept and record the transmitted signal. We consider only the third type—concealment systems are primarily a psychological problem and privacy systems a technological one.[45]

Yet although cryptography was a crucial element of military communications, espionage had few uses for it, as spies' main concern laid in the concealment of communication itself. There were abundant methods to choose from—some devised by the ancient Greeks and used by German spies: prick holes in a book or a newspaper above the letters of the secret message. Detecting such covert communication over multiple carriers—newspapers, letters, movies, telegrams, and so on—became a major concern of the United States after Pearl Harbor. The censorship service created in aftermath of the attack employed close to 15,000 examiners who listened to phone conversations; scanned movies, magazines, and radio scripts; and opened up to a million pieces of overseas mail *each day*:

> To plug up as many steganographic channels of communication as possible, the Office of Censorship banned in advance the sending of whole classes of objects or kinds of messages. International chess games by mail were stopped. Crossword puzzles were extracted from letters, for the examiners did not have time to solve them to see if they concealed a secret message, and so were newspaper clippings which might have spelled out messages by dotting successive letters with secret ink. . . . Listing of students' grades was tabooed. One letter containing knitting instructions was held up long enough for an examiner to knit a sweater to see if the given sequence of knit two and cast off contained a hidden message. . . . A stamp bank was maintained at each censorship station; examiners removed loose stamps, which might spell out a code message, and replaced them with others of equal value, but of different numbers and denomination. Blank paper, often sent from the United States to relatives in paper-short countries, was similarly replaced from a paper bank to obviate secret-ink transmissions. Childish scrawls, sent from proud parents to proud grandparents, were removed because of the possibility of their covering a map. Even lovers' X's meant as kisses, were heartlessly deleted if censors thought they might be a code.[46]

This display of imagination from both spies and censors points to the enormously varied ways in which the materiality of media can be leveraged to transmit information. Indeed, as detailed in the next chapter, cryptographers themselves would eventually resort to such methods to evade and ridicule efforts by the intelligence establishment to police the spread of cryptographic knowledge.

Networked Computers

The advent of networked computers signaled a remarkable expansion of the cryptographic field, as the financial and governmental sectors began to assess their needs for secure electronic transactions. In the early 1970s, IBM researcher Horst Feistel—at the time one of the few private-sector cryptographic researchers—began work on an algorithm that would, he argued, safeguard individual privacy in the coming computer society. Feistel proposed that ciphers could be used to encrypt databanks in order to guard their contents from anyone but authorized individuals. Feistel presented these ideas and the design principles of his Lucifer cipher in a 1973 *Scientific American* article, at the time one of the most explicit discussion of modern cryptographic principles ever presented to the American public.[47]

The design of Lucifer was remarkably simple: like the Vernam cipher, it worked directly with the binary representation of messages: "We shall tacitly assume that the messages we wish to handle cryptographically have first been translated into a sequence of binary digits. Any kind of information, be it letters, musical sounds, or television signals, can be represented by binary coding. We shall no longer worry about the original meaning of the messages. We shall deal only with their binary representation."[48]

It relied on Shannon's suggestion in *Communication Theory of Secrecy Systems* that strong and practical ciphers could be constructed from two simple methods—*diffusion* and *confusion*—which, when combined, made difficult any statistical (i.e., frequency) analysis of the ciphertext.

Diffusion dissipates the redundancy found in natural languages by spreading it throughout the ciphertext.[49] A simple permutation of the letters of the plaintext, for example "hello" to "lohel," breaks the frequencies of bigrams and trigrams. Confusion makes the relation between the key and ciphertext as involved as possible, so that statistical analysis of the cipher text will not yield much information about the key. Mono- and polyalphabetic substitution are both methods of achieving confusion. Permutation and substitution are inadequate methods of encryption by themselves, but Shannon showed that their combination yields practical ciphers of great speed and resilience. The Lucifer ciphering process consisted precisely in the interleaving of successive operations of diffusion and confusion. The algorithm performs sixteen rounds of such operations on the plaintext, sixty-four bits at a time. Because they are performed directly at the binary level, each operation necessitates only the simplest hardware to implement it, yet their composition yields a cipher of remarkable strength while achieving speeds yet to be met by any cipher based on algebraic properties.[50]

If Feistel's goal of protecting individual's privacy did not seem to be associated with any specific market, protecting banking transactions clearly was. IBM quickly realized the business potential of integrating cryptographic technologies into the data processing infrastructure undergirding the deployment of networked ATM machines (introduced in the United States in 1968). Aware of the increasing needs for a cryptographic algorithm suitable for industry purposes, the National Bureau of Standards (NBS) solicited proposals for a standard in 1973. Selection as a federal standard would be premised on meeting two distinct conditions: the algorithm would be forwarded to the National Security Agency (NSA) for evaluation, and the winner would grant nonexclusive royalty-free licenses to design, build, use, and sell hardware and software implementing the cipher.[51] The only game in town at the time, Lucifer was selected and the details of the algorithm published in March 1975 in the *Federal Register* as the Data Encryption Standard (DES, pronounced *dez*), with requests for comments from the industry and the public.[52]

Almost immediately, critics pointed to the suspicious reduction of the original 64 bits keys length to 56 bits, with the assignment of 8 bits to error correction. The move seemed to suggest an attempt "to intentionally reduce the cost of exhaustive key search by a factor of 256."[53] Martin Hellman, a soon-to-become-famous Stanford professor of electrical engineering, wrote to the NBS that "Whit Diffie and I have become concerned that the proposed data encryption standard, while probably secure against commercial assault, may be extremely vulnerable to attack by an intelligence organization."[54] Diffie and Hellman subsequently published an extensive analysis of the standard, claiming that "using the simplest cryptanalytic attack [exhaustive key search], a $20 million machine can be built to break the proposed standard in about 12 hours of computation time . . . major intelligence agencies possess the financial resources and the interest to build such a machine."[55] Worse still, critics pointed that the design criteria for the "S-boxes"—eight fixed tables dictating the specific bit substitutions—was not publicly clarified, an omission that suggested the existence of a *trapdoor*, a weakness known only to the designers, who would thus have the ability to cryptanalyze messages at will.

Rumors abounded. Was DES an authentically secure cipher, or was the entire process a sophisticated funkspiel cleverly devised by intelligence agencies? The academic community worried that its expertise was effectively coopted to certify the validity of technological mole planted by the NSA. In response, the NBS organized two workshops in September and December of 1976 to discuss concerns with both a trapdoor and key size, and subsequently approved it unchanged as a Federal Information Processing Standard (FIPS) on January 15, 1977, with the provision that it be revised every five years. No evidence of government tampering has ever surfaced: "Claims which have repeatedly arisen and been denied over the past 20 years regarding built-in weaknesses of DES remain unsubstantiated."[56]

As the first cryptographic algorithm ever to be officially endorsed by the United States government and the first to be openly exposed to cryptanalytic scrutiny by the cryptographic community, DES played a major role in forging the structure and identity of modern cryptography on at least three distinct levels: (1) the development of a civilian market for cryptographic products; (2) the structuring of that market through standardization; and (3) a validation process falling somewhat short of full technical disclosure, resulting in increased suspicion from academic cryptographers toward the intelligence establishment. The gap between these two communities was soon to broaden into a wide gulf.

Conclusion

This short overview highlighted a number of recurring tensions in the historical development of cryptographic theory and practice, namely the importance of understanding security in relation to context, the practical difficulties of fielding large-scale cryptosystems, the material embodiment of cryptographic techniques, and the special conditions that obtain in a scientific field of such import for national security.

The "Best" Method Depends on Context

Through different communication epochs, different cryptographic techniques have been favored based on specific conditions, perceived security needs, cultural preferences, legal environment, usability, and so on. A seemingly primitive technology, nomenclators, ruled the cryptographic world longer than any other technique, but could not be adapted to the military requirements of the Civil War, while commercial codes provided "good enough privacy" for business use. The effectiveness of any cryptographic method can only be evaluated based on careful evaluation of the totality of such factors rather than mere mathematical strength.

Cryptography Is Brittle and Key Distribution Difficult
Large-scale deployment of cryptographic systems, mostly observed in the context of warfare, demonstrates the enormous practical difficulties in ensuring their proper functioning. In particular, procedures for key distribution, while integral to the security of these systems, must be precisely adhered to. As a result, the practice of cryptography demands rigorous discipline, rarely met even by trained operators. Cryptanalysis thus sometimes proceeds by direct attack on the mathematical properties of ciphers, but mostly thrives on inevitable procedural errors. This is in part due to the structural contradiction between the demand for systematic production of *randomness* in cryptographic procedures and cognitive needs of cryptographic operators to *routinize* their behaviors, whether motivated by productivity or fatigue. As Kerckhoffs's desiderata highlighted as early as 1883, in cryptographic design, "easy" and "secure" exist in a space of constant trade-offs.

Cryptography Is a Material and Embodied Activity
Cryptography cannot hide the very existence of a message, which communicates the desire for secrecy. Traffic analysis reveals the origin, destination, and size of messages, as well as overall communication patterns. A Morse operator's "fist" is embedded in a radio signal. Computing and communication always occur through some kind of material means, and—as subsequent chapters will explore—the material basis of modern networked computing offers new resources and challenges to cryptographic algorithms. Steganography and cryptography thus exist in a more symbiotic relationship than modern taxonomies of the field have allowed for.

Certainty Is Elusive
Cryptographic knowledge seems to constantly oscillate between the three states succinctly articulated by Donald Rumsfeld in 2002 in a press confer-

ence on the Afghan conflict: "There are known knowns. These are things we know that we know. There are known unknowns. That is to say, there are things that we now know we don't know. But there are also unknown unknowns. These are things we do not know we don't know." Although this is perhaps an inescapable condition of all systems of knowledge production, few fields share cryptography's historical predicament, whereby unknown unknowns are an explicit product of structural conditions, including national security interests and the control and censorship of scientific literature. As the next chapter discusses, this dialectic of openness and secrecy has strongly shaped the relationship between the scientific establishment and intelligence agencies. Furthermore, the entire edifice of modern cryptography is based on an explicit balancing act between mathematical "known knowns" and "known unknowns"—for example, the relative computational difficulty of performing certain algorithms.

Yet Rumsfeld's tripartite classification of knowledge is incomplete without the (appropriately occulted) fourth term of the equation, the "unknown knowns." Philosopher Slavoj Žižek defines them as "the disavowed beliefs and suppositions we are not even aware of adhering to ourselves."[57] One aim of this book is to allow some of these beliefs and suppositions to float to the surface so that cryptography can become a more reflective form of technical practice.[58] Of particular import is the implicit association of computer and mathematics, as it endows digital information with the special cultural authority that has historically accrued to mathematics as pure symbolic expression of natural laws. One contemporary form of that association was cemented in 1976 by the publication of modern cryptography's defining manifesto, Diffie and Hellman's "New Directions in Cryptography."

3 On the Brink of a Revolution

By all accounts, 1976 marks one of the most important dates in the history of cryptography: the birth of the public-key paradigm. Two Stanford researchers, Whitfield Diffie and Martin Hellman, presented a set of innovative cryptographic ideas in a landmark publication, "New Directions in Cryptography," a paper that stands out not only for its scientific content but also for its self-awareness as a potential game-changer.[1] Opening with a prophetic "We stand on the brink of a revolution in cryptography," it made an eloquent case that cryptographic devices would soon leave the confines of the military world to become ubiquitous fixtures of computing networks, embedded in everything from computer terminals to cash dispensers. In turn, this emerging civilian context would require the development of new cryptographic methods to achieve, among others, easier distribution of keys and authentication of electronic contracts. "New Directions" proposed innovative techniques addressing both of these issues. Furthermore, the authors provided a new mathematical framework for ascertaining the security of these techniques, suggesting that theoretical developments in information theory and computer science offered the promise "of providing provably secure cryptosystems, changing this ancient art into a science."[2] It was quite a program, and in large part, the paper delivered.

What perhaps secured "New Directions" such a lofty place in the pantheon of cryptography was its authors' ability to situate their discoveries in the context of a broad historical progression. The public-key paradigm offered not only a new mode of key distribution, but also a new mode of doing cryptography altogether, one in which the design and evaluation of cryptographic algorithms, standards, and products would be vetted through a public process. The technical and the social were intimately fused in this new approach. Diffie and Hellman's methods for accessing keys and for the social organization of cryptography both explicitly eschewed centralized authority as inherently opaque and thus corruptible. In its place, they proposed the transparency of publicly verifiable mathematical knowledge and the resilience of the peer-review process. Cryptographic tools and knowledge would thus move from a dysfunctional institutional context, dominated by the needs of states for self-protection, to one regulated by the scientific ethos of openness.

In the following two decades, cryptographers would tap into these technical and symbolic resources to develop an exceptionally rich research program, with explicit motivations to shape the politics of the emerging socialities of computer networks. In this chapter, I revisit some episodes of this vibrant period, when the emergence of Internet politics, the feverish pace of the dot-com gold rush, and the scientific possibilities unleashed by the public-key paradigm uniquely combined to form an unusual experiment in mathematics as agent of social change.

Some of these episodes have already been well documented. The "crypto wars," a series of public clashes between the cryptographic and intelligence communities over censorship of scientific communication, public access to strong encryption tools, and governmental wiretapping of the digital infrastructure, regularly made the headlines throughout the 1980s and the 1990s. It is not my purpose here to revisit debates that have been extensively covered elsewhere.[3] Instead, I want to highlight some of the less visible tensions that accompanied the spectacular growth of the cryptographic community, from the publication of "New Directions" to the end of the first Internet bubble.

First, although the cryptographic community political identity was most visibly associated with cyberlibertarianism, this proposition was far from self-evident within the community itself. In particular, the various research agendas that emerged as the field sought to define its future course included a broad range of positions on the social role of cryptography, including conservative law-and-order ones. Second, though prominent cryptolibertarians argued extensively that access to strong cryptography was essential to secure the potential of the Internet as a political tool, they also very much understood that potential in terms of new opportunities for business and commerce. As well, the vibrancy of the field originated in no small part from the ambition of prominent figures (e.g., David Chaum) to develop research agendas explicitly motivated by social concerns such as privacy and anonymity. These, however, coexisted with more conservative approaches that sought to define the foundations of the field in purely mathematical terms, motivated only by scientific needs for internal coherence and objectivity. Finally, the relationship of cryptography to steganography remained unsettled. The mathematical manipulation of binary digits as an abstract quantity seemed to imply the chains that bound information to its material substrate had been finally vanquished. Yet the public-key cryptography framework generated surprising new possibilities and challenges for information hiding.

I begin by outlining the case for the public-key paradigm as argued by Diffie and Hellman in "New Directions" and its first successful realization by Rivest, Shamir, and Adleman. I then review the main episodes of the "crypto wars," as well as some of the defining research programs that emerged in the 1990s, including Gustavus Simmons's "Science of Information Integrity," Oded Goldreich's quest for proper foundations, and David Chaum's inquiry into authentication and anonymity.

Decentralized Cryptography

The problem of key distribution was, in Diffie and Hellman's analysis, *the* central problem to overcome if electronic networks were to fulfill their potential for business:

> In order to use cryptography to insure privacy, however, it is currently necessary for the communicating parties to share a key which is known to no one else. This is done by sending the key in advance over some secure channel, such as private courier or registered mail. A private conversation between two people with no prior acquaintance is a common occurrence in business, however, and it is unrealistic to expect initial business contacts to be postponed long enough for keys to be transmitted by some physical means. The cost and delay imposed by this key distribution problem is a major barrier to the transfer of business communications to large teleprocessing networks.[4]

Using traditional (secret key) cryptography, in a computer network comprising a large number of users (say, n), each pair of users must establish a common key (see figure 3.1). Doing so requires a quadratic (n^2) number of key pairs, because each of the n users needs to establish a key with $n-1$ other users, along with a corresponding number of communication rounds between users to establish the keys. Diffie and Hellman argued

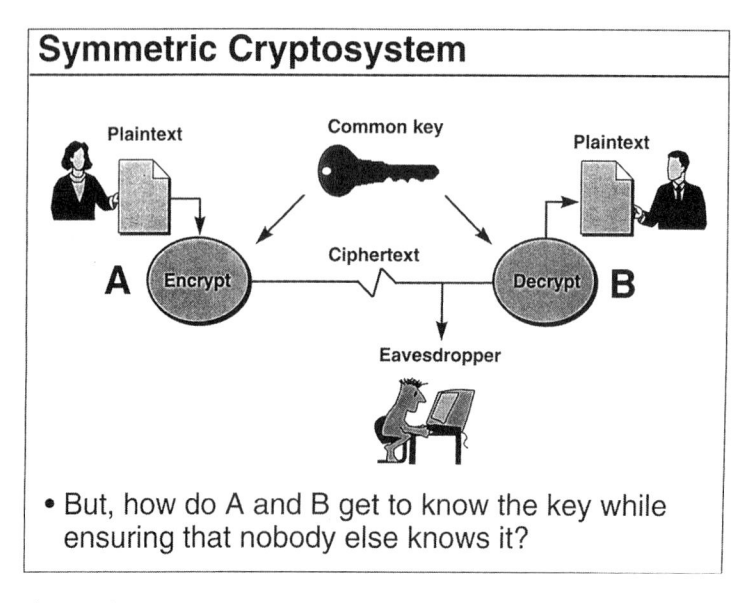

Symmetric Cryptosystem

- But, how do A and B get to know the key while ensuring that nobody else knows it?

Figure 3.1
Secret-key (symmetric) cryptography. To illustrate the definition of the cryptographic signature model, I use slides representative of the kinds that were ubiquitous in cryptography-related conferences in the 1990s. They are meant to serve both as pedagogical aids and exhibits of the process I seek to illuminate. The slides feature the legitimate participants to the protocol (Alice and Bob), as well as the adversary that seeks to defeat the security objectives of their communication. Image courtesy of Dr. Warwick Ford.

that this would be, in effect, a burden so significant as to all but negate the benefits of electronic communications.

One solution lay in equipping networks with centralized key distribution centers, "trusted third parties" that could provide each pair of users with the required key pairs without the need for prior interaction. As he later explained, Diffie viewed such solutions with suspicion: "The virtue of cryptography should be that you don't have to trust anybody directly involved with your communications."[5] He felt that any system that relied on centralized authority put the user at risk of having her personal information disclosed, even if that authority was well intentioned. The very existence of the keys in a centralized system would inevitably lead to their compromise, as authorities could simply present the system operator with a subpoena: "That person would sell you out because he had no interest in defying the order and going to jail to protect your data."[6]

Centralized systems thus involved institutions devoted to their own protection, rather than users' privacy. Diffie envisioned the solution as the development of cryptographic privacy-protection tools which would effectively put the user at the wheel: "Diffie believed in what he called 'a decentralized view of authority.' By creating the proper cryptographic tools, he felt, you could solve the problem—by transferring the data protection from a disinterested third party to the actual user, the one whose privacy was actually at risk."[7]

In "New Directions," Diffie and Hellman proposed two new methods for transmitting keys over public (i.e., insecure) channels without compromising their security: the first method, which they called *public key distribution system* (now commonly known as Diffie-Hellman key agreement), enabled users to establish a common key over a public channel in such a way that an eavesdropper could not deduce the key even though it had access to the entire exchange.[8] The second method, *public-key cryptography*, would write a new and defining chapter in the contemporary evolution of the field.

Diffie and Hellman's system was deceptively simple. The solution lay in splitting the key in two components: a *public* and a *private* part. Each user on the network is assigned such a pair of keys. The private part is kept secret by each user; the public part is made available to all other users on the network. Imagine two such users, Alice and Bob (see figure 3.2). If user Alice wants to send a confidential message to user Bob, she obtains his public key and uses it as the enciphering key before sending him the resulting encrypted message. The message can then be decrypted by Bob using his private key. The trick lies in the mathematical relationship between the public and the private part of the key: although each key provides the inverse function of the other, even with significant computational resources it would require considerable time to deduce the private from the public portion of the key.

The system effectively solved the problems identified by Diffie with respect to secret key cryptosystems. It relieved users from having to establish a common key with every other user in the system prior to communicating with them. As the need for interaction arose, a user could simply fetch other users' public keys, which would be conveniently stored in a public directory indexed by their names. Theoretically, key distribution was thus reduced to the problem of correctly maintaining the public directory and protecting it against malicious modifications.

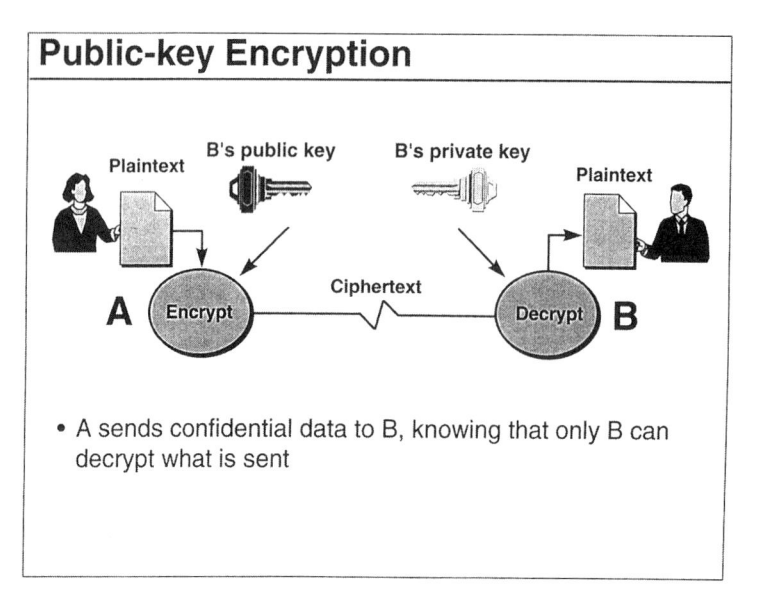

Figure 3.2
Public-key (asymmetric) cryptography. Image courtesy of Dr. Warwick Ford.

Diffie and Hellman suggested that the *one-way functions* used in login procedures provided a useful example of the mathematical basis of public key cryptography. When a user enters her password *pw* for the first time on the system, a function *f(pw)* is calculated, Rather than the actual password, it is the result of this function that is stored in the system. When the user logs in again, the same function is applied to the typed password, and the result is compared with that stored in the system. For the system to be secure, it must be hard to *invert f*. That is, given the stored information *f(pw)*, it must be difficult to find *pw*. Such functions are called one-way functions "if for any argument *x* in the domain *f*, it is easy to compute the corresponding value *f(x)*, yet, for almost all *y* in the range of *f*, it is computationally infeasible to solve the equation *y* = *f(x)* for any suitable argument *x*."[9] Diffie and Hellman characterized public key cryptosystems as *trapdoor one-way functions*: "These are functions that are not really one-way in that simply computed inverses exist. But given an algorithm for the forward function, it is computationally infeasible to find a simply computed inverse. Only through knowledge of certain trapdoor information can one easily find the easily computed inverse."[10]

Thus, a public-key cryptosystem was achievable if one could find functions that could be efficiently computed in forward mode (using the public key) but were computationally infeasible to invert unless one knew of a certain trapdoor (the private key). Diffie and Hellman could not, however, offer a practical realization of the principle. Although they examined a number of possible solutions to the problem, including matrix inversion, none proved sufficiently hard to invert. The honor of finding a suitable candidate for the first trapdoor one-way function would instead befall in 1978 to three MIT computer science researchers, Ronald Rivest, Adi Shamir, and Leonard Adleman (whose last names would provide the RSA acronym).[11] Their solution tapped into classical number theory problems, the computational differential between multiplication and prime decomposition (factoring) of integers.

The fundamental theorem of arithmetic states that every positive integer *n* can be written as the product of prime factors, that is, numbers no further divisible. 1, 2, 3, 5, 7, 11, 13, 17, and 19 are prime numbers; 20 is a composite number that can be written as the product $2 \times 2 \times 5$. The interest of this lies in the fact that though there are known efficient procedures for multiplying two numbers, no similarly efficient procedure is known to exist for calculating the *inverse function*, that is, finding the prime decomposition of a composite number. In computational terms, it is "easy" to multiply any two numbers and obtain their product, but it is "difficult" to reverse the procedure and find the prime factors of a number, unless of course one happens to know this decomposition in advance. In the RSA system, this decomposition is Diffie and Hellman's trapdoor: Alice generates the public key by multiplying two large prime numbers, but because she has knowledge of the prime decomposition of the public key, she can easily compute the inverse, yet anyone who has access to only the public key is forced to attempt to calculate its prime decomposition. Although such a calculation is conjectured to be "computationally infeasible," the absence of formal proof of the difficulty of factoring integers constitutes one of cryptography's most famous "known unknown."[12]

Regardless of this uncertainty, the RSA paper established number theory as the new practical foundation for the mathematics of cryptography. It spurred a gold rush for the discovery of additional suitable problems—discrete logarithms, quadratic residuosity, factorization of polynomials over finite fields, and so on—on which to base public-key cryptographic schemes. Each of these problems involves different *computational assumptions*, distinct conjectures about the difficulty of calculating inverse functions for the scheme. The RSA paper also spurred immediate interest in several hitherto obscure areas of applied mathematics: factoring, prime number generation, and modular exponentiation, the main numerical operation in RSA encryption and decryption.[13]

To cryptography's public image as an esoteric alchemical experiment with the mathematics of language, number theory added an equally powerful mystique: prime numbers and their mysterious Platonic properties. No other mathematical object conjures such powerful feelings among mathematicians: "Upon looking at these numbers, one has the feeling of being in the presence of one of the inexplicable secrets of creation."[14] In his final collection of essays, popular scientist Martin Gardner uses them to justify his unwavering commitment to mathematical Platonism: "If all sentient beings in the universe disappeared," he writes, "there would remain a sense in which mathematical objects and theorems would continue to exist even though there would be no one around to write or talk about them. Huge prime numbers would continue to be prime even if no one had proved them prime."[15] Combined with binary encoding, they are the purest expression of signal versus noise, enabling the creation of messages "that makes communication transparently simple."[16] Indeed, the binary encoding of prime numbers forms the basis for the messages sent by extraterrestrial beings in Carl Sagan's *Contact* and part of the message sent to potential alien life forms by the Arecibo radio telescope.

The publication of the RSA paper (first as a technical report) was immediately picked up by science journalists: Gina Kolata reported on it in *Science*, and Martin Gardner devoted a column to the "MIT cipher" in the August 1977 issue of *Scientific American*.[17] Gardner's column, "A New Kind of Cipher That Would Take Millions of Years to Break," gave birth to an enduring genre of cryptographic research rhetoric, the *key factorization contest*, as he called readers to a challenge to break a message enciphered with RSA using a key of 129 bits by recovering the factors p and q of the public key. "Millions of years" turned into the slightly shorter period of seventeen years, as the ciphertext "the magic words are squeamish ossifrage" was revealed in 1994.[18] Spurred on by the increase of interest in public key cryptography, mathematicians had significantly improved the efficiency of existing factoring algorithms, and in the ensuing decades, performance anxiety based on key size would become a recurrent theme in cryptographic culture.

Cryptography and National Security

The successive publication of David Kahn's *The Codebreakers* in 1967, Feistel's overview of Lucifer in *Scientific American* in 1973, Diffie and Hellman's "New Directions" in 1976, the DES standard in 1977, and the RSA paper in 1978 fostered the rapid development of an academic cryptographic research community. It gathered in August 1981 at the University of California, Santa Barbara, for the first academic conference devoted to cryptographic research, CRYPTO '81. The following year, a group of attendees, including David Chaum, Whitfield Diffie, and David Kahn, met to establish the International Association for Cryptologic Research (IACR).[19]

The conferences were the theater of some dramatic exchanges between this burgeoning community and the NSA, which viewed with increasing anxiety public dissemination and discussion of technologies with direct relevance to national security.[20] The NSA warned the community that public presentations of cryptographic research might be in possible violation of the 1954 Munitions Control Act. It followed up with attempts to control researchers' NSF funding.[21] In 1982, then director of the NSA Admiral Bobby Imann proposed a truce to the community in the form of a *mandatory review agreement*, arguing that

> If the scientists did not agree to the voluntary review of their work by the intelligence agencies, they would face a "tidal wave" of public outrage that will lead to laws restricting the publication of scientific work that the government might consider "sensitive" on national security grounds. . . . Imann warned a meeting of the AAAS that "the tides are moving, and moving fast, toward legislated solutions that in fact are likely to be much more restrictive, not less restrictive, than the voluntary censorship system."[22]

Such warnings stood in stark contrast to the cryptographic community's embrace of the scientific ethos of open communication: David Kahn's report on CRYPTO '82 features a picture of a broadly smiling Adi Shamir shaking hands with Len Adleman (respectively, the S and A of RSA), congratulating him over the break of the Graham-Shamir knapsack public-key algorithm.[23] The handshake powerfully symbolized the new ethics of codemaking and codebreaking, activities now openly performed in public forums by scientists allied in the common pursuit of objective knowledge.

In 1986, further restrictions on public dissemination were attempted through the use of the patent secrecy system, which enables the Patent and Trademark Office to prevent the disclosure or publication of any subject matter deemed detrimental to national security.[24] By the 1990s, however, cryptography enjoyed amounts of public attention rarely experienced by an esoteric mathematical field, emerging as the "first political movement in the digital era."[25] Cryptographers appeared on the cover of the *New York Times Magazine* and *Wired*, and articles on the use of cryptography for privacy protection appeared in *Scientific American* and *Communications of the ACM*.

It was thus with a renewed sense of purpose that the community embarked in the mid-1990s in another round of confrontation with the intelligence establishment. This time, the battle concerned the social and technical adequacy of a system known as the *Clipper chip* and a set of rules restricting the export of cryptographic products outside of the United States. The issues, collectively known as "the crypto debate," spawned a small policy industry, sharply divided along pro–law enforcement and cyberlibertarian lines. Because widespread access to encryption technologies would result in diminish wiretapping capabilities for law enforcement, the Clipper proposal sought to ensure that every communication device in the United States be equipped with capabilities for *key escrow*, to be accessed by authorities as required by circumstances. Export controls sought to diminish the dissemination of technologies felt to be an essential element of national security, by limiting the export of so-called strong cryptography, that is, products with key lengths thought sufficient to defeat the capabilities of intelligence agencies.

The cryptographic research community largely espoused the cyberlibertarian position. It argued that access to cryptography was essential to a democratic society increasingly structured around computer networks and provided the only effective tool to escape the looming onslaught of Big Brotherism.[26] Some saw even greater potential for public-key encryption. Timothy May, an Intel engineer and founder of the "Cypherpunk" mailing list, prophesied that free cryptography would act as "the wire clippers which dismantle the barbed wire around intellectual property" and unleash an age of digital anarchy.[27] Some academics even concurred: "With the widespread availability of various technologies (such as public-key cryptography), it now appears that certain anarchist ideals may be possible, if not inevitable."[28] The idea that mere regulation could prevent the spread of such powerful technologies seemed positively quaint, a point the community drove home through a series of highly publicized and spectacular pranks.

Strong Cryptography Wants to Be Free

Throughout the crypto debate, cryptolibertarians engineered practical demonstrations that regulation could not, so to speak, stuff the cryptographic genie back into the bottle. One particular software package, PGP (for *Pretty Good Privacy*), became the movement's *cause célèbre*, and its author, Phil Zimmerman, its first martyr, after becoming in 1993 the target of a three-year criminal investigation over possible breach of export laws. Freely downloadable from the Internet and relatively easy to install, PGP brought military strength public-key cryptography to personal computers. Using PGP, individuals could set up public key pairs and exchange encrypted files over email. To underline the incoherence of export laws, which prohibited the distribution of the program on electronic media but not in book form, Zimmerman and the MIT Press published the source code of PGP in book form, in a format designed to aid the scanning and optical character recognition of the entire book.[29]

Taking the idea of embedding programming code into a material artifact one step further, another prank coded the RSA algorithm in a mere three lines of the Perl programming language (figure 3.3). Printed on a T-shirt (figure 3.4), affixed to emails as a signature, or even tattooed on a forearm (figure 3.5), the lines of code instantly transformed the messenger into an international arms trafficker, demonstrating the irrelevance of antiquated export laws to the reality of modern information flows.

```
#!/bin/perl    -sp0777i<X+d*lMLa^*lN%0]dsXx++lMlN/dsM0<j]dsj
$/=unpack('H*',$_)  ;$_= `echo 16dio\U$k"SK$/SM$n\EsN0p[lN*1
lK[d2%Sa2/d0$^Ixp"|dc`;s/\W//g;$_=pack('H*',/((..)*)$/)
```

Figure 3.3
The RSA algorithm in three lines of Perl. Figure by the author.

Figure 3.4
Munitions T-shirt, front. Printed on clothing, the RSA in Perl algorithm promised to instantly transform ordinary citizens into international arms traffickers. Available at http://www.cypherspace.org/adam/uk-shirt.html, used by permission.

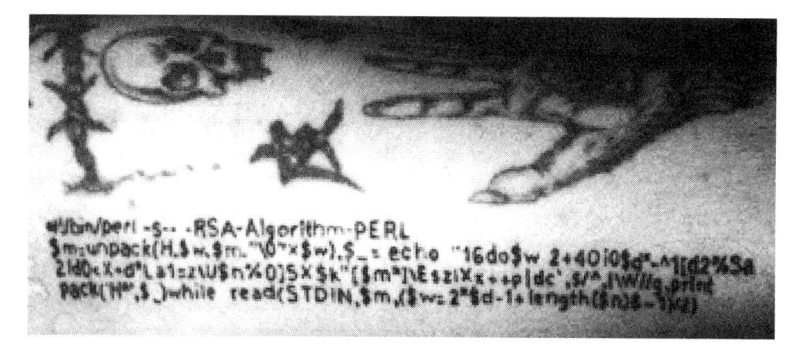

Figure 3.5
Richard White's RSA tattoo. Available at http://www.cypherspace.org/rsa, used by permission.

In another demonstration of this irrelevance, Ron Rivest proposed a mechanism that performed encryption using authentication and steganographic techniques, both of which lay outside the scope of export regulations. He commented: "As usual, the policy debate about regulating technology ends up being obsolete by technological innovations. . . . Mandating government access to all communications is not a viable alternative. The cryptography debate should proceed by mutual education and voluntary actions only."[30]

The never-ending suspicions over the inadequacy of DES were also given renewed vigor by John Gilmore, a cofounder of the Electronic Frontier Foundation (EFF). Taking up a suggestion in Diffie and Hellman's 1977 analysis of the standard, he funded the development of a "DES Cracker" machine, designed specifically to break the cipher through exhaustive key search. Relying on 1,500 custom chips, the machine broke DES in 1998 and 1999, the first time in three days, the second time in less than twenty-four hours through collaboration with a distributed computing initiative. Breaking DES underlined how the then-current 56-bit key length was inadequate, the same key length above which products were deemed "strong" and consequently restricted by export regulations.[31] Both breaks were winning entries in the "DES Challenges" sponsored by RSA Data Security, the business entity holding the patents to the public-key RSA algorithms. By providing actual metrics for the strength of DES, the "Cracker" was explicitly designed to influence policy makers: "The Electronic Frontier Foundation hopes that this book inspires a new level of truth to enter the policy debates on encryption. In order to make wise choices for our society, we must make well-informed choices. Great deference has been paid to the perspective and experience of the National Security Agency and Federal Bureau of Investigation in these debates. This is particularly remarkable given the lack of any way for policy-makers or the public to check the accuracy of many of their statements."[32]

To further highlight the incongruence of encryption regulation, the Electronic Privacy Information Center, an advocacy group based in Washington, published in 1998, 1999, and 2000 a review of encryption regulation across the globe, noting that "there are a small number of countries where strong domestic controls on the use of cryptography are in place. These include Belarus, China, Israel, Pakistan, Russia, and Singapore. . . . The policies of the United States are the most surprising, given the fact that virtually all of the other democratic, industrial nations have few if any controls on the use of cryptography. The position may be explained, in part, by the dominant role that state security agencies in the U.S. hold in the development of encryption policy."[33]

Collaborators

A few cryptographers sought more conciliatory positions, most famously Dorothy Denning, then a professor of computer science at Georgetown. Denning saw crypto anarchy as a undesirable threat, arguing "Our information superways require responsible conduct just as our interstate highways require. Key escrow encryption has emerged as one approach that can meet the confidentiality and data recovery needs of organizations while allowing authorized government access to fight terrorism and crime."[34]

Silvio Micali, a colleague of Ron Rivest in the theoretical computer science group at MIT, also felt there was room for compromise between the ability to protect one's conversations and the legitimate needs of law enforcement. Arguing that cryptographic technologies could in fact provide the means to satisfy both camps, he proposed the concept of *fair cryptosystems*, in which the power of law enforcement is mitigated by the split of the private key into two parts, with one part recoverable solely in cooperation with a trusted third party. His paper began with a lengthy exposé on the merits of a conciliatory approach:

> There is a legitimate concern that wide-spread use of public-key cryptography may be a big boost for criminal and terrorist organizations. Indeed, many bills propose that a proper governmental agency, under the circumstances allowed by the law, be able to obtain the clear text of any communication over a public network. . . . It is not surprising that such alternatives have legitimately alarmed many concerned citizens, generating the feeling that privacy should come before national security and law enforcement.[35]

Micali's solution consisted in splitting the secret key into a number of shares to be entrusted to independent trustees (i.e., "federal judges, Congress . . . a civil rights group"). In the event of a court order, the shares could be united to reconstruct the private key and thus decrypt encrypted communications. The idea was, in Micali's word, to improve "the security of the existing communication systems, while *keeping the legal procedures* already holding and accepted by the society."[36] Micali argued that fair cryptosystems were, in fact, "close in spirit to Democracy itself, in that power is not trusted to any chosen individual (read "trustee") but to a multiplicity of delegated individuals."[37] Micali's patents were eventually bought by the U.S. government and the concept of "fairness" has enjoyed a respectable career as a design feature of various cryptographic protocols—for example, anonymous electronic cash whose traceability can nevertheless be switched back on to meet the needs of law enforcement.

Perhaps the most surprising compromise was offered by none other than Whitfield Diffie and Susan Landau. In *Privacy on the Line*, a review of the crypto policy debates, they provided extensive arguments that any attempt to regulate the spread of encryption technologies was at best futile, and at worst antidemocratic. Yet the authors suggested to the intelligence community that the ensuing loss of wiretapping capabilities might be offset by an unexpected consolation:

Tactical communications intelligence will probably improve despite the prevalence of encryption. Cryptography is much less successful at concealing patterns of communication than at concealing the contents of messages. In many environments, addresses (and, equally important, precedences) must be left in clear so that routers will know how packets are to be forwarded. In most environments, the lengths and timings of messages are difficult to conceal. SIGINT organizations are already adept at extracting intelligence from traffic patterns and will adapt to extract more. The resulting intelligence product, abetted by increases in computer power, may not give as detailed a picture in some places but will give a more comprehensive overview.[38]

In other words, although individual communications might become untappable, communication patterns will fill in the missing intelligence glue. Even better, this new form of intelligence will increase in quality, as social intercourse increasingly takes place over computer networks, providing intelligence agencies endless opportunities for traffic analysis and electronic profiling.

Similarly, law enforcement would find its losses greatly mitigated by the enhanced opportunities for low-level social control offered by information technologies. Diffie and Landau pointed out that "the police are a mechanism of social control, and their work goes hand in hand with other mechanisms of social control. . . . Employees in many jobs are now monitored by machines. Workers who once had substantial autonomy, such as truck drivers, find that they are subject to the same sort of close monitoring that might have been expected on a factory floor."[39] Thus, fears that the spread of strong cryptography would wreak havoc on intelligence gathering and law enforcement were greatly exaggerated. What government control of cryptography would inexorably defeat was "the great vision of electronic commerce," "an orgy of buying and selling over the Internet." Fortunately for all parties, "the fight for cryptographic freedom ... is a fight in which privacy and commerce are on the same side."[40]

In many respects, the crypto debate comfortably fitted with traditional understandings of science-based innovation in which its scientific, technical, and social dimensions are understood to operate in largely distinct and consecutive phases. In contrast, and in the same period, the cryptographic research community articulated several distinct research programs, programs defining much more complex relationships between the content of cryptographic research itself, the physical artifacts it sought to reproduce in electronic environments, and the social contexts in which such artifacts would eventually operate.

Cryptographic Research Programs

By the beginning of the 1990s, the cryptography community had seemingly turned on its head a centuries-old relationship with the state, a relationship that had committed the field to obscurity, secrecy, and national security. Even better, cryptographers found themselves celebrated as heroes of the coming Internet's revolution and rode a wave of exciting scientific innovation unleashed by the public-key paradigm. This profound shift in their public and professional image was also reflected in a newfound sense of purpose. As articulated by leaders in the field, the research program for contemporary cryptography defined areas of investigation vastly larger than cryptography's historical dedication to the design of tools for confidentiality. I highlight four important research orientations that emerged during that period: (1) designing the full range of information security analogues; (2) establishing firm theoretical foundations for the field; (3) preventing leakage through subliminal channels; (4) and reconciling authentication and anonymity.

The Science of Information Integrity

In "New Directions," Diffie and Hellman noted that the coming emergence of data networks would require appropriate substitutes be found to the paper records required for business intercourse. Unlike previous electronic authentication schemes, they argued public-key cryptosystems could provide a "purely digital replacement" for signed written contracts. The use of cryptography to "sign" digital documents seemed to point to a more general role it might play in providing other analogues to paper-based evidence. An important collection of papers published in 1992, *Contemporary Cryptology: The Science of Information Integrity*, signaled this shift away from narrower concerns with confidentiality. In his introduction, Gustavus Simmons contextualized at length the basis for this conceptual shift:

> The conduct of commerce, affairs of the state, military actions, and personal affairs all depend on the parties to a transaction having confidence in there being means of accomplishing such functions as privacy, proof of identity, authority, ownership, license, signature, witnessing or notarization, date of action, certification of origination and/or receipt, etc. As a result, an elaborate, and legally accepted, collection of procedural and physical protocols have evolved that specify how to create records (information in documentary form) in such a way that later disputes as to who is liable, or of the nature of that liability, or of when a liability was incurred, etc., can be arbitrated by a third party (typically in a court of law). The essential point is that existing precedent depends on information having a physical existence in the form of a document which have been signed, witnessed, notarized, recorded, dated, etc. The "proof" process, if it must be invoked, depends almost entirely on the physical instrument(s) as the means for establishing the integrity of the recorded information.[41]

In this view, digital information no longer had any material existence that could provide means for its authentication. In the context of electronic networks, the various forms of resistance provided by the intimate binding of ink to paper fibers cease to obtain. Only mathematical (i.e., cryptographic) transformations of the information itself could and would provide the constraints necessary for information to achieve the same functions:

> In an information-intensive society however, in which the possession, control, transfer, or access to real assets is frequently based on incorporeal information—that is, information whose existence is not essentially linked to any physical record, and in which a license (to use, modify, copy, etc., valuable or sensitive information) is similarly determined, it is essential that means be found to carry out all of the functions associated with establishing the integrity of information mentioned above, based only on the internal evidence present in the information itself . . . as distinguished from other non-information-dependent means such as documentary records, physical security, etc.[42]

Simmons thus saw the business of cryptography as the design of analogues for the wide range of methods, protocols, and artifacts with which to "prevent cheating." The entire range of information integrity functions—identification, authorization, license, certification, signature, notarization, concurrence, liability, receipts, endorsement, validation, time of occurrence, authenticity of files, vote, proof of ownership, and of course, privacy—were in need of such cryptographic analogues.

The *Handbook of Applied Cryptography*, the defining summary of the field as it stood in 1997, reiterated much of Simmons's analysis of the immateriality of digital information: "What is needed then for a society where information is mostly stored and transmitted in electronic form is a means to ensure information security which is independent of the physical medium recording or conveying it and such that the objectives of information security rely solely on digital information itself."[43] It also made the call for cryptography to provide "analogues of the 'paper protocols' currently in use," arguing that the shift to the digital presented "a unique opportunity for society to introduce new and more efficient ways of ensuring information security."[44] Information security would require a mixture of technical and legal skills, and the technical means would be "provided through cryptography." Such concerns with ensuring law and order on the electronic frontier stood in vivid contrast with cryptography's renegade, cyberlibertarian image.

Firm Foundations

Another important research direction sought to continue Diffie and Hellman's initial impetus to establish solid mathematical foundations to the ad hoc collections of techniques generated over the years by the community. Not only were cryptographers facing a much broader range of security goals than mere encryption, but the security afforded by the number theoretic problems underlying public-key cryptography remained largely undefined. Even while working from a much more mathematical framework, much of the proofs for cryptographic primitives and protocols still appeared unsystematic. Beginning in the early 1990s, Oded Goldreich, cryptography's most famous advocate of foundationalism, has called on cryptographers to develop a coherent framework for proving the security of cryptosystems: "It is our opinion that the design of cryptographic systems has to be based on firm foundations; whereas ad-hoc approaches and heuristics are a very dangerous way to go."[45]

In a similar vein to Simmons's "information integrity" program, Goldreich's quest for firm foundations appears a primarily conservative endeavor. It proceeds from a definition of cryptography committed to the prevention of cheating: "Cryptography is concerned with the construction of schemes which are robust against malicious attempts to make these schemes deviate from their prescribed functionality." These prescribed functionalities would originate from cryptographers' "definitional activity," which Goldreich describes as "the identification, conceptualization and rigorous definition of cryptographic tasks which capture natural security concerns."[46] The simple and elegant lines of such a characterization stand in contrast with the inherent complexity of Simmons's project: could the myriad issues inevitable in the design of digital analogues to paper-based protocols—from signatures to voting and cash—be reduced to the capture and identification of "natural security concerns"?

In any case, cryptographers heeded the call and embarked on the arduous task of providing clear definitions of the entire cryptographic toolbox. The toolbox included simple primitives (e.g., block ciphers, hash functions), the building blocks from which more complex systems could be built, but also protocols, whereby several participants interact in order to realize a security objective, for example, the creation and verification of a signature. Although the task of proving the security of basic primitives has met with some levels of success, proving the security of protocols has proved more challenging, a process I discuss at more length in chapter 7.

Notably, none of the major reference works and textbooks published during this period—that is, Doug Stinson's *Cryptography: Theory and Practice*, Ron Rivest's "Cryptography" entry in the *Handbook of Theoretical Computer Science*, and the *Handbook of Applied Cryptography*—include steganography as part of these foundational efforts.[47] In spite of these disciplinary commitments, issues relative to the concealment of information would make a surprising reappearance, in fact, within the very heart of public key cryptosystems.

Subliminal Channels

If cryptography is indeed about communication in the presence of adversaries, then it also about the perhaps less intuitive cases in which the communicating parties *themselves* are the adversaries. In 1981, Manuel Blum proposed a protocol enabling cryptography's most famous couple, Alice and Bob, to flip a coin over the phone ("They have just divorced, live in different cities, want to decide who gets the car").[48] In 1991, Simmons, a cryptographer working at Sandia National Laboratories,—a R&D facility specialized in nuclear security and nonproliferation—reported on a similar issue: how could the Soviet Union and the United States collaborate and agree on methods for verifying compliances with SALT treaties requiring test bans and reduction in nuclear arsenals?[49]

Implementing Reagan's famous quip, "trust but verify," required placing unmanned seismic sensors monitoring Russia's compliance with the test ban. Though such sensors would return precisely delimited information back to the United States, how could the Americans be sure that the Russians would not tamper with the information emitted by the censors? Encryption would work, but how could the Russians then be assured that no extra strategic information would be communicated by the sensors? The issue required two mutually distrustful parties to engage in a collaborative process yet achieve security goals to their mutual satisfaction.

In his wide-ranging investigation of these issues, Simmons discovered that the authentication mechanisms used for such purposes could be subverted to provide a hidden communication channel, which he called a "subliminal channel." He further demonstrated that various digital signature schemes could be used to communicate secret information through such a high-capacity subliminal channel and that the very existence of the channel could be proved only by breaking the digital signature scheme itself.[50] He eventually concluded that "any time redundant information is introduced into a communication to provide an overt function such as digital signatures, error detection and/or correction, authentication, etc., it may be possible to subvert the purported function to create a covert (subliminal) communications channel."[51]

Adam Young and Moti Yung further developed Simmons's discovery as it applied to the covert operation of encryption systems, developing a research agenda they humorously named "Kleptography."[52] In a series of papers, they demonstrated that "black-box" cryptosystems—that is, cryptographic systems embedded in closed hardware devices—can be subverted by their manufacturers so as to capture and "subliminally" transmit users' private keys in the output of the system itself. Young and Yung showed that important digital signatures algorithms such as RSA, El-Gamal, and even the DSA federal standard could be subverted to effectively turn cryptographic devices against their users.

Young and Yung's research was motivated by the U.S. government's "Capstone" proposal to develop cryptographic algorithms for encryption, signature, key exchange, and hashing and embed them in a hardware chip. Given that the specifications of the encryption algorithm were classified, "kleptography" provided additional arguments for the essential function for peer review of cryptographic code by the scientific community: "Capstone, cryptographic servers, and cryptographic libraries are all guards used to prevent system infiltration . . . measures need to be taken to guard these guards."[53]

Reconciling Authentication and Anonymity

Another strand of the problem of mutual cooperation in the absence of trust was picked up by David Chaum, one of cryptography's most visible figure in the 1980s and 1990s. Unlike Simmons, Chaum did not view cryptography's role as merely replicating existing paper-and-pen protocols. Rather, he envisioned it as an active intervention in severing the link between increased computerization and data collection practices.

In several widely read publications, Chaum articulated a broad-reaching research program seeking to provide the mathematical foundations for the design of computer systems supportive of transactional anonymity—for example, pseudonym systems and anonymous cash.[54] Whereas Simmons had sought to unlink authentication from secrecy, Chaum sought to unlink authentication from identification and developed a series of cryptographic techniques whereby participants could perform information exchange protocols with surprising properties. Chaum called his central technique for ensuring transactional anonymity "blind signatures," which could be applied to payment, voting, or credentials systems. A blind signature is a verifiable digital signature on a document (say, a bank note), with the property that the signatory has seen neither the document nor the resulting digital signature. A bank could, for example, issue such signed bank notes and provide customers with the assurance that it could not trace its subsequent use.[55] The implications of Chaum's work were important for global networking, suggesting ways to make traffic analysis difficult for several types of transactions.

Chaum's entrepreneurial ambitions led him to secure numerous patents on his ideas. He founded DigiCash in 1990, a celebrated start-up that sought to commercialize anonymous electronic cash but eventually filed for bankruptcy in 1999.[56] Although Chaum seemingly could not quite bring his proposals into lasting commercial success, his work opened up not only durable research avenues but also—more importantly—a certain design space. That space suggested that computers need not necessarily be linked with images of surveillance and social control and that coherent and creative scientific research programs could be driven by explicitly social goals—in this case, privacy protection, anonymity, and their implications for democratic participation.[57]

At the same time, Chaum shared in some of the assumptions that have come to characterize the culture of modern cryptographic research. First, the joining of networked computers and cryptography would vastly outperform paper-based security technologies: "Coupling computers to telecommunications technologies creates what has been called the ultimate medium—it certainly is a big step up from paper."[58] Second, cryptographic methods would provide the means to altogether avoid centralized trust mechanisms: "With modern cryptology, we can solve any information security problem just by letting each person have their own computer. Let them use their own computer to protect their own interests. There is no need at all to have any mutually trusted mechanisms."[59]

Conclusion

"New Directions" indeed ushered in a new era in the world of cryptography, on multiple levels. Most visibly, in the wake of the public-key revolution, it led to the emergence of an independent academic community, eager to distance itself from the "Dark Side" of intelligence agencies and state controls over cryptographic research. Yet beyond the media-friendly image of cryptographers as defenders of electronic freedoms, multiple agendas operated simultaneously within the field. These agendas encompassed a broad spectrum of relationships to state authority and power— from May's "crypto anarchy" to Simmons's "science of information integrity," Goldreich's foundationalist project, and Diffie's trade-offs between individual privacy and population controls. They also differed in their conceptualization of the role of cryptography proper: should it be concerned with the crafting of digital analogues of paper-based security protocols, with the identification of cryptographic tasks that capture "natural security concerns," or with a more explicit commitment to value-driven design of cryptographic tools?

Whatever their position on these issues, cryptographers exhibited the firm convictions that technology trumps regulation every time and that encryption as code could not be caged and—once released—would inevitably roam free, spreading security, freedom of speech, and democracy in its wake. In making their case, the community developed a playful style of policy interventions, deriding attempts at controlling encryption through regulation. Ironically, to craft these interventions, they often dipped into the steganographic toolbox, embedding code into material carriers to demonstrate the invincibility of the digital. Indeed, though mostly shut out of the official modern cryptography canon, steganography continued to demonstrate its relevance, as public-key mechanisms exhibited surprising properties of concealment, with the potential to blackmail users with their own keys. The possibility of funkspiels, of hidden trapdoors, thus continued to threaten public confidence in cryptographic technologies, even as cryptographers struggled with establishing the coherent mathematical foundations that would ground their own trust.

Regardless of these debates, by the mid-1990s, cryptography's agenda had expanded far beyond its traditional focus on military applications of encryption. Instead, it concerned itself with the design of mathematical analogues to the complex paper-based artifacts and protocols that have evolved over centuries to realize a broad range of security objectives. Of these analogues, signatures seemed to have the most promising future, the best chance of leaping from the serene pages of scientific journals into the hustle and bustle of the real world. In short, signatures might just become crypto's killer app. Such an achievement would first involve designing a fuller model of digital signatures and determine its relationship to paper-based signatures. Eventually, it would also involve determining the legal status of such an object.

4 The Equivalent of a Written Signature

The success of the public-key paradigm gave much impetus to Simmons's research program for cryptography, one that sought to define and create digital analogues to the paper-based artifacts and protocols that provide for information integrity in the social world. Such analogues would have to perform in a radically different material environment than their paper-based counterparts, an environment where information objects are accessible only through the mediation of computing hardware and software, where the usual associations between the materiality of those information objects and their evidential value could no longer be presumed, where parties to the transactions would not be physically present to each other but instead communicating through networks. In the case of cryptographic signatures, performance would have to be measured not only for their viability as a mathematical object, but also as a legally codified means of evidence. In Diffie and Hellman's words, "In order to develop a system capable of replacing the current written contract with some purely electronic form of communication, *we must discover a digital phenomenon with the same properties as a written signature.*"[1]

But what exactly *is* a written signature? Its utter banality seems to require no explanation, yet also raises suspicions of greater complexity. As Béatrice Fraenkel notes, "For us moderns, this sign presents itself over a background of tenacious forgetting."[2] The distant origins of the signature in antiquity and the Middle Ages, its historical evolution and current incarnation as the idiosyncratic writing of one's name, and its relationship to other signs of identity have received little attention from scholars. Its association with another mundane artifact, the record—at once the fundamental instrument of bureaucratic rationalization, and, as Bruno Latour has quipped, "the most despised of all ethnographic objects"—has not helped signature's overall standing.[3]

It is against this background of a seemingly familiar yet potentially mysterious object that the "discovery" of a digital analogue would take place. The process would involve defining a *model*, some specification of the multidimensional physical artifact that would aim to capture the characteristics deemed most pertinent to the digital context. In this chapter, I tease out the gradual construction of the cryptographic signature model, a process that largely took place without explicit recognition of the representational nature of models.

Beginning with Diffie and Hellman's initial suggestion that public-key cryptography could provide the basis for a suitable "equivalent" to handwritten signatures, I review how cryptographers came to define the services that cryptographic signatures would be expected to provide, namely *authentication, integrity,* and *non-repudiation*. I also review the gradual elaboration of a solution to the problem of secure and efficient distribution of public keys, that of *public-key infrastructures* (PKI).

Another window on the modeling practices of the cryptographic community is provided by an activity that extends cryptographic work beyond the mere design of digital analogues to paper-based protocols. The definition of signatures as a cryptographic object with specific mathematical properties opens the possibility for the creation of entirely new types of signatures with unheard-of security properties. I describe some of these new kinds of signatures and the real-world scenarios provided by cryptographers to justify their design. Finally, the various *proof models* under which the security of cryptosystems is mathematically proved are discussed in chapter 7.

My goal here is to map as precisely as possible the contours of digital signatures as an object, usable by cryptographers, users, and the legal process. Which problems did the model solve for each of these groups? Which features of the "real world" artifact did the model encompass, and which were deemed irrelevant? What disciplinary assumptions were brought to bear on the model? How did the practical logic of cryptographic work constrain the scope of the model? How did cryptographers experience and debate the relationship of mathematical work to the "real world"? A precise picture of digital signatures as eventually defined by the cryptographic community will provide the necessary foundation from which to investigate the reception of this object by the legal community in subsequent chapters.

The Early History

Authenticating messages, rather than ensuring their confidentiality, formed the primary motivation for Diffie and Hellman's work on public-key encryption. Working in John McCarthy's AI lab at Stanford, Diffie had been stimulated by discussions over the possibility of computers becoming mainstream appliances and the numerous issues in electronic communications this would bring, including the problem of duplicating customary methods of authentication:

> What would be the computerized version of a receipt? How could you get a computer-generated equivalent of a signed contract? Even if people were given unique "digital signatures"—say a long randomly generated number bequeathed to a single person—the nature of digital media, in which something can be copied in milliseconds would seem to make such an identifier pointless. . . . Diffie began to wonder how one could begin to fix this apparently inherent flaw in the concept of digital commerce.[4]

"New Directions" thus makes the case for solving the problem of authentication in electronic networks at some length, arguing that it presented "perhaps an even more serious barrier to the universal adoption of telecommunications for business transactions than the problem of key distribution."[5] Diffie and Hellman point out to the major shortcoming of symmetric cryptography for the purposes of such transactions: "In order to have a purely digital replacement for this paper instrument [written contracts], each user must be able to produce a message whose authenticity can be checked by anyone, but which could not have been produced by anyone else, even the recipient."[6]

That is, because in symmetric cryptosystems the sender and the receiver share the same secret key, both are confident that no third party has been able to modify the message while in transit. However, because they share the same secret key, there is nothing to prevent either party from modifying the message after it was first sent and reencrypting the message with the secret key. The common secret key will still correctly decrypt the message and both sender and receiver would thus be able to exhibit different versions of the message and claim them to be the original one. Symmetric cryptosystems would thus enable parties to a contract to produce *contradictory evidence* of their commitments. Diffie and Hellman thus argued that the solution to the problem of providing signatures in an electronic environment lay in providing messages *verifiable* by third parties: "Current electronic authentication systems cannot meet the need for a purely digital unforgeable message-dependent signature. They provide protection against third-parties forgeries, but do not protect against disputes between transmitter and receiver."[7]

In these two short sentences, Diffie and Hellman laid out the essential design of cryptographic signatures, a design that has remained largely untouched to this day: a digital signature is (a) *purely digital*; (b) *unforgeable*, in the sense of being uniquely linked to its author; (c) *message-dependent*, that is, uniquely linked to each message; and (d) providing *protection against disputes* between the contracting parties.

Public-key cryptography fulfilled just such properties, if one inversed the procedure required for encryption: to produce a signature, Alice must use her *private key*, and to verify Alice's signature, Bob must use Alice's *public key* (see figures 4.1 and 4.2). That is, Alice encrypts her message using her private key and sends the resulting ciphertext to Bob. Note that the procedure does not provide for confidential communication: because Alice's

Public-key — Authentication Mode

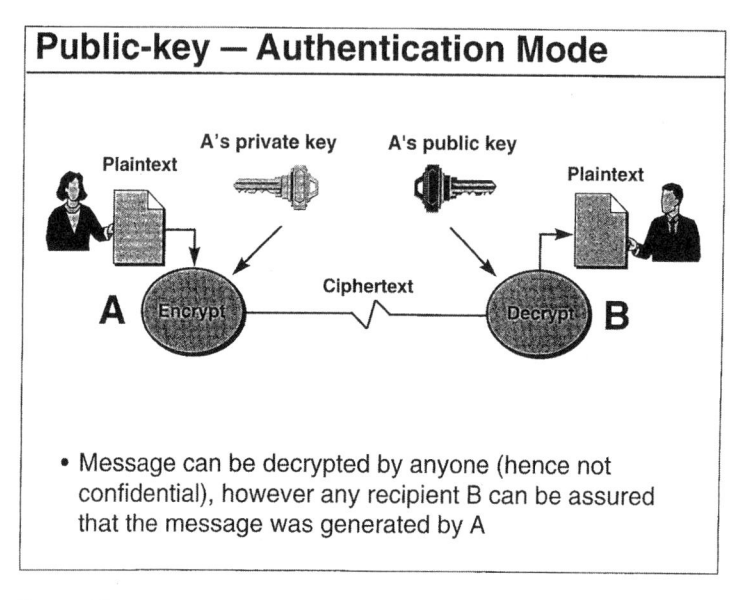

- Message can be decrypted by anyone (hence not confidential), however any recipient B can be assured that the message was generated by A

Figure 4.1
Public-key cryptography, authentication mode. By reversing the order of the keys used to encrypt and decrypt, one obtains an entirely different set of security properties. Image courtesy of Dr. Warwick Ford.

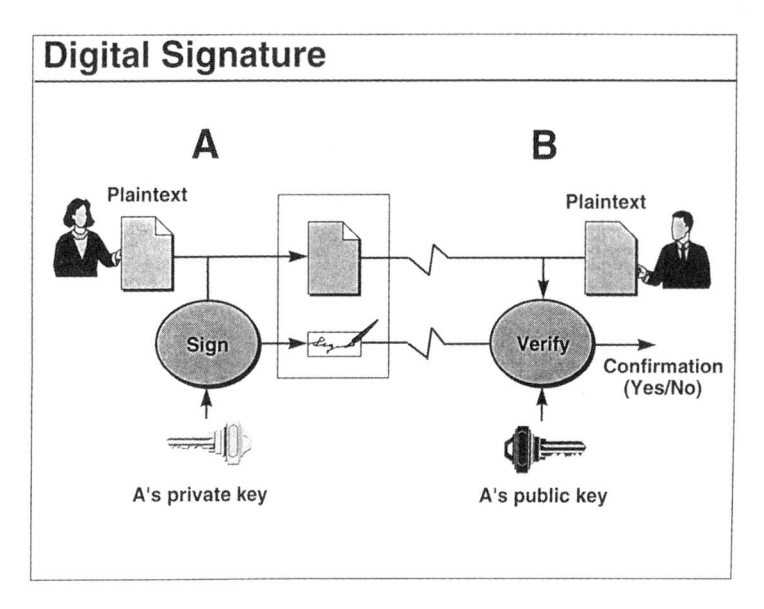

Figure 4.2
The digital signature model. Image courtesy of Dr. Warwick Ford.

public key is publicly available, anyone can decipher the message. But given the unique mathematical relationship that obtains between the public and the private keys, the receiver has confidence the message was encrypted with the private key corresponding to Alice's public key and furthermore, that it was not modified in transit, because otherwise the decryption process would fail.

As noted before, Diffie and Hellman could not offer a concrete realization of trapdoor one-way functions and thus, of digital signatures. The RSA paper, "A Method for Obtaining Digital Signatures and Public-Key Cryptosystems," focused explicitly on the potential of public-key cryptography for digital signatures. The signature algorithm it proposes fulfills the three requirements outlined by Diffie and Hellman: (1) *unforgeability*: if the verification is successful, only the private key corresponding to the public key obtained by Bob could have produced the signature; (2) *message dependence*: if the message is modified after it is signed, the verification will fail; (3) *evidence in case of disputes*: neither Alice nor Bob can hope to modify the message after it has been sent without the verification failing. The authors recognized however that the translation of traditional concepts of "signature" and "proof" into the mathematical context required the cautionary reserve of scare quotes: "Therefore, Alice has received a message 'signed' by Bob, which she can 'prove' that he sent, but which she cannot modify."[8]

A few issues had to be resolved before RSA signatures could become a practical reality, among them computational performance. A major disadvantage of public-key algorithms is their relative inefficiency: in contrast to secret-key algorithms, the arithmetic operations required by RSA are orders of magnitude more computationally intensive. Furthermore, in 1982, cryptographer George Davida discovered an attack against RSA signatures that would eventually prove of considerable import.[9] Under the assumption that it could get a user to sign arbitrary messages (see "chosen-message attacks" in "The Threat of Forgery," later in this chapter), an adversary could break the system and obtain valid signatures on any message of his choice. In 1984, Dorothy Denning proposed to resolve both issues at once.[10] To improve the efficiency of the signing process and thwart Davida's attack, messages should be first compressed using *hash functions* and signed in a single application of the public-key algorithm.

Cryptographic hash functions are algorithms that compress messages into fixed-length strings of bits (usually called hashes, message digests, or fingerprints). That is, given as input a digital object of arbitrary length (e.g., a document, an image, a software program), the hash function will output a fixed-length (e.g., 128- or 160-bit) fingerprint. Because there are only a finite number of strings of 128 or 160 bits, multiple digital objects are bound to have identical fingerprints, in what is a called a "collision." Cryptographic hash functions are designed to be resistant to an adversary taking advantage of such collisions: given an object x and its fingerprint h, it is presumed computationally infeasible to find another object y with the same fingerprint h. Additionally, given a fingerprint h, it is presumed computationally infeasible to reverse the function, that is, to find an object x that hashes to h. In both cases, collision resistance means the best strategy available to an adversary is that of exhaustive search, that is, trying all objects one at a time.[11]

Cryptographic hash functions are now an integral part of the mechanics of RSA signatures, both in theory and practice.[12] Davida's attack and its solution underlined an issue that would become increasingly important over time: the provable security of number-theoretic *algorithms* did not translate without effort in that of cryptographic *protocols*. As Denning noted, "it is not enough to have an encryption algorithm that is computationally hard to break; the procedures for using the algorithm must also withstand attack."[13] Indeed, the breaking of the World War II Enigma machine by the Allies had already powerfully demonstrated the wisdom of such an insight.

Security Services

By the mid-1990s, the expected properties of cryptographic signatures had crystallized in the scientific literature.[14] Remarkably, these had remained largely unchanged from Diffie and Hellman's initial proposal: *certifying the origin of the message* (authentication), *certifying its integrity* (data integrity), and the more vaguely defined *provision of evidence that can be used by an unbiased third party to settle a dispute* (non-repudiation).

Authentication

To authenticate something means, according to the Oxford Dictionary, "to verify its claimed origin or authorship." Digital signatures involve two distinct types of authentication: *message* and *entity authentication*. The former is defined as "a type of authentication whereby a party is corroborated as the (original) source of specified data created at some (typically unspecified) time in the past."[15] The latter is equivalent to identification; that is, one party (the verifier) gains assurance that the identity of another (the claimant) is as declared, thereby preventing impersonation (the term "entity" is used to signify that both claimants and verifiers may be individuals or computational devices). Techniques for identification are typically divided into three classes, depending on the kind of evidence the claimant provides:[16]

1. Something the claimant *knows*: passwords, PINs, or cryptographic keys, the knowledge of which is demonstrated in *challenge-response* protocols.

2. Something the claimant *possesses*: passports, smart cards, magnetic strip cards, or similar. In this case, identity is demonstrated by control of an object, usually (but not necessarily) functioning as a container for other identifying information, such as a smartcard containing cryptographic keys.

3. Something the claimant *is*: physical characteristics, such as fingerprints and retinal patterns, or behavioral characteristics, such as handwritten

signatures, voice, or typing patterns. This class of identification techniques is usually referred to as *biometrics*.

However, digital signatures do not as such provide for identification of a signatory. Instead, they provide for *message authentication*, that is, evidence that a given message has been encrypted with a certain private key at some time in the past (see figure 4.3). The link between an individual and her private key must thus be *presumed*. In practice, this is a multilayered presumption: because users cannot be expected to remember 160-digit-long prime numbers (category 1), these must be stored on smart cards or computers (category 2), and access to the keys often granted through biometrics mechanisms (category 3) or PINs (category 1). Nevertheless, by and large, the field has not concerned itself with the means whereby users achieve agency over their cryptographic keys and the risks associated with such means. Indeed, given the overall orientation of modern cryptography toward information in digital form, concerns with authentication through passwords, physical documents, or biometrics are largely absent from the cryptographic canon, relegated to the distinct field of *physical security*.

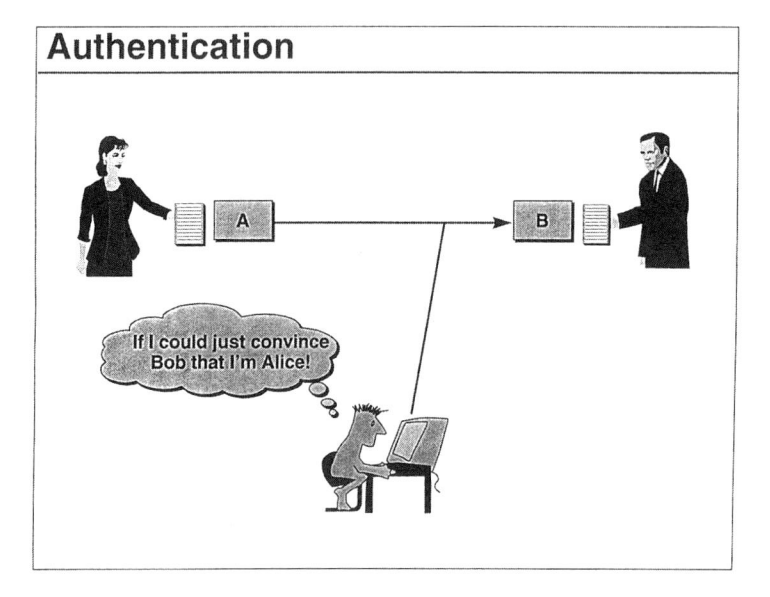

Figure 4.3
Authentication and the corresponding threat of key substitution. Image courtesy of Dr. Warwick Ford.

Data Integrity

The cryptographic definition of data integrity is a fairly straightforward one: "the property whereby data has not been altered in an unauthorized manner since the time it was created, transmitted, or stored by an authorized source."[17] However, the advent of the digital computer as the primary engine of cryptographic computation has meant that cryptographic algorithms operate on data solely at the binary level. As Feistel declared with respect to the design of the Lucifer cipher, "We shall no longer worry about the original meaning of the messages. We shall deal only with their binary representation."[18] It is thus important to note that in the context of digital signatures, the specific focus of data integrity is on the *bitwise* composition of data. This entails that integrity is defined at the finest, binary level of electronic information coding (see figure 4.4). Given this, operations that invalidate integrity include "insertion of bits, including entirely new data items from fraudulent sources; deletion of bits; re-ordering of bits or groups of bits; inversion or substitution of bits; and any combination of these."[19] In digital signature systems, the use of hash functions provides the cryptographic safeguard against attempts to alter the integrity of messages after

Figure 4.4
Data integrity and the corresponding threat of forgery. Image courtesy of Dr. Warwick Ford.

their signature: because of their resistance to collisions, if a *single bit* of the message is changed, the hash function will generate a different fingerprint, ensuring that signature verification will fail.

Non-repudiation

In Diffie and Hellman's original formulation, a cryptographic signature attests not only to the origin of the signed message (the private key that produced the signature) and its integrity (no modification was possible, as otherwise the verification would have failed), but also a third, essential, effect: *no other party than the signer, including the verifier, could have produced the signature*. Thus, the final security service of digital signatures requires that they provide a form of *evidence* external to the two parties engaged in the transaction, from which an authorized third party—in particular, a judge—may draw conclusions. Rivest, in a 1990 survey of the field, synthesized the difference between mere authentication and signature: in the first case, "the recipient of a message can *convince himself* that a message as received originated with the alleged signer," while in the second case, "the recipient of a message can *convince a third party* that the message as received originated with the alleged signer."[20] Over the years, this putative power to convince has become referred to as *non-repudiation*, a term whose origin and gradual evolution warrants closer examination (see figure 4.5). This evolution is characterized by a constant ambiguity over the extent of signatures' evidential power: with respect to third parties' evaluation of the authenticity of the signed message, does the signature merely serve as one element among many, or is it instead of such a compelling nature that this evaluation is reduced to mere confirmation of the signature's verification process?

Although the early scientific cryptographic literature does not directly employ the term of non-repudiation, the figure of the judge seems to make its first appearance in the RSA paper: "The recipient of a signed message has proof that a signed message originated from the sender. This quality is stronger than mere authentication (where the recipient can verify that the message originated from the sender); the recipient can convince a 'judge' that the signer sent a message."[21]

The RSA patent is already positioned slightly differently, stating that public-key cryptography provides a "recognizable, unforgeable, document-dependent, digitized signature whose authenticity *the signer cannot later deny*."[22] Ron Rivest's 1990 survey of the field proceeds along a similar line,

The Equivalent of a Written Signature   73

Figure 4.5
Non-repudiation and the corresponding threat of denial of commitments. Image courtesy of Dr. Warwick Ford.

introducing the concept of "repudiation": "A signature scheme provides a way for each user to *sign* messages so that the signatures can later be *verified* by anyone else. The verifier can convince himself that the message contents have not been altered since the message was signed. Also, the signer cannot later repudiate having signed the message, since no-one but the signer possesses his private key."[23]

The concept of non-repudiation as a well-defined property of technical systems seems to have originated with the ISO/IEC 1388 standard series for security in open systems. Published in the mid-1990s, the standard defines *non-repudiation of origin* as "protection against the originator's false denial of having created the content of a message and of having sent a message."[24] This protection comes from cryptographic signatures' ability to provide "irrefutable evidence to support the resolution of any such disagreement."[25] The demonstration of this evidence occurs through the signature verification process (see figure 4.6). By the power of the mathematics of public-key cryptography, when a signature is verified, all parties to the process (signer, recipient, judge, etc.) can conclude only that the signer's private key has been used to sign the document (authentication)

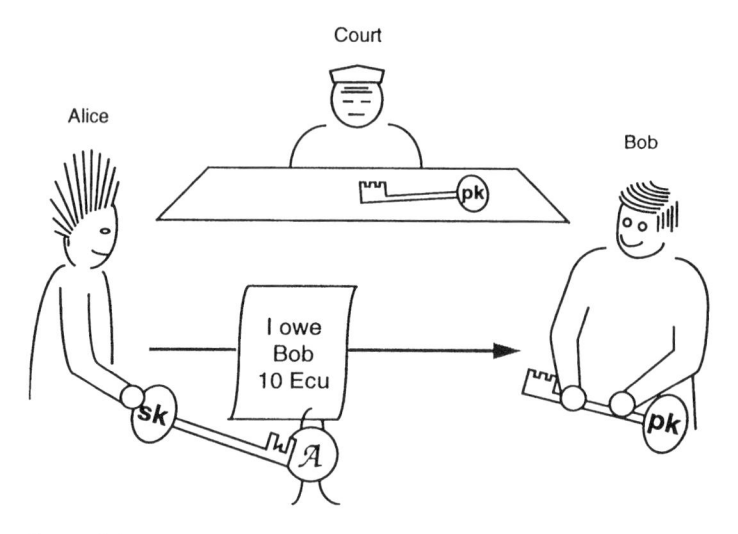

Figure 4.6
The scene at the courtroom during evaluation of signed documents. From Birgit Pfitzmann, *Digital Signature Schemes: General Framework and Fail-Stop Signatures* (Berlin: Springer, 1996), 13. Used by permission.

and that the document has not been modified since the signature's creation (data integrity).

Non-repudiation has subsequently migrated back from the standardization universe into the scientific cryptography literature. To the three objectives of historical concern to the discipline—confidentiality, data integrity, and authentication—the *Handbook of Applied Cryptography* adds a fourth, non-repudiation, defined as "a service which prevents an entity from denying previous commitments or actions."[26] This is an ambitious goal. Legal scholar Jane Winn humorously notes, "As anyone with children knows, you cannot prevent someone from 'falsely denying' an action."[27] Nevertheless, it is under the umbrella of non-repudiation that cryptography has staked a claim as a forensic science essential to the network society.

Attacks and Adversaries

To these security services, cryptographers would add a taxonomy of *attacks*, a taxonomy that models an adversary's resources as he tries to break the system and defeat the security properties of signatures. That is, if signatures provide authentication, then a corresponding threat is the ability for an adversary to *substitute* someone's identity for his own (see figure 4.3). If signatures provide data integrity, a corresponding threat is the ability for an adversary to *forge* signatures on messages of her choice (see figure 4.4). If signatures must "convince a judge" and "protect against false denials," a corresponding threat is the ability for the signer to create signatures that can be easily *denied* and fail to convince a third party (see figure 4.5). The development of means to effectively protect against these threats has significant implications for the design and usability of cryptographic signature technologies and the infrastructure necessary for their large-scale deployment.

The Threat of Substitution

Diffie and Hellman argued that public-key cryptography solved a fundamental obstacle to electronic commerce by eliminating the need for parties for prior communication in order to establish common keys. If Alice wants to send a confidential message to Bob, she acquires Bob's public key and encrypts her message with it. If she wants to send him a signed message, she encrypts it instead using her private key, and Bob can verify the resulting signature using Alice's public key. But how exactly do Alice and Bob gain access to each other's public key? In both scenarios, Diffie and Hellman proposed that the public key simply "be made public by placing it in a public directory along with user's name and address."[28] Provided with access to such a centralized telephone book, each user could simply obtain the necessary public key whenever required.

But such a scenario prompted the question of how Alice and Bob can be certain they have obtained each other's *authentic* public keys. A simple subversion of the public directory seemed immediately possible: by substituting Bob's public key with his own, an adversary may send messages to Alice that will appear to have originated from Bob, given that the signature verification process will proceed using the subverted public key. The precise details of how parties might obtain authentic public keys would turn out to have great practical import for the implementation of public-key cryptosystems. To understand why, it is useful to retrace the history of the technical design of what came to be known as public-key infrastructures.

Rivest, Shamir, and Adleman addressed the issue in their RSA paper, suggesting that the authority managing the public file be assigned its own public/private key pair with which to authenticate its communications with users. They proposed the following scenario: whenever a user joins a network, she (a) registers her public key with the public file in person or through any suitable offline channel; in return, she (b) receives (in similar offline manner) the public key of the public file authority. Each time the user requires the public key of another user, she (c) requests it from the public file authority. The authority (d) sends a copy of that key, itself signed with the public file authority's private key. The user then (e) verifies the public file's signature on the key, using the public file's public key obtained in step (b).

The advantages of such a system were to minimize offline interactions to "a single secure meeting between each user and the public-file manager when the user joins the system."[29] However, users would still need to interact with the public file for each and every signature verification. Alternatively, Rivest, Shamir, and Adleman suggested that users might be provided at the time of their joining the system with "a book (like a telephone directory) containing all the encryption keys of users in the system."

Loren M. Kohnfelder, an undergraduate student of Adleman at MIT, noted the practical difficulties posed by such a system. In his 1978 honor's thesis, he remarked that it presented a single point of failure: "An enemy that has broken the Public File encryption function could authoritatively pass out bogus encryption functions and thereby impersonate any communicant in the system." The system would also introduce considerable inefficiencies: "Continually referencing the Public File is a nuisance. . . . If it is frequently used, it will need to be a very large and complex system. Securely updating such a large system will be difficult. The communications equipment will be very expensive since it must be secure against tampering."[30]

Kohnfelder proposed to improve on the concept by eliminating the need for users to communicate with the public file beyond their initial registration into the system, though the use of *public key certificates*. A certificate is simply a document that associates a user's identity to a public key. For each user in the system, the public file authority issues and signs such a certificate, using its own private key. To verify the authenticity of a user's public key, users need only obtain the public key of the public file authority, presumably through offline means.

Public-key certificates thus offered interesting improvements over Diffie and Hellman's original scheme: using certificates, public keys can be distributed and stored using insecure channels and systems, as any attempt at subverting them will be detected through verification of the public file authority's signature. That is, individuals can exchange their certificates through email and store them on their computers, confident in the fact that their authenticity can be verified at any time; furthermore, users need not interact with the public file for every signature verification, but need only obtain its public key once.

However, as Kohnfelder noted, distribution of public keys through certificates introduced new risks and security/efficiency trade-offs. The power of public-key cryptography rests equally on ease of access to public keys and on users' control of their private key. If the spread of public key certificates over the network reduces the need to interact with a central repository, it becomes more difficult to recover from the compromise of user's private key. Indeed, if, through loss or theft, users have lost control over their private key, the corresponding public key should no longer be used, either to verify signatures or encrypt messages. Such *key revocation* is difficult in Kohnfelder's system, given that the certificates containing the key are now disseminated over the entire network. He suggested three different solutions, each with different risk and efficiency trade-offs:

1. Require each user to periodically download a list of revoked certificates. Because it would always be partially out of date, the list would allow some revoked certificates to slip through.

2. Assign expiration dates to certificates. This limits the damage a compromised key might cause but requires periodic renewal of public-key pairs for all users, a complex logistical process.

3. At the time of signature verification, contact the public file for an up-to-date report on the status of the public key. This step provides for maximum security at the cost of increased resources for the operation of the public file.[31]

With only minor variations, the essential elements of Kohnfelder's system—public-key certificates, a centralized public file authority, and revocation mechanisms—would remain as the basis for the infrastructure necessary to society-wide deployment of digital signatures. Throughout the 1990s, the business opportunities entailed by such a deployment would be repeatedly predicted explosive growth, in spite of lethargic market uptake. In 1999, business analysis firm Datamonitor commented, "Public key infrastructure has been predicted to boom since 1997. However, so far this prediction has consistently failed to become a reality."[32] Yet it could not help but join the chorus of well-wishers, itself claiming that "PKI will experience sustained growth over the next four years," with predictions of global market growth from a mere $79 million in 1997 to $1.4 billion in 2003.

The Threat of Forgery
Of most concern to cryptographers are threats to the mathematical integrity of the digital signature scheme. These threats are modeled according to two parameters:

1. The information at the adversary's disposal. This information ranges from the user's public key to message/signature pairs of the adversary's choosing.

2. The level of success the adversary can achieve against the signature scheme. This success ranges from the ability to forge a signature on some random message to computation of the private signing key.

The combination of these two parameters forms the basis of a taxonomy that classifies the relative strengths of cryptographic signature systems against forgery, given the relative resources of attackers.[33]

The taxonomy distinguishes three different flavors of attacks based on the resources of the attacker, listed in order of increasing strength: in a *key-only attack*, the adversary's only resource is the public key of the signer, and he is therefore restricted to checking the validity of signatures on messages presented to him; in a *known-signature attack*, the adversary has access to the public key of the signer and has seen message/signature pairs chosen and produced by the signer; in *chosen-message attacks*, the adversary is allowed to ask the signer to sign a number of messages of the adversary's choice; finally, in the *adaptative* context, the choice of these messages may depend on previously obtained signatures.

There are four levels of success, listed in increasing order: (a) *existential forgery*: the adversary succeeds in forging a signature on one message, not necessarily of his choice; (b) *selective forgery*: the adversary succeeds in forging signatures on some messages of his choice; (c) *universal forgery*: the adversary, although unable to determine the private key of the signer, is able to forge signatures on any messages of his choice; (d) *total break*: the

The Equivalent of a Written Signature

adversary can compute the signer's private key and thus sign any messages he wishes to.

At a minimum, any public-key signature scheme should be resistant against total break under a key-only attack (that is, an adversary shouldn't be able to compute the private key, given only access to the public key). At the other end of the spectrum, signature schemes aim to resist against existential forgery under an adaptively chosen message attack (that is, an adversary shouldn't be able to create a single signature, even with access to signatures on any document of his choice).[34] Proof of a cryptographic signature scheme thus entails two distinct elements: on the one hand, the specific computational assumptions on which the scheme is based (e.g., integer factorization is difficult); on the other hand, the attacks and resources against which it is resistant.

The Threat of Repudiation

Both substitution and forgery are concerned with an adversary seeking to abuse Alice's signing instrument, trying to produce valid signatures on messages not of her own. But given signature schemes aim to produce "undeniable" evidence that is binding on Alice, the threat model must also consider that she herself might try to subvert the signature process and produce valid signatures while somehow undermining their evidential value. Throughout the 1980s and 1990s, cryptographers debated whether Alice might be able to use the *key generation* process for such a purpose. By deliberately creating a public key from which the private key could easily be deduced, Alice could cast doubt on the strength of the evidence generated by the signature mechanism and consequently provide herself with an opportunity to renegade on her commitments.

The attack would rely on a special-purpose "$P-1$" method, an algorithm that can rapidly factor the public key n if its prime factors p and q possess a certain "weak" structure.[35] In order to prevent against such attacks, p and q can be specially chosen to be "strong" and thus resistant to the $P-1$ method. But given that users may generate public key pairs themselves (e.g., using software on their computers), what if they *deliberately* generated a "weak" prime?

The user could do so by repeatedly generating RSA key pairs until one of the primes output as part of the RSA private keys was obviously weak (to detect the weakness, the user need only try to factor $p-1$ or $q-1$, perhaps by the Elliptic Curve Method).

A user might be motivated to do this if the user later could claim that, because the prime was weak, the resulting RSA modulus could easily be factored. The user could thereby attempt to repudiate a previously verified signature.[36]

Standardization committees repeatedly argued over whether key generation algorithms for RSA signature schemes should test for strong primes.[37] The arguments attempted to evaluate how the generation of weak primes might provide the basis for repudiating signatures:

> On the one hand, it was argued that a user would have a difficult time convincing a judge that the supposed weakness was the result of chance. Since it is unlikely that a random prime would be weak against the $P - 1$ method, the claim would be suspicious, particularly as to why an opponent would choose this one RSA modulus to factor with the $P - 1$ method without knowing in advance where the effort would succeed (although the user could know in advance whether a modulus could be factored by the $P - 1$ method, there is no way for an outsider to determine this without actually trying to factor it). On the other hand, it was pointed out that the mere possibility that such a ruse might succeed was sufficient justification to prevent it.[38]

What is perhaps most interesting about these arguments is cryptographers' vision of the court process as one in which judges appreciate the evidential value of the signatures based on their mathematical properties. The design of cryptographic systems actively involved a priori imagination of how the evidence they produced might hold up in court. These debates add additional layers of complexity to cryptography's project of constructing evidence usable in court: "A general consensus was emerging by the late 1990s that is was important to consider not only security against outside opponents, but security against insiders—the users—when constructing requirements for key generation."[39] Although digital signature users must obviously exert control over their keys if they are to claim them as signing instruments, they must simultaneously be prevented from having *too much* control over them.

Mutations

The preceding sections highlighted some of the work necessary to bridge the gap between digital signatures and their handwritten counterparts. As communicated by Rivest, Shamir, and Adleman's initial bracketing of "signature," "proof," and "judge" within the protected space of quotes, cryptographic algorithms are not transparently assimilable to the writing of one's name on paper. On every level documented in this chapter, mathematical constructions cannot simply be assumed to coincide with the material and social world. Yet by applying the "real world" concept of signature to their new mathematical construction, Diffie and Hellman performed a powerful move: "an account of the new and unfamiliar in terms of the familiar and intelligible."[40]

This reaching out to familiar "real-world" concepts would continue in the context of even more unfamiliar mathematical objects. As cryptographers expanded their repertoire of cryptographic primitives, interactive protocols, desirable design features, proof models, and security objectives, these activities constituted a rich toolbox from which new and surprising mathematical objects could be creatively assembled. This creative activity has resulted in new configurations of the original signature protocol, most of which cannot easily be related to paper-and-ink counterparts. These include:

One-time signatures   The private/public key pair can be used to sign at most one message.[41]

Proxy signatures   In proxy schemes, the signer delegates her signing power to a designated third party. Delegation comes in several flavors: full, partial, and by warrant, differing in their efficiency and security properties. Among the many variants are *one-time proxy signatures*, *anonymous proxy signatures*, *multiproxy signatures*.

Group signatures   Any member of the group can sign a document, but it is not possible to identify which one. If a dispute arises over the legitimacy of a signature, a group manager (who controls membership) can be called on to identify the signer.[42] Among the many variants proposed are *threshold-type signatures*, in which given a group of size n, any subgroup of k members can produce a signature, but it is not possible to identify the specific members of the subgroup;[43] *multisignatures*, in which the size k of the subgroup need not be specified in advance; *ring signatures*, which require no group managers and no prespecified group size;[44] and *proxy threshold signatures*.

Blind signatures   In these schemes (the basis of Chaum's anonymous cash system), the signer affixes her signature to a document but cannot later link the two together.[45] Variants include, among others, *fair blind signatures*, in which the judge may be called on (e.g., by authorities) to link together signature and document, and *proxy blind signatures*.[46]

Forward-secure signatures The private key of the signer is updated at regular time intervals, with the security property that if the key is compromised, an adversary can forge only signatures dated within the time period pertaining to the compromised key. Only one public key is required to validate signatures from all private keys, thus mitigating the inconvenience of key exposure.[47] Variants include *group, threshold, and proxy forward-secure signatures*.

Undeniable signatures The signature can be verified only with the cooperation of the signer.[48] Variants include *convertible undeniable signatures*, an undeniable signature with the additional property that the signer can eventually release a secret that can convert all his undeniable signatures into ordinary signatures; and *designated confirmer signatures*, whereby a third party designated by the confirmer can cooperate in (and only in) the verification step, should the signer be unable to do so.[49]

Designated verifier signatures Bob can convince himself that a message indeed originates from Alice, but cannot transfer that conviction to a third party; that is, the scheme does not provide for non-repudiation.[50]

Fail-stop signatures Such schemes provide an additional layer of security. In conventional schemes, if the underlying computational assumption of the scheme is broken, the adversary can produce forged signatures at will. In fail-stop signatures, the supposed signer can nevertheless prove that the signatures are forgeries.[51]

These signature schemes represent fascinating new configurations of responsibility, liability, trust, and power within the signing process. In most cases, there are no obvious "real-world" equivalents to these mathematical constructs, and in most cases, it is difficult to imagine the specific context in which they might be applied. Nevertheless, it is standard practice for cryptographic papers to justify such schemes with a "motivation" narrative, a "real-world" scenario that aims to suggest a plausible practical application of the signature scheme. These justificatory narratives form a unique genre in the mathematical literature, worth quoting at length. The *Handbook* for example describes a potential application of *convertible undeniable signatures*:

As an application of this type of signature, consider the following scenario: Entity *A* signs all documents during her lifetime with convertible undeniable signatures. The secret piece of information needed to convert these signatures to self-authenticating signatures is placed in trust with her lawyer *B*. After the death of *A*, the lawyer can make the secret information public knowledge and all signatures can be verified. *B* does not have the ability to alter or create new signatures on behalf of *A*.[52]

These justificatory narratives are also remarkable with respect to their integration of broad assumptions about the litigation process, in particular the ability of courts to appreciate the evidential power of signatures based on their underlying mathematics. Fail-stop signatures, for example, are precisely designed to provide supplementary evidence to the judge, in the case where a signature scheme's computational assumptions are broken:

> If a signature scheme is broken although one had reasons to hope it would not, the supposed signer of a message with a forged signature is defenseless: The forged digital signature looks exactly like an authentic one. If it is presented to a court, the court decides, still with the public test key T, that the signature is valid. Thus the supposed signer will be held responsible. (The recipient of a signed message, however, is absolutely secure: If he has checked that the signature passes the test with the public test key, he knows that it will also do so in court, no matter if it is authentic or forged.) At least this is the technical view of what a court should do. A real court is not obliged to comply with this view. (At least German courts are not obliged to acknowledge a handwritten signature either.) It could believe the protestation by the supposed signer that the signature is a forgery, the more so since the signer can adduce that the signature scheme relies on an unproven assumption, no matter how long it has been examined. However, if this were the case, recipients would not be secure at all any more: Even if the assumption is perfectly correct and no signature is ever forged, the real signers could now deny their signatures in court, just like the supposed signer above. It is impossible for the court to distinguish the two cases.[53]

The scenarios are sometimes extremely detailed. For example, in "How to Leak a Secret," Rivest, Shamir, and Tauman propose the following with respect to potential applications of ring signatures:

> To motivate the title for this paper, suppose that Bob (also known as "Deep Throat") is a member of the cabinet of Lower Kryptonia, and that Bob wishes to leak a juicy fact to a journalist about the escapades of the Prime Minister, in such a way that Bob remains anonymous, yet such that the journalist is convinced that the leak was indeed from a cabinet member. Bob cannot send to the journalist a standard digitally signed message, since such a message, although it convinces the journalist that it came from a cabinet member, does so by directly revealing Bob's identity.
>
> It also doesn't work for Bob to send the journalist a message through a standard "anonymizer," since the anonymizer strips off all source identification and authentication: the journalist would have no reason to believe that the message really came

from a cabinet member at all. A standard group signature scheme does not solve the problem, since it requires the prior cooperation of the other group members to set up, and leaves Bob vulnerable to later identification by the group manager, who may be controlled by the Prime Minister.

The correct approach is for Bob to send the story to the journalist (through an anonymizer), signed with a ring signature scheme that names each cabinet member (including himself) as a ring member. The journalist can verify the ring signature on the message, and learn that it definitely came from a cabinet member. He can even post the ring signature in his paper or web page, to prove to his readers that the juicy story came from a reputable source. However, neither he nor his readers can determine the actual source of the leak, and thus the whistleblower has perfect protection even if the journalist is later forced by a judge to reveal his "source" (the signed document).[54]

This small sample of justificatory scenarios is sufficient to reveal some recurrent tensions in cryptographer's creative production. New cryptographic objects are generated through more or less straightforward combinations of elements of the cryptographic toolbox, such as threshold, proxy, or fairness properties. Like so many modular Lego pieces, cryptographic primitives and design patterns are assembled in new schemes and protocols exhibiting security properties with no obvious real-world equivalents. This creative process is one of the core professional activities of cryptographers, rewarded through conference presentations, journal publications, and commercial patents. Yet the cryptographic paper genre seems to require that these products of mathematical creativity be justified in some "real-world" setting, motivated either by their potential application, their evidential value, or the new threats they identify. These justificatory scenarios are remarkable in their assumptions that the properties of cryptographic objects, as designed and discussed by cryptographers, will translate transparently into the complex social settings they describe. In effect, the various characters that populate these scenarios (users, adversaries, judges, etc.) understand the properties of cryptographic technologies exactly as cryptographers themselves would. The enormous challenges inherent in turning these cryptographic constructs into forensic and security technologies able to perform in the context of users' everyday lives is thus simply glossed over, assumed away. At the heart of this oversight, I will argue, lies a fundamental difficulty in coming to terms with a crucial intermediary between mathematics and the "real world," that of models.

Mathematics and the Real World

The gradual development and refinement of the digital signature model provides a useful window from which to examine the cryptographic research community's conceptualization of their mathematical practices. In the aftermath of the publication of "New Directions," these practices sat at the intersection of several trends: Diffie and Hellman's call for increased mathematization of the field; the practical concerns that have historically given the field its identity, that is, the construction of effective systems that afford confidential communications; and Simmons's program for a broader disciplinary identity, centered on the design of digital analogues to paper-based security protocols. The challenges in reconciling these divergent trends registered, among other symptoms, as a certain ambivalence in dealing with the relationship between mathematics and the "real world" and the role of models in mediating that relationship. At times, that world seems immediately and self-evidently at hand, as in Diffie and Hellman's succinct definition of the signature, a definition whose fundamental features were never challenged or improved upon again. At other times, it seems reluctant and remote, forcibly summoned through the scenarios that justify, with various degrees of realism, the practical utility of the mathematical objects created by cryptographers. Both cases reveal a problematic encounter with the practice of modeling, and the attendant issue of *representation*. Even though modeling clearly formed an integral dimension of cryptographic practice, by and large, cryptographers did not and could not explicitly articulate its specific possibilities and constraints.

This issue shouldn't necessarily come as a surprise. Models have remained a largely tacit dimension of scientific practice. The twelve-volume *Encyclopedia of Mathematics* entry is content to define modeling as "a (rough) description of some class of events of the outside world, expressed using mathematical symbolism."[55] Philosophers Mary Morgan and Margaret Morrison point out that "there appear to be no general rules for model construction in the way that we can find detailed guidance on principle of experimental design or on methods of measurement."[56] Indeed, it is only in last decade that historians, philosophers, and sociologists of science have begun examining models with the same degree of attention they previously lavished on other dimensions of the scientific process. These investigations have raised models' epistemological profile to the point where together with "measuring instruments, experiments, theories and data," they can today be acknowledged "as one of the essential ingredients in the practice of science."[57]

Models resist easy categorization however: they form a highly heterogeneous class that includes, among others, physical objects (e.g., a wooden scale model of a bridge, Watson and Crick's model of DNA), analog models (e.g., modeling the mind in computational terms), idealized models (e.g., rational economic actors in markets), and mathematical models (e.g., equations that model economic processes or climate change).[58] In fact, they often combine these elements in "gerrymandered ontologies" that freely mix the pictorial, the narrative, and the mathematical.[59] Whatever form they take, models endure as part of a discipline's worldview, enshrined and transmitted through textbooks, core texts, and other apparatus of disciplinary culture.

Models provide a crucial intermediary link between the abstraction of theories and the concreteness of observable phenomena: "Models become a form of glue, simultaneously epistemic and social, that allows inquiry to go forward, by connecting the ideal and the material. To do that, they need to make compromises: they must simultaneously look like theory—because they have to explain and predict, and give structure—and like practical knowledge—because they have to connect to real world features."[60] This connection with the real world is, in fact, the defining characteristic of models: they "should *behave* in the same way as the things they represent behave. Models are thus different from theories not only in being applied, but in being analogues."[61]

These analogues function by eliminating the superfluous, focusing on the significant dimensions of the modeled phenomena. The selection of relevant dimensions is often described in terms of reaching for "essences," such as "the analysis of a mathematical model allows the essence of a phenomenon to be penetrated."[62] Giere suggests the more pragmatic criteria of "fitness":

Models need only be similar to particular real-world systems in specified respects and to limited degrees of accuracy. The question for a model is how well it "fits" various real-world systems one is trying to represent. One can admit that no model fits the world perfectly in all respects while insisting that, for specified real-world systems, some models clearly fit better than others. The better fitting models may represent more aspects of the real world, or fit some aspects more accurately, or both. In any case, "fit" is not simply a relationship between a model and the world. It requires a specification of which aspects of the world are important to represent and, for those aspects, how close a fit is desirable.[63]

This fitness should not be understood as an inherent feature of the models themselves: "It is not the model that is doing the representing; it is the scientist using the model who is doing the representing. One way scientists do this is by picking out some specific features of the model that are then claimed to be similar to features of the designated real system to some (perhaps fairly loosely indicated) degree of fit."[64]

Recent scholarship in science studies has produced insightful analyses of two scientific communities whose practices are intimately bound with modeling—climatology and mathematical finance. The empirical material obtained through extended fieldwork engagement with both communities suggests the complex relationships that obtain between scientists, their models, and the real-world systems they investigate. In his historical analysis of climatology and global warming, Paul Edwards demonstrates that models and data can never be cleanly separated but should instead be understood as mutually constitutive. Models are not "pure theories, ungrounded in observation" and data are never model-independent. In fact, *"everything we know about the world's climate—past, present, future—we know through models."*[65]

In his investigation of the mathematization of financial markets that began in the 1960s, Donald Mackenzie argues that the success of the new and contested discipline of financial economics was dependent on a certain epistemological stance with respect to the "fitness" of mathematical models. For this new breed of economists, the goal of theory was to perform as an "engine of inquiry," not as "an (infeasible) camera faithfully reproducing all empirical facts."[66] Such an approach did not imply a "commitment to the literal truth of economics' models": even if they trusted the model as "identifying an economic process of great importance," they also recognized its empirical limitations, as well as the "economically consequential ways in which the model's assumptions were unrealistic." Their approach was, at heart, pragmatic:

For Black, Scholes, and Merton . . . a model had to be simple enough to be mathematically tractable, yet rich enough to capture the economically most important aspects of the situations modeled. Models were resources, not (in any simple sense) representations: ways of understanding and reasoning about economic processes, not putative descriptions of reality. If the latter is the criterion of truth, all of the financial economists discussed here would agree with their colleague Eugene Fama that any model is "surely false."[67]

MacKenzie tracks how the Black-Scholes-Merton model of option pricing became a material resource in the "scrum of human bodies on trading floors," through the simple technology of printed paper: "Away from the hubbub, computers were used to generate Black-Scholes prices. Those prices were reproduced on sets of paper sheets which floor traders could carry around, often tightly wound cylindrically with only immediately relevant rows visible so that a quick squint would reveal the relevant prices."[68] Such immediate access to the numerical models created a form of "feedback loop from the theory." By becoming part of the distributed cognitive processes of traders, models—instead of merely representing the world—became an essential element of its performance: "The availability of convenient material implementations of the Black-Scholes-Merton model . . . most likely had the effect of reducing discrepancies between empirical prices and the model . . . there was thus an homology between the way the model was tested econometrically and options market practices based on the model. Use of the model does indeed seem to have helped to create patterns of prices consistent with the model."[69]

MacKenzie argues that the success of the models depended in no small part on their simplicity. Floor traders were in no particular awe of academics, but found the "cognitive simplicity" of Black-Scholes-Merton's attractive, as its "one free parameter (volatility) was easily grasped, discussed, and reasoned about."[70] This was a marked advantage over competing models: "When numbers of free parameters are larger, or parameters do not have intuitive interpretations—as is often the case with more complex models—communication and negotiation become much harder."[71]

Clearly, not all disciplines relate to their models in the same way. If, as MacKenzie reports, mathematical finance embraced the feedback loops between its equations and actual markets as a form of creative tension, pure mathematics has followed an opposite trajectory. Historian of mathematics Herbert Mehrtens tracks this process in a paper on to three-dimensional models, physical objects commonly used at the end of the nineteenth century to represent geometrical entities and today mostly confined to the (elementary) classroom.[72] Such models, he argues, pointed to a certain ontological ambiguity of mathematics, an ambiguity that was resolved with the embrace of modern conceptual mathematics, whose purism "excluded corporeality and visuality from the discursive universe of mathematics." The disappearance of three-dimensional models, and the troubled epistemological status of diagrams in contemporary mathematical practice is, according to Mehrtens, "closely related to the dominance of mathematical modernism with its preference for general theory, symbolic formalism, and the treatment of mathematical theories as worlds of their own without any immediate relation to the physical world around us."[73]

The switch to axiomatic mathematics thus enforced, among other things, a strict demarcation between applied and pure mathematics: "If mathematics rests in itself, no other science can legitimately discuss the mathematical principles of truth, existence, and value. A mathematics that takes *Anschauung* or intuition as essential will have to face questions from philosophers, psychologists, and maybe neurologists. Modernist purism restricted mathematics to the construction of strictly regulated worlds of meaning made from formal typographical sign systems. For other tasks there is the applied mathematician."[74]

It should then come as no surprise that in adopting the ideals, methodologies, and standards of a modern, theory-oriented mathematical discipline, cryptographers found few available concepts from which to engage with the possibilities and constraints of modeling real-world systems. No language presented itself that might have provided some reflexive awareness of this inescapable dimension of their practice. For example, as noted earlier, Goldreich has argued cryptographic practice proceeds through "the identification, conceptualization and rigorous definition of cryptographic tasks which capture *natural security concerns*."[75] Di Crescenzo, another foundationalist, argues that modern cryptography is based on "mathematically rigorous design requirements."[76] But where do these requirements come from? How does one identify such "natural security concerns"? On these questions, the literature remains silent. Furthermore, neither of these approaches provide a rationale for the definitions of the "mutant" signatures described in the preceding section, which can hardly be accounted for on the basis of "natural requirements."

It is one argument of this book that the inability to discuss models *as models*, as necessary and inevitable components of scientific practice, has hindered the development of cryptographic technologies. When the mediating role of models goes unrecognized, scientific practice becomes blind to the trade-offs inherent in the process of abstracting away the unruliness of the phenomenal world. Phil Agre has articulated the consequences of such an epistemological stance in his analysis of the role of metaphor in the field of artificial intelligence: "Any practice that loses track of the figurative nature of its language loses consciousness of itself. As a consequence, it becomes incapable of performing the feats of self-diagnosis that become necessary as old ideas reach their limits and call out for new ones to take their place. No finite procedure can make this cycle of diagnosis and revision wholly routine, but articulated theories of discourses and practices can certainly help us to avoid some of the more straightforward impasses."[77]

Such articulated theories might prove quite relevant to cryptographers. They might help them account for how models evolve and mutate in response to the constantly shifting boundaries between theory and practice. Indeed, such shifts have already occurred with respect to the proof model under which the correctness of cryptographic schemes is ascertained. Chapter 7 investigates the struggles of the community as it debates how to best adjust the model while maintaining the epistemological integrity of its practices.

Conclusion

This chapter gradually built a fuller picture of the cryptographic signature model. Based on the mechanics of public-key encryption, the model involves distinct steps of signature creation and verification, supposes an underlying infrastructure for key distribution and revocation, and posits specific threats to which cryptographic signature schemes must be resistant. Without yet attempting to evaluate the *fitness* of the model, we are nevertheless in a position to examine some of the (inevitable) abstractions and simplifications built into it. In attempting to create a digital analogue of handwritten signatures, what did the definitions of the signature process, of the three security services, and of the threat model foreground, what did they relegate to the background?

First, in the model, the evidential value of signatures is wholly derived from the verification process. Though it merely outputs a binary answer—either the signature is valid or it is not—the verification process encompasses broader semantic and technical complexity. On the one hand, though there may be multiple causes to a signature's failure to verify, (i.e., incorrect key or modifications to the signed message), it is not possible to distinguish these causes given the output of the verification process itself. On the other hand, a fundamental dimension is strikingly absent from the scene of signature as portrayed by the model (see figure 4.1): *time*. Bob may well verify Alice's signature shortly after she produced it, but verification in the context of litigation may occur years afterward. Signed documents and their evidential qualities will have to be *digitally preserved* for durations that will vary according to record-keeping requirements. These durations may range from a few years (tax documents) to the lifetime of individuals and institutions (blueprints for nuclear reactors).

Furthermore, cryptographic signatures model *data integrity* at the bit level; that is, modification of a *single bit* of a digitally signed document results in failed verification. However, the extreme sensitivity of this measure poses significant challenges. The conflicting mechanics of digital preservation and signature verification will have important implications for the forensic usability of cryptographic signatures, implications that I further examine in chapter 6 in the context of the French notarial profession.

The taxonomy of *entity authentication* partitions identification techniques in three distinct classes: something the claimant *knows*, *possesses*, or *is*. The literature classifies cryptographic keys in the first category; yet, accessing and manipulating 300-digit numbers necessarily requires that they be stored on a computing device (desktop, smart card, mobile phone), itself secured through password or biometric identifiers. Users' agency over their private signing keys is thus likely to be more complex than assumed by the model. Furthermore, the taxonomy fails to account for the specificity of handwritten signatures as the bodily performance of a certain secret knowledge. Unlike a fingerprint or a retina pattern, a signature results from a volitional act. Handwritten signatures are something someone *does* to express assent or commitment in a performance paradoxically each time unique, yet identical.

The third security service provided by digital signatures, *non-repudiation*, modeled evidential qualities of written documents and their use in court—their ability to "convince a judge." As the following chapters further document, the status of non-repudiation would remain ambiguous throughout the process of legal codification: should it be considered an inherent characteristic of cryptographic systems or something to be adjudicated within the legal domain proper? Furthermore, non-repudiation would eventually serve as a powerful rhetorical resource in apportioning burdens of proof, an issue with important consequences in establishing the power relationship between litigating parties—consumers, businesses, service providers.

Finally, in the threat model inherited from the analysis of cryptosystems, both users and adversaries are endowed with the resources and motivations of national security agencies. The model does not provide for finer gradients of risks that would account for a cost-risk analysis of contractual relationships and the appropriateness of distinct security solutions for different risk factors. Such a one-size-fits-all approach eventually proved a liability. In spite of repeated predictions to the contrary, the market for public-key infrastructures never took off, as businesses could not account for the costs and organizational complexity of applying military-grade technology to civilian-grade risks.

This then was the ground covered by the cryptographic signature model in the mid-1990s, as it prepared to make its debut on the legal scene. The next two chapters account for the reception of the model, first by the legal scholars and regulators tasked with updating centuries-old rules of evidence for the information age and later by the professions centered around the production of documentary evidence—including contracts, identification, and property.

5 Written Proof

On March 13, 2000, France—the country that gave bureaucracy its name, where citizens must carry at all times their *papiers d'identité*, where administrative procedures are synonymous with intricate theatrical performances of forms, stamps, signatures, and countless *pièces justificatives*—finally got around to legally defining written proof: "Civil code, art. 1316—Documentary, or written, evidence, results from a series of letters, characters, numbers, or any other signs or symbols endowed with an intelligible signification, whatever their media or the means of their transmission."

The clarification came hot on the heels of Henri III's 1566 *Ordonnance de Moulins*, France's previous comprehensive response to innovation in evidential technologies. Concerned with reducing both the quantity and duration of litigation, the 1556 *Ordonnance* mandated that the emerging technology of written documents would henceforth supplant witness testimony in all contractual disputes.

The scope of the 2000 reform—its perceived need to reexamine and rearticulate fundamentals—was spurred on by an event that seemed to shake *l'état de droit* to its very core, the emergence of the Internet. In the late 1990s, at the height of the dot-com boom, French media breathlessly reported on the Internet's power to upend traditional business models, flatten social hierarchies, foster scientific innovation, and stimulate political change, while generating massive wealth in the process. Tapping deeply into France's anxieties over its declining global powers, the Internet seemed to throw into sharp focus everything that was wrong with the French model. Inherently horizontal, adaptable, and capital-friendly, the Internet was driven by a new type of business culture, feverish yet relaxed, as removed as could be from the French traditions of elitism and reverence for the state perpetuated by the *Grandes écoles*. Indeed, in every office and home, the dark screens of *Minitel* terminals—France's first stab at cyberspace—stood as silent reproaches to the technological ineptitude of French "dirigisme" and its excessive thirst for regulation.[1] Worse, the Internet's ability to evade censorship, mock copyright, and seamlessly cross borders made nation-states and their reliance on the rule of law seem positively antiquated, institutional relics of a past ill equipped to deal with the utter modernity of electronic networks.

The issue was not particular to France. In the United States, legal scholars and practitioners debated whether the lawlessness of cyberspace could be tamed using existing statutes and concepts, or whether it required something completely new: a body of *cyberlaws*. In a famous debate, Frank Easterbrook, a judge, and Lawrence Lessig, an academic, articulated the positions of, respectively, the rearguard and the vanguard. Easterbrook argued that cyberlaw advocates treaded treacherous ground: "Beliefs lawyers hold about computers, and predictions they make about new technology, are highly likely to be false. This should make us hesitate to prescribe legal adaptations for cyberspace. The blind are not good trailblazers."[2] If American law had barely begun catching up with the impact of photocopying on intellectual property, "What chance do we have for a technology such as computers that is mutating faster than the virus in *The Andromeda Strain*?" His recommendations for future action were strikingly conservative: "Well, then, what can we do? By and large, nothing. If you don't know what is best, let people make their own arrangements. Next after nothing is: keep doing what you have been doing."[3]

Lessig responded that in fact, electronic networks operated in ways that required careful analysis of law's ability to regulate behavior. Regulation, he proposed, is effected through four simultaneous yet distinct mechanisms: law obviously, but also markets, social norms, and *architecture*. Although regulation by architecture is common in "real space" (e.g., speed bumps or automatic seatbelts), it acquires a special valence in networks: "The software and hardware that make cyberspace what it is constitute a set of constraints on how you can behave. . . . The code or software or architecture or protocols set these features; they are features selected by code writers; they constrain some behavior by making other behavior possible, or impossible. The code embeds certain values or makes certain values impossible. In this sense, it too is regulation, just as the architectures of real-space codes are regulations."[4]

Lessig and others argued that such code constitutes a "Lex Informatica" unto itself, "the set of rules for information flows imposed by technology and communication networks."[5] For regulators to devise effective cyberspace policies, the normative implications of code writing and information technology design must be consciously recognized, harnessed, and harmonized with market forces, social norms, and law.

In this analysis, cryptography holds a unique role. If software architecture, hardware design, or protocols induce constraints on cyberspace as side effects of their primary engineering purposes (say, the delays associated with Internet packet switching), cryptography is code *created with the sole purpose of regulating behavior*. Cryptographic technologies are specifically designed to provide confidentiality, authentication, anonymity, accountability—in short, to implement the locks and keys of cyberspace architecture. In Lessig's vision, this granted cryptography an extraordinary role in the building of the Information Society: "Here is something that will sound very extreme, but is at most, I think, a slight exaggeration: encryption technologies are the most important technological breakthrough in the last one thousand years. No other technological discovery—from nuclear weapons (I hope) to the Internet—will have a more significant impact on social and political life. Cryptography will change everything."[6]

Indeed, the early days of cyberlaw saw much discussion of cryptography export controls, key escrow, and other assorted topics relative to ensuring freedom of encryption.[7] As the Internet gradually mutated from a scientific research network into a commercial one, the focus shifted to encryption's less controversial sibling, digital signatures. Sustained growth of e-commerce, it was claimed, depended on consumers trusting that effective technologies and a clear legal framework could guarantee the security of electronic transactions. Conveniently, public-key technologies provided precisely the required infrastructure. Their deployment demanded only that evidence law statutes be modernized to grant admissibility and legal value to electronic records and signatures—with perhaps some economic incentives thrown in to jump-start the necessary infrastructural investments.

Yet there were good reasons to believe that reform might proceed less straightforwardly than the previous scenario suggested. In both common and civil law, the rules of evidence have, over centuries, coevolved together with the technical possibilities of paper, ink, and signature, and litigation proceeds on the basis of considerable tacit knowledge about their relationship. Indeed, law is "predominantly a textual enterprise" and paper, ink, and signatures are the material technologies from which the legal process itself is crafted and ultimately signals its authority.[8] Furthermore, as documented in the previous chapter, the cryptographic signature model brings its own expectations to the litigation process and its own understanding of itself as a forensic object.

This chapter provides an on-the-ground account of evidence law reform from the vantage point of the French system. I trace the process starting with the 1980 reform, a reform that sought to account for the expanding reliance of the business world on photocopies, faxes, and microfilms, and for the challenges these new documentary technologies presented to the courts. The 1980 reform is significant because it introduced *evidentiary presumptions* as a potential solution to the problem of ascertaining the *trustworthiness* of the mechanisms that produce and mediate access to these documents. I then survey the discussions that took place among French legal scholars through the 1980s and 1990s over the necessity of a more extensive reform that could fully account for born-digital documents. These discussions were informed by similar ones occurring at the same time within several international bodies, including the United Nations Commission on International Trade Law, the European Union, and the American Bar Association.

I conclude by tracking the proposed text of the 2000 reform through committees and legislative bodies, and subsequent modifications to the rules of civil procedure with respect to the admissibility of electronically signed documents. Throughout, I pay attention to the conciliation of the inner logic of cryptographic signatures with that of the French evidence system—in particular, the role of evidentiary presumptions in providing the glue for the realization in law of the principle of non-repudiation.

Contracts

Much of the conceptual structure and material practices of the French evidential system can be traced back to Roman law.[9] As early as the early first century AD, private parties began writing down the terms of small contractual obligations—loans, sales, leases—on wax-covered wooden tablets, *tabulae ceratae*, in a documentary genre known as the *chirograph*. In contrast to *tabulae signatae*, written testimonies signed and sealed by seven witnesses as evidence of legally significant transactions, chirographs were written and sealed by the parties themselves and thus enjoyed little power to compel. They were "based on agreement, on faith, and on the threat of an appeal to the praetor."[10] Still, chirographs were not without efficacy. On the one hand, parties had a significant stake in defending the reputation attached to properly honoring their *bona fides*; on the other hand, the writing down of agreements by the parties brought into play the power of performance:

> Physical form and special language connected individual documents with other well-known, venerable acts performed by Romans: the wooden *tabulae*, along with its customary rhythmic and formulaic language, was characteristic not only of political acts like the creation of treaties, magisterial edicts, *leges*, *senatusconsulta*, or the census, but also of religious acts like vows and prayers and important household acts like the entering of accounts, the making of a will, or the sending of a curse. These acts relied on tablets' understood capacity—as part of a protocol in which each step had to be performed and performed correctly—to bring an act to completion and to make it perceptibly real.[11]

In the Middle Ages, the material qualities of parchment enabled significant technical innovations to chirographs. Contractual agreements were written out in duplicate (sometimes triplicate) on a single piece of parchment. Between each copy of the agreement, parties would write in capital letters the word "chirographum" and cut across the word in a wavy line: "each party received a copy of the agreement, authenticated by the seal of the other party, and the cut enabled the copies to be checked against one another."[12] The medieval chirograph provided an elegant solution to the problem of fairly apportioning the *burden of proof*: by providing each other with an authenticated confession of the contractual terms, prior to both execution and litigation, parties collaborated in constituting evidential ammunition against themselves.[13]

These basic principles—the freedom of private parties to contract on the sole basis of their good faith (*consensualisme*), use of form requirements in the production of written evidence (*formalisme*), and fair apportionment of the burden of proof (*préconstitution de la preuve*)—continue to characterize the French evidential regime of private contracts.[14] The Napoleonic codification of 1803 restated the principles of the 1566 *Ordonnance* as article 1341 of the Civil Code: "A written document must be established, either by a notary or as a private act, for any dealing over a sum or value of 50FF [French francs], and no proof by testimony is admissible against or beyond the content of this document, nor with regard to what could have allegedly been said before, during, or since the writing of the document."

By the power of consensualism, parties are free to contract to their hearts' content, but in order to *prove* their obligations, parties must constitute, prior to litigation, a written document.[15] The specification of the hierarchical superiority of written proof over witness testimony illustrates a key element of the civilist approach to evidence: though *all* evidence is potentially admissible, the rules of its evaluation are formally specified by the law. The judge is responsible for determining to which legal category—authentic (notarized) act, private contract, *prima facie* evidence—a given document belongs, based on its formal characteristics. Once this operation of *qualification* has been performed, the judge's appraisal of the evidence is determined by the formal rules specifying the evidential arithmetic that obtains between these categories, rather than by his inner conviction.[16]

As a consequence, the power of a written document to testify to the events of the contractual scene and its resilience in the face of contradictory evidence will vary according to the various *formal requirements* it fulfills, such as date, signature of the parties, or of notary. For private contracts, the only form required is that they be signed in the parties' own hand. Yet these signatures do not, in and of themselves, testify to the identity and consent of the parties, who must first formally recognize or disavow their authorship of the contract. If parties do not acknowledge the signature as theirs, a procedure of formal document examination by a court-appointed expert is ordered by the judge. Furthermore, though the content and date of private contracts may not be opposed by testimony, other written documents of equal or higher evidential grade may present contradictory evidence. Finally, though copies may be relied upon in court, only originals have evidential value, and must be available if the authenticity of the copy is contested.

In spite of the eminently Cartesian spirit of the civilist approach, not only are the principles of the Code considerably extended by case law addressing omissions, ambiguities, and loopholes, but there are also substantial exceptions to the arithmetic of preconstituted proof. First, a written document may fail to fulfill its form requirements: for example, that it be signed. Such failure does not imply that the contract is void, or that it cannot be proven, but rather that the document qualifies only as *prima facie* evidence, and the arithmetic of its value is left to the appraisal of the judge. In fact, a judge may admit under the same conditions any written document "emanating from the party against which claims are made and which makes plausible the alleged fact" along with any testimony that may further support it. The judge may also consider the record of the sworn testimonies of the parties as such written *prima facie* evidence. As well, in cases where parties are unable to produce a written document due to theft, war, natural destruction, loss, or social norms (e.g., a debt between husband and wife), proof may obtain by any means, including testimony.

By requiring adherence to basic rules of form, and by specifying the arithmetic of their evidential value, the Civil Code ensures contracting parties a certain amount of predictability and a more level playing field in litigation. Yet judges have remained pragmatically aware of the many limitations of written proof instruments; their susceptibility to tampering, loss, and accidental destruction; or even their absence between parties who expected to be primarily bound by their *bona fides*. The courts have consequently protected the ability of judges to rule based on their inner conviction, and it is indeed one of the sovereign powers of French judges to evaluate the relative strength of all evidence presented to them—an evaluation protected from challenge on appeal.

To Reform or Not to Reform

In the 1970s, new communication technologies (telephone, telex, fax) and new methods of reproducing and archiving documents (photocopiers, microfilms, microforms) simultaneously extended and challenged the primacy of paper as contractual instrument. In particular, Computer Output Microfilm (COM) found widespread use in France as a cost-effective way for the storage and retrieval of the "paperwork explosion" experienced by the military, scientific, financial, and insurance fields.[17] Yet the formal requirements of written proof posed significant hurdles to their adoption in the business world: on the one hand, the obligation to preconstitute proof for all transactions over 50FF imposed a heavy administrative burden on transactions of small value; on the other hand, the requirement to keep originals meant that the advantages of microfilming could not be leveraged to bring about reductions in storage costs of records. In 1980, the French Senate proposed to address both issues through a limited reform of evidential rules.[18] The first restriction was easily addressed: the reform raised the ceiling so that transactions under 5000FF could be proved by any means.

Determining the evidential status of copies proved more complex however, requiring a subtle balancing act between the formal rules of pre-constituted proof and the judge's sovereign powers over the evaluation of the evidence presented to him. It also required confronting the problem of *technological mediation*: between the document originally witnessed by the parties and the one presented in court, a series of highly technical processes—electronic, optical, chemical—had intervened. How could the courts gauge their reliability or susceptibility to fraud? Who was best equipped to provide this expertise? The initial proposal from the Senate suggested copies be granted an evidential value equivalent to the original, as long as it could be demonstrated that the copy be a *faithful* and *durable* one. Given the burden of such a demonstration, however, it proposed that a copy would be *presumed faithful* if it provided a reproduction "of the integral content and of the exact form of the original title," and *presumed durable* if it was "established on a media of a quality offering every guarantee of conservation."[19]

The mechanism of evidentiary presumptions allows a court to assume a plausible fact is true until rebutted by some contrary evidence. A classic legal presumption is that the child born of a husband and wife living together is considered the natural child of the husband, and parties alleging the contrary bear the burden of providing a paternity test. In decreeing what the law considers common sense, presumptions thus affect a shift in the burden of proof.[20] The Senate proposal would thus have two main consequences: on the one hand, instead of having to demonstrate the faithfulness of the copies themselves, parties would merely have to use a technology that meets the criteria of the presumption; on the other hand, the legal endorsement of the presumption would confer considerable legitimacy and a significant market advantage to the evidentiary technology in question.

Despite recognizing that admitting copies as self-standing evidence would increase the opportunities for fraud, the Senate emphasized that judges would still have latitude in deciding whether a copy did indeed qualify for the presumption. Furthermore, in most cases, the judge would be faced with several versions of the same title—some originals, some copies—and thus be able to compare their relative faithfulness. The National Assembly's legislative commission strongly disagreed. However faithful and durable reproductions might be, it argued, they are *not* originals. Given constant innovation in counterfeiting techniques, technical experts, rather than presumptions, could assist the judge in assessing the authenticity of a copy. Thus, when determined faithful and durable, copies should be admissible as evidence without the original title but their value left to the judge's appraisal.[21]

During parliamentary debate, the National Assembly scrapped both proposals. Rather than grant copies explicit standing as evidence, it took advantage of the existing exceptions to preconstituted proof allowing parties to rely on copies when originals have been lost. Copies were required to be faithful and durable reproductions of the originals, with a presumption of *durability* granted when the reproduction is indelible and "entails an irreversible modification of the media." The law provided no explicit criteria for faithfulness, nor specified the evidential status of the copies. In theory, copies could thus be opposed by all means, including testimony, and their value left to the judge's appraisal.

In the end, then, the reform performed minimally invasive surgery on the evidential system while still allowing businesses to rely on the new technologies. It avoided dealing with the metaphysics of proof that a deeper consideration would necessarily entail. It adopted a highly conservative technical presumption—that the chemical processes of exposure and development irremediably alter photographic film—and left the rest to the judgment of the court.

Throughout the 1980s and 1990s, the French legal community resounded with repeated calls for a more thorough reexamination of evidence law than had been afforded by the reform. Conflicting jurisprudence over the admissibility of faxes, photocopies, and electronic messages seemed to threaten the overall rationality and coherence of the French evidential regime. Scholars and practitioners were unanimous in arguing that the current system, founded on the primacy of paper-based writing, could not be interpreted so as to admit born-digital materials, documents produced, transmitted, or stored in electronic form.

Under the 1980 reform, admissibility could only be granted as exceptions to written proof—either by arguing that electronic documents were admissible as prima facie evidence, as copies for which originals no long existed, or as falling under private proof conventions. Such exceptions effectively assigned electronic documents a lower status in the proof hierarchy. Admitting electronic documents as full-fledged means of proof seemed to require a more thorough reworking of the system than provided by the reform, one that would address head-on the deeper questions raised by nonpaper writing.

In 1988, Jacques Larrieu, a law professor at the University of Toulouse, published an extensive and influential analysis of the issue with a surprising conclusion. Larrieu argued the probative value of a particular evidence had historically never been based on its intrinsic technical qualities. Rather, the probative value of a written document is inferred from the qualities of its author (e.g., a representative of the state), the forms and procedures required for its production, and the severity of the punishment threatening those who abuse it. Following Levy-Bruhl's sociological analysis, Larrieu argued that the preeminence of writing in French evidence law could not be explained by its material qualities but rather by the extensive symbolic capital it enjoys in French culture and the far-reaching protection it is afforded by the legal system.[22] Granting electronic records the same evidential value as paper-based writing would plausibly heighten their symbolic worth, but legislative intervention by itself would not suffice "to grant to these modern techniques the 'social endorsement' which alone can establish confidence in a means of proof."[23]

It is with these considerations in mind that in November 1996, the Ministry of Justice entrusted a small group of prominent jurists with the task of outlining a possible reform of evidence law fully integrating electronic documents within its scope. One year later, the group submitted a proposal for a bill "relative to the adaptation of evidence law to new technologies," which began circulating in October 1998 as an *avant-projet de loi*.

Defining Writing

The group noted with Larrieu that arguments for or against reform did not primarily focus on the technical issues of affording legal recognition to electronic documents. Rather, they sparred over the need to foster trust in new technologies or, conversely, the dangers of producing legislation destined to age prematurely in light of a rapidly moving technological horizon. Indeed, several members of the group feared the reform would undermine the philosophy of the existing system. Even if reform proved eventually necessary, it should remain careful "not to betray the spirit of the Civil code," in particular the preconstitution of written proof and the protection it provides in evenly sharing the burden of proof between the parties.[24]

What kind reform should then take place? The group weighed the relative merits of several approaches, including the status quo. One could widen the scope of the free proof regime—that is, admit all and any electronic writing—but leave the evaluation of its evidential qualities to the court. One could also continue the current practice of admitting electronic documents as exceptions to written proof. However, this approach continued to relegate electronic evidence to a second-class status, and in any case, it was conceptually difficult to define born-digital documents as faithful reproductions of paper originals, when these never existed in the first place. Finally, one could also formally recognize the right for parties to conclude private proof conventions, a mechanism already admitted by jurisprudence and widely employed for debit and credit cards. Such private agreements did not, however, guarantee an even playing field with respect to the burden of proof.

Thus, although French legislation and jurisprudence did not formally deny admissibility and legal effects to electronic documents, it lacked a clear definition of their status. Like Larrieu, the members of the group agreed that a reform would mostly perform a symbolic function. Yet inasmuch as "in the citizens' practice and imaginary, writing remains assimilated to paper," the law could also serve a pedagogical purpose, by introducing a new characterization of written proof that would emphasize its independence from any particular media, paper or electronic. It is in this spirit that the group suggested the new article 1316 that defined written evidence as *any sequence of intelligible symbols, whatever its media and means of transmission*. Though the authors underlined that case law had never restricted writing to a specific physical media or sets of symbols, critics were quick to point out that the definition was so abstract as to include within its scope a broad range of ephemeral traces: "'*Loulou pour la vie, Riri*' engraved on a tree trunk or on a wooden desk, words traced out on a misty window, in addition to writing on sand or an advertisement traced in smoke by a plane, all constitute, in application of article 1316, written proof."[25]

In its attempt to provide a modern definition of writing as fully independent from any specific material basis, the new article 1316 thus seemed to potentially sacrifice an essential property of written proof, that is, its fixity and durability over time.

Proving by Electronic Writing

If the reform were to grant electronic writing full status as a means of proof, several difficult issues would need to be addressed: (a) the conditions under which such a status would be granted; (b) the probative value of electronic writing; and (c), its relationship to other means of proof, that is, its place within the evidence hierarchy, with the specific problem of how to adjudicate conflicts between paper-based and electronic writing.

The group proposed to add two new articles to the Civil Code to follow the new article 1316. They defined the conditions necessary for electronic writing to be granted probative value: "Electronic writing is considered as having probative value, provided that the person from which it emanates is duly identified and that it is drawn up and preserved under conditions able to guarantee its trustworthiness." That is, electronic writing would have to fulfill three separate conditions: (a) *imputability*—the possibility of linking it to its author, producer, or originator; (b) *formalism*—having been drawn up under appropriate conditions; (c) *integrity*—having been preserved following appropriate procedures. Although the specific nature of the link between author and document and the criteria for evaluating appropriate "conditions" would be left to the sovereign appraisal of the judge, once those conditions were satisfied, electronic writing would be writing, period. As the group stated, "electronic writing is elevated to the rank of written proof. No longer will we ask ourselves whether it must considered a beginning of written proof, or an exception to written proof. It is a written title, affording to the one who uses it a full and complete proof."[26]

The group felt, however, that the boldness of granting electronic writing full probative value should be tempered by a more cautious approach in establishing the degree of that force and, in particular, the question of establishing the burden of proof. That is, presented with an electronic document, how could a party challenge its trustworthiness? The working group pondered whether, given his access to the inner workings of the computerized system, "the burden must lie on the one who controls the technology, i.e., the operator of the computerized system, to prove the proper functioning of this system?" On the other hand, such a burden would lead, in effect, to a presumption of the system's untrustworthiness until proof of the contrary by the operator. The working group thus preferred a middle-ground approach that would distribute the burden of proof among the parties: it granted neither negative or positive presumptions to the technical system and required parties to gather "serious, precise, and concordant" evidence to convince a judge that the system malfunctioned. The balance of power between the parties and the technology was thus achieved by providing specific criteria for the admissibility of evidence against electronic writing and ultimately relying on the judge's evaluation of how specific evidence met these criteria.

Still, granting electronic writing standing equal to paper seemed risky. Rather than leaving the matter entirely to the judge, the group preferred to establish a hierarchy within written proof that would distinguish between the "classical writing of the Civil Code" and new technologies: electronic writing would not be able to prove against properly preconstituted paper instruments. For all other cases, "the courts solve conflicts of written evidence by determining, by any means, the most credible title."

The question of the signature, which, like writing, the Civil Code had never seen fit to define, remained. Jurisprudence had however repeatedly ruled that depending on context and type of document, a wide range of methods could fulfill the role of a handwritten signature, as long as they provided for identification and manifestation of consent. The working group thus sought to define "the ordinary function of signatures" in those two terms: "The signature necessary to complete a private act identifies the person to which it is opposed and manifests his consent to the obligations which result from the act. It is understood as the affixing of one's name or other personal signs, or the use of a mechanism of identification incorporated to the act or constituting a whole with it."

Defining electronic signatures required only an extension of this basic definition. Rather than rely on an explicit technology, the extension merely required that they consist "in the use of a trustworthy process, guaranteeing its link with the act to which it is affixed." The group underlined that such trustworthy technologies already existed, namely cryptographic signatures, but expressed some doubts that "the ordinary tasks of everyday life would accommodate its complexity."[27]

Global Signatures

The French jurists were not alone in attempting to update their antiquated evidential systems. In the late 1990s, in the span of a few short years, dozens of countries, from Estonia to Tunisia, from Singapore to the United States, adopted laws mandating courts to admit electronic signatures as evidence. Historical precedent suggests that such reform should have proceeded slowly: ancient, often arcane, rules for framing the admissibility and adjudication of written evidence would have to be rewritten; new formulations for long-standing concepts of originals, authentic copies, signatures, and records would have to be devised. However, the explosion of the New Economy in the mid-1990s insured that all over the world, governments lent a much readier ear to calls for adapting their legislation in order to ensure the most favorable environment for the blossoming of e-commerce.[28]

A broad range of institutions—professional, state, national, international, and supranational—worked at producing the new concepts and strategies needed to foster the legislative adoption of digital signatures. Among others, the United Nations Commission on International Trade Law, the American Bar Association, and the European Union produced policies, guidelines, and legislation, documents extensively shared and discussed among the small of community of experts that worked on the issue. As these institutions attempted to design a workable framework for electronic evidence, the cryptographic signature model offered itself as a particularly comprehensive conceptualization of the issue, complete with extensive mathematical analysis, patents, standards, business models, and working implementations. The question of how to take advantage of the maturity of this particular solution while developing concepts and legislation that would stand the test of time presented itself over and over, as the following brief overview demonstrates.

United Nations Commission on International Trade Law

The mandate of the United Nations Commission on International Trade Law (UNCITRAL) is the promotion of "the harmonization and unification of international commercial law." In 1996, the Commission's electronic commerce working group published a Model Law on E-Commerce with the aim of broadly facilitating "the use of modern means of communications and storage of information, such as electronic data interchange (EDI), electronic mail and telecopy, with or without the use of such support as the Internet."[29] Model Laws are meant to serve as "ready-to-enact" legislation, transposable by legislatures in their national context with little modification.

The Model Law on E-Commerce introduced several influential concepts and analytical strategies. The most important one is that of *nondiscrimination*, which states that "information shall not be denied legal effect, validity or enforceability solely on the grounds that it is in the form of a data message."[30] That is, to dismiss electronic evidence, courts must rely on other criteria than its mere electronic nature. The Model Law further proposed that within statutes of evidence law, three requirements typically prevent the realization of the nondiscrimination principle: the obligation to provide information in the form of *written document*, the obligation to *sign* such documents, and the obligation to provide *originals*. To overcome these obstacles, the Model Law suggested the definition of "functional equivalents" to writing, signature, and originals, "based on an analysis of the purposes and functions of the traditional paper-based requirement with a view to determining how those purposes or functions could be fulfilled through electronic-commerce techniques." For each requirement, the Model Law defined the following functional equivalents:

1. *Writing* "Where the law requires information to be in writing, that requirement is met by a data message if the information contained therein is accessible so as to be usable for subsequent reference."

2. *Signature* "(a) The signing method must enable one to identity the signer, and indicate that the signer manifests his consent; (b) the trustworthiness of the signing method must be proportional to the value or object for which the data message was created in the first place" (principle of proportionality).

3. *Originals* "A data message is considered to be an original if there is (a) a reasonable guarantee as to the integrity of the information from the moment of its creation, and (b) the information can be shown to the person who requires it."[31]

The Model Law has been cited as a reference by most electronic signature legislation. Although the principles of nondiscrimination and functional equivalence have enjoyed wide dissemination, the significance of the principle of proportionality and the cost-risk trade-offs it entails has been more rarely acknowledged.

American Bar Association
In 1996, the Information Security Committee of the American Bar Association (ABA) published a set of recommendations, "Digital Signature Guidelines: Legal Infrastructure for Certification Authorities and Secure Electronic Commerce," directed at American state legislatures. The *Utah Digital Signature Act*, the first American statute to legislate digital signatures, was directly inspired by the ABA guidelines, itself becoming a "model law" for other state legislatures. The Guidelines' editorial committee was chaired by Michael Baum, an attorney and vice president of PKI vendor VeriSign, and also included three representatives of CertCo, another PKI vendor. It is thus no surprise that, in contrast with the UNCITRAL Model Law, the Guidelines were not concerned with establishing a broad legal framework for electronic authentication technologies. Rather, they advocated for legislation that literally hard-wired cryptographic signatures into the law to the exclusion of all other possible authentication technologies:

> In a digital setting, today's broad legal concept of signature may well include markings as diverse as digitized images of paper signatures, typed notations such as /s/ John Smith, or even addressing notations, such as electronic mail origination headers. From an information security viewpoint, these simple electronic signatures are distinct from the digital signatures described in this tutorial and in the technical literature. . . . These Guidelines use digital signature only as it is used in information security terminology, as meaning the result of applying the technical processes described in this tutorial.[32]

The defining contribution of the Guidelines however is its introduction of a number of evidentiary presumptions concerning the validity of digital signatures: "In resolving a dispute involving a digital signature, it is rebuttably presumed that: . . . (2) a digital signature verified by reference to the public-key listed in a valid certificate is the digital signature of the subscriber listed in that certificate; (3) the message associated with a verified digital signature has not been altered from its original form."[33]

The effectiveness of two security services provided by digital signatures—authentication and integrity—is thus presumed as a matter of law. What is the basis of such a presumption? Quite simply, that "certificates issued by certification authorities and time-stamps provided by a trustworthy system *are likely to be reliable*; therefore, presuming their correctness will conserve resources by not requiring routine proof of what is generally true."[34] The issue then becomes one of establishing procedures to distinguish between trustworthy and untrustworthy cryptographic systems, an issue on which the Guidelines provided little guidance.

Furthermore, although it is always possible to overcome a rebuttable presumption and "repudiate" the signature, it is up to the party contesting its validity to provide convincing evidence to the contrary. The third characteristic of the cryptographic signature model, non-repudiation, is thus (partially) realized, not as a consequence of the inherent qualities of cryptographic signatures, but as an effect of the burden of proof borne by those wanting to contest their validity. The consequences are important, as one attorney warned: "Consumers who participate in the infrastructure developed under the Utah act subject themselves to a far greater risk of liability than they face in other electronic transactions, such as credit card or debit card transactions. The liability allocations and evidentiary burdens of the Utah act contradict the spirit, and in certain circumstances . . . the letter, of consumer-protection statutes such as the Electronic Fund Transfer Act and the Truth in Lending Act."[35]

By combining these evidentiary presumptions with a liability cap for certification authorities, the Utah Digital Signature Act did provide an attractive legal environment for one group: entrepreneurs contemplating the business opportunities of the nascent market for public-key certificates.[36]

The European Union
As they observed the rapid spread of the Internet across the European landscape in the mid-1990s, EU legislators pondered what kind of regulatory framework might best usher in the "European Information Society." The development of the European Common Market requires abolishing all obstacles to trade among member states, yet must be achieved in the least intrusive way possible with respect to their national sovereignty. The resounding success of the European GSM mobile phone infrastructure gave

regulators good reason to think they might strike again the appropriate balance. The harmonization of technical standards and economic frameworks across member states had succeeded in giving the European Union a unified market for phone services, along with a considerable technological head start over the United States, whose own industry struggled with the market fragmentation wrought by competing technical standards.[37]

Martin Bangemann, then the European commissioner responsible for information technology, saw the success of the GSM directive as a blueprint for a "market-driven revolution" in which "technological progress and the evolution of the market mean that Europe must make a break from policies based on principles which belong to a time before the advent of the information revolution. The key issue for the emergence of new markets is the need for a new regulatory environment allowing full competition." Because of the network effects that characterize information services, it was important to rapidly establish first-to-market positions and thus "identify and establish the minimum of regulation needed, at the European level, to ensure the rapid emergence of efficient European information infrastructures and services."[38] Given authenticated electronic exchanges were presumed to form an essential requirement for the blossoming of the coming European Information Society, the Commission moved quickly to avoid any internal market obstacles to the development of such exchanges.

In 1997, the Commission began to take steps toward an harmonized legal framework for electronic signatures across all member states. The framework was to be enacted through a *directive*, a uniquely European regulatory instrument. A directive "is binding, as to the result to be achieved, upon each Member State to which it is addressed, but shall leave to the national authorities the choice of form and methods."[39] That is, a directive carries obligations of results, not of means. It is thus the primary legislative instrument for legal harmonization among member states. Though it is up to the member states to decide which measures should be adopted in order to comply with a directive, they are obligated to repeal all contradictory national legislation.

In drafting the directive, the Commission's biggest concern related to the issue of "technological neutrality." The explanatory memorandum attached to the initial proposal explained:

While there is much discussion and work on digital signature technologies which employ public-key cryptography, a Directive at the European level should be technology-neutral and should not focus only on these kinds of signatures. Since a variety of authentication mechanisms is expected to develop, the scope of this Directive should be broad enough to cover a spectrum of "electronic signatures," which would include digital signatures based on public-key cryptography as well as other means of authenticating data.[40]

The regulatory framework should thus, on the one hand, "create a clear framework for generating trust in digital signatures, while, on the other hand, remain sufficiently flexible to react to new technological developments."[41] The reconciliation of these two objectives—capitalizing on the "most recognized form of electronic signature" to rapidly establish a thriving market and establishing a framework flexible enough to accommodate a broad range of technological solutions to authentication—proved a major tension in the successive versions of the directive that circulated between the various European bodies responsible for its enactment.

The final version, adopted on December 13, 1999, settled on a two-tiered approach that distinguished between two kinds of electronic signatures with different legal effects.[42] It first defined electronic signatures as a generic method for providing authentication (without providing a definition of that term): "Electronic signatures means data in electronic form which are attached to or logically associated with other electronic data and which serve as method of authentication."[43] To this generic definition, it added one for "advanced electronic signatures": "An electronic signature which meets the following requirements: (a) it is uniquely linked to the signatory; (b) it is capable of identifying the signatory; (c) it is created using means that the signatory can maintain under his sole control; (d) it is linked to the data to which it relates in such a manner that any subsequent change of the data is detectable."[44]

The definition succinctly captured the three security services of the cryptographic signature model outlined earlier: requirement (b) provides for the identification of the signatory, requirements (a) and (c) provide for non-repudiation, through a presumption of control over the private key, and requirement (d) provides for data integrity, through the ability of the verification algorithm to detect modifications of a single bit to the message after creation of the signature.

Each type of electronic signatures was attributed its own conditions for admissibility and resulting legal effects. On the one hand, generic electronic signatures provided the baseline case for nondiscrimination:

"Member States shall ensure that an electronic signature is not denied legal effectiveness and admissibility as evidence in legal proceedings solely on the grounds that it is . . . in electronic form."[45] On the other hand, member states were required to amend their national laws so that cryptographic signatures "satisfy the legal requirements of a signature in relation to data in electronic form in the same manner as a handwritten signature satisfies those requirements in relation to paper-based data; and are admissible as evidence in legal proceedings."[46] In contrast with generic electronic signatures then, the directive mandated that member states go beyond mere admissibility and grant cryptographic signatures equal standing to handwritten ones.

Like the presumptions of the ABA's Guidelines, this evidentiary advantage was meant to motivate the development of a European industry of cryptographic signature services, including certification, hardware and software devices, time-stamping, and so on. So as to guarantee the trustworthiness of such services, the directive required member states to transpose four annexes specifying minimal requirements that such services and devices would be expected to meet. For example, given that non-repudiation is based on users' ability to control their cryptographic keys, requirement III.1.c stated that "secure signature-creation devices must, by appropriate technical and procedural means, ensure at the least that the signature-creation-data [i.e., keys] used for signature generation can be reliably protected by the legitimate signatory against the use of others." Remarkably, the directive issued only nonbinding recommendations for "secure signature-verification devices." That is, although manufacturers of signature creation devices had to meet specific quality requirements, for signature verification—the second and essential part of the signature process—manufacturers were literally left to their own devices.

Cryptographic signatures were thus given a head start in the form of a well-defined legal status (fulfilling the same requirements as handwritten signatures); any other technology falling under the generic category would be admissible, but with unspecified legal effects. Beyond these baseline requirements however, member states were still free to define the evidential value of these signatures in any manner they preferred. Indeed, the Commission was careful to include a disclaimer that the directive "does not affect national rules regarding the unfettered judicial consideration of evidence."[47]

La Loi du 13 mars 2000

In August 1997, Prime Minister Lionel Jospin formally acknowledged that the Minitel, France's telematic pride and joy, had been superseded by the Internet. The Minitel embodied a distinctively French approach to the development of information networks in which state-owned telecoms commanded the design of the entire network—software, hardware, infrastructure, and services. Yet Jospin could conclude only that "Minitel, as a network bounded by the nation, is technologically limited and threatens to constitute a progressive hindrance to the development of new and promising applications of information technologies."[48]

In spite of the symbolic weight of this announcement, Jospin's speech argued for the relevance of "a political vision of the Information Society," one that would contest "discourses presenting the inevitable effacement of the State." At stake was nothing less than "the economic power and the cultural influence of France in the coming century." And because such power and influence would involve the development of new regulatory and legal instruments, Jospin mandated the *Conseil d'état* to conduct an extensive study that would fully consider any and all necessary adaptations to French legislation. The *Conseil* did things thoroughly: 50 experts, meeting in 3 subcommissions (protection of the individual, electronic commerce, intellectual property), conducted more than 230 interviews between October 1997 and June 1998, including a one-week visit to Washington and New York by a delegation.

The report began with an assessment of the new map of regulatory institutions associated with global computing networks. It highlighted that France had only reluctantly intervened in such institutions, in effect leaving plenty of elbow room for American economic and cultural imperialism: "This debate is international, and time for reflection is running out. Very important international negotiations are already under way and, for some of them, about to conclude. These negotiations, for the most part conducted under the initiative of North American public and private interests, threaten to structure practices and behaviors over digital networks. Tomorrow, it will be too late to defend a different conception of human or consumer rights."[49]

The challenges to such a defense were significant. The bottom-up and distributed organization of these new networks seemed to directly and profoundly question the French attitude to power, the pervasive impulse to regulate from above. As the *Conseil* further noted, "This implies a profound disruption of our modes of thinking and working: to a vertical and centralized approach must be substituted transversal and decentralized orientations." Such disruption did not imply however that existing legislation was inapplicable, and the report firmly emphasized that "there does not exist and there is no need for Internet- and network-specific laws."[50]

In spite of this declaration of faith, the report did include a new legislative proposal for evidence law reform, one that combined elements of the working group's *avant-projet de loi*, and of the forthcoming European directive. The *Conseil d'état* went further than either proposal when it suggested applying a *presumption of trustworthiness* to cryptographic signatures: "When an electronic message is presented in order to establish the proof of an act, it is presumed endowed with the probative value of a private act if it is accompanied by a certificate delivered by an accredited certification authority, independent of the signatory, under conditions specified by decree, which guarantee the integrity of the message, the imputability to the designated author, and its durable preservation."[51]

So much for France defending a "different conception of consumer rights." VeriSign's shareholders couldn't have been more pleased with the apportionment of liability proposed by the *Conseil d'état*.

The Final Bill

In August 1999, a mere two years after officially embracing the Internet age, Jospin took stock of the situation in another speech, stating that the preceding two years had been nothing less than a "profound collective mutation: the entry of France into the information age."[52] Indeed, France seemed on the brink of a profound cultural, economic, and technical revolution. The miraculous healing powers of the New Economy brought a soothing relief to a public more accustomed to its daily dose of energetic strikes, public-health disasters, and corruption scandals. Information technologies seemed to be about not only new ways of connecting with other people but also new ways of making, having, and spending (and eventually losing) money. The Internet start-up was celebrated not only as an economic triumph but also as a model that French entrepreneurs could use to their competitive advantage, if only enough regulatory red tape were to be removed.

Indeed, the government had recently decreed lawful the free use of strong cryptographic products, a decision Jospin described as "of the utmost importance, since [such products] guarantee both confidentiality of messages and security of transactions." Such a decree was only one example of the work accomplished by the government in order to adapt the French legislative framework to the Information Society, and Jospin announced that "the proposal for a bill 'regarding the adaptation of evidence law to information technologies and relative to electronic signatures' will be presented at the next meeting of the Ministerial Council. The main legal obstacles to the development of dematerialized transactions should thus be lifted."[53]

Jospin further announced that the government would soon propose a comprehensive bill that would define the social charter of the French Information Society. At that point, however, the electronic signature bill constituted the only clearly defined element of that charter and was submitted to the Senate on September 1, 1999. Built on the *avant-projet* drafted by the working group, the new version incorporated several of the recommendations from the *Conseil d'état*. It largely adopted the working group's definition of writing and requirements for admissibility, its proposal for resolving conflicts between paper-based and electronic written proof and its recognition of private proof agreements. However, instead of establishing an evidential differential between paper-based and electronic written proof, it resolutely affirmed the directive's nondiscrimination principle:

Art. 1316-3—Writing on electronic media has the same evidential value as writing on paper.

The bill also disregarded the working group's proposals with regard to apportionment of the burden of proof, taking up instead the *Conseil d'état* proposal to shift the question over to the signature mechanism's trustworthiness:

Art. 1316-4—The signature necessary to perfect a juridical act identifies the one who affixes it and manifests his consent to the obligations which flow from this act. When it is electronic, it consists of the use of a trustworthy identification mechanism guaranteeing the link with the act to which the signature is attached. The trustworthiness of this mechanism is presumed, until proof of the contrary, when the signature is created, the identity of the signatory ensured, and the integrity of the act guaranteed, under conditions established by a decree from the *Conseil d'état*.

The bill thus introduced a rebuttable presumption of trustworthiness of electronic signature mechanisms subject to their conformance to criteria to be laid out in a forthcoming application decree from the *Conseil d'état*. The final bill (see figure 5.1) was adopted unanimously by both chambers of the Parliament, with a single significant modification, the inclusion of *authentic acts* within the scope of the bill, an event whose consequences are discussed at length in the next chapter.

The application decree was published a short year later, in March 2001.[54] It was entirely devoted to the transposition of the four annexes of the European directive and listed the minimal quality requirements that cryptographic signatures devices and certification service providers would need to meet in order to qualify for the presumption. The technical and legal machinery required for accreditation was bewildering: no fewer than thirty-five distinct criteria were listed just for certification services, with multiple additional executive orders required, including those necessary for the creation of a committee responsible for the accreditation of the bodies responsible for the accreditation of the providers, along with all relevant rules and procedures for these brand new regulatory bodies.

The byzantine technicity of the decree spurred a small industry of legal analyses attempting, appropriately, to decipher its structure and consequences.[55] Several scholars could not help but comment that the mechanics of the presumption had turned into *une usine à gaz*—"bloatware"—that clashed with the elegant lines of both the French evidential system and the mathematics of public-key cryptography. As France's most eminent evidence law scholars put it, "It seems doubtful that the purpose of the Civil Code is to pilot the economy."[56] Perhaps the most disconcerting feature of the decree was, in accord with the directive, its failure to regulate signature verification. After all, verification constitutes the single locus of the signature's mathematical and forensic truth, the primary justification for embracing the complex mechanics of public-key infrastructures in the first place. A "secure signature-verification device" that failed to ensure with reasonable certainty any of the recommendations—including "that the signature is reliably verified and the result of that verification is correctly displayed"—could still benefit from the presumption of trustworthiness, as long as it met the other requirements.

Another legislative reform was to provide the escape route out of this cryptographic labyrinth. In 2002, the New Code of Civil Procedure updated

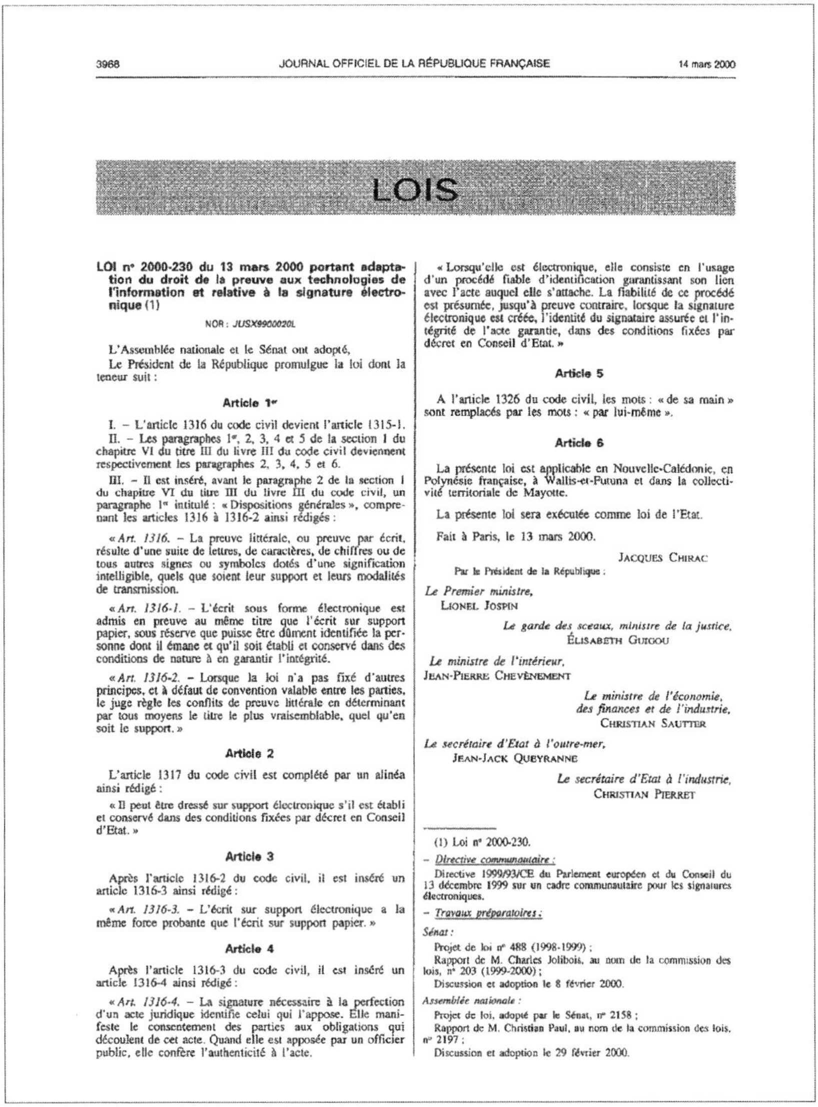

3968 JOURNAL OFFICIEL DE LA RÉPUBLIQUE FRANÇAISE 14 mars 2000

LOIS

LOI n° 2000-230 du 13 mars 2000 portant adaptation du droit de la preuve aux technologies de l'information et relative à la signature électronique (1)

NOR : *JUSX9900020L*

L'Assemblée nationale et le Sénat ont adopté,

Le Président de la République promulgue la loi dont la teneur suit :

Article 1er

I. – L'article 1316 du code civil devient l'article 1315-1.

II. – Les paragraphes 1er, 2, 3, 4 et 5 de la section 1 du chapitre VI du titre III du livre III du code civil deviennent respectivement les paragraphes 2, 3, 4, 5 et 6.

III. – Il est inséré, avant le paragraphe 2 de la section 1 du chapitre VI du titre III du livre III du code civil, un paragraphe 1er intitulé : « Dispositions générales », comprenant les articles 1316 à 1316-2 ainsi rédigés :

« *Art. 1316.* – La preuve littérale, ou preuve par écrit, résulte d'une suite de lettres, de caractères, de chiffres ou de tous autres signes ou symboles dotés d'une signification intelligible, quels que soient leur support et leurs modalités de transmission.

« *Art. 1316-1.* – L'écrit sous forme électronique est admis en preuve au même titre que l'écrit sur support papier, sous réserve que puisse être dûment identifiée la personne dont il émane et qu'il soit établi et conservé dans des conditions de nature à en garantir l'intégrité.

« *Art. 1316-2.* – Lorsque la loi n'a pas fixé d'autres principes, et à défaut de convention valable entre les parties, le juge règle les conflits de preuve littérale en déterminant par tous moyens le titre le plus vraisemblable, quel qu'en soit le support. »

Article 2

L'article 1317 du code civil est complété par un alinéa ainsi rédigé :

« Il peut être dressé sur support électronique s'il est établi et conservé dans des conditions fixées par décret en Conseil d'Etat. »

Article 3

Après l'article 1316-2 du code civil, il est inséré un article 1316-3 ainsi rédigé :

« *Art. 1316-3.* – L'écrit sur support électronique a la même force probante que l'écrit sur support papier. »

Article 4

Après l'article 1316-3 du code civil, il est inséré un article 1316-4 ainsi rédigé :

« *Art. 1316-4.* – La signature nécessaire à la perfection d'un acte juridique identifie celui qui l'appose. Elle manifeste le consentement des parties aux obligations qui découlent de cet acte. Quand elle est apposée par un officier public, elle confère l'authenticité à l'acte.

« Lorsqu'elle est électronique, elle consiste en l'usage d'un procédé fiable d'identification garantissant son lien avec l'acte auquel elle s'attache. La fiabilité de ce procédé est présumée, jusqu'à preuve contraire, lorsque la signature électronique est créée, l'identité du signataire assurée et l'intégrité de l'acte garantie, dans des conditions fixées par décret en Conseil d'Etat. »

Article 5

A l'article 1326 du code civil, les mots : « de sa main » sont remplacés par les mots : « par lui-même ».

Article 6

La présente loi est applicable en Nouvelle-Calédonie, en Polynésie française, à Wallis-et-Futuna et dans la collectivité territoriale de Mayotte.

La présente loi sera exécutée comme loi de l'Etat.

Fait à Paris, le 13 mars 2000.

JACQUES CHIRAC

Par le Président de la République :

Le Premier ministre,
LIONEL JOSPIN

Le garde des sceaux, ministre de la justice,
ÉLISABETH GUIGOU

Le ministre de l'intérieur,
JEAN-PIERRE CHEVÈNEMENT

Le ministre de l'économie, des finances et de l'industrie,
CHRISTIAN SAUTTER

Le secrétaire d'Etat à l'outre-mer,
JEAN-JACK QUEYRANNE

Le secrétaire d'Etat à l'industrie,
CHRISTIAN PIERRET

(1) Loi n° 2000-230.

– *Directive communautaire :*

Directive 1999/93/CE du Parlement européen et du Conseil du 13 décembre 1999 sur un cadre communautaire pour les signatures électroniques.

– *Travaux préparatoires :*

Sénat :

Projet de loi n° 488 (1998-1999) ;

Rapport de M. Charles Jolibois, au nom de la commission des lois, n° 203 (1999-2000) ;

Discussion et adoption le 8 février 2000.

Assemblée nationale :

Projet de loi, adopté par le Sénat, n° 2158 ;

Rapport de M. Christian Paul, au nom de la commission des lois, n° 2197 ;

Discussion et adoption le 29 février 2000.

Figure 5.1

The March 13, 2000, law, "bearing on the adaptation of evidence law to information technologies and relative to electronic signatures," available at http://www.legifrance.gouv.fr. From the public domain.

the rules relative to questioned document examination, the procedure that kicks in place when litigating parties deny authorship or signature of a document presented to them. In the case of electronically signed documents, the updated rules now state that the judge begins the procedure by ascertaining whether the signed document meets the conditions required for the presumption of trustworthiness. However, "when an electronic signature is presumed trustworthy, it is the prerogative of the judge to determine whether the elements under his consideration are sufficient to rebut this presumption." By simply refusing to acknowledge an electronic document, parties could automatically call the judge's inner conviction to the rescue. In the end, even when confronted with technologies claimed to possess extraordinary powers of conviction, judges continued to enjoy significant latitude in considering the evidence presented to them.

Conclusion

The process of carving out a place for electronic documents in French evidence law thus repeatedly stumbled on a tension: should the appraisal of their evidentiary qualities belong to the realm of the (Cartesian) arithmetic of preconstituted proof, or to that of the (subjective) inner conviction of the judge? Behind this question looms a larger one: can there be a technology whose material characteristics and whose evidentiary qualities are so exceptional that it may be said to utterly compel the conviction of the parties and judge, indeed, to be "non-repudiable"?

An historical look at the organization of paper-based written proof and the evaluation of its forensic qualities by French courts suggests that in fact, these never relinquished their power to rule to the formal qualities of evidence. In his overview of the development of handwriting analysis in the French system, Ken Alder points to a curious fact: a legal system founded on the primacy of written evidence relied on and accommodated a dubious forensic science of handwriting analysis. Indeed, common-law legal scholars have often marveled at the exceptional career of handwriting expertise in France, when its vague scientific basis and demonstrated unreliability have afforded it a much more limited purview in other legal systems. Alder suggests that the choice was primarily pragmatic in that "there was often no other way to superintend script culture." That is, "insofar as the French state sought to earn its legitimacy by acting as the guarantor of the stability of the social order, it also sought to assure its citizen-subjects of the reliability (and enforceability) of written contracts," and handwriting expertise provided a key element of that reliability.[57]

Indeed, even though the methods of handwriting expertise never matured sufficiently to garner the respectability due to a properly scientific forensic method, this was not in and of itself a fundamental problem. Most of the time, handwriting analysis worked well enough, "If by 'worked' one means that it bolstered judgments from the magistrate's bench by appealing to the impartiality of science (without necessarily offering any of the public accountability or reproducibility that the term "science" usually implies). For this reason, the experts' reports were a powerful tool which the magistrates kept under their discretionary control—to confirm judgments they sought on other grounds."[58] For this reason, the failure of handwriting experts to meet modern scientific criteria did not disqualify it as a useful adjunct to the judicial process, insofar as it served to reinforce that most essential element of a judge's decision: its legitimacy.

It is of course tempting to impute this to just another example of "junk science," the historical failure of the legal process to require and match the exacting standards of the scientific method, perhaps combined with a case of, you know, *"the French . . ."* This is indeed a position adopted by some scholars:

> It is not surprising that the foundations of today's "science" handwriting analysis came out of 19th century Continental thought. Western Europe was then a hotbed of extreme rationalism on the fringes of science, where theories were spun out to satisfyingly mystical complexity and experience was expected to conform or be damned. The same intellectual climate that gave us phrenology, Lombrosian physiognomy and, as previously noted, "graphology," gave us "chirography," or handwriting identification as a "science."[59]

Yet dubious but widely accepted forensic sciences are not exclusive to the French: the lie detector has enjoyed a successful career in American courts (and in the public imagination), despite a similarly dubious scientific foundation.[60]

In the final analysis, just like handwriting expertise, the presumptions of trustworthiness advocated by both the ABA and the *Conseil d'état* deal in the currency of legitimacy. As expressions of dominant norms, presumptions and the judicial decisions based on them draw their legitimacy from the standardization of social relations. By reversing the burden of proof, presumptions imply that if a party must bear the burden of proof, it is because it tries to prove a situation contrary to the presumed acceptable norm.[61] Yet presumptions must be used sparingly: "The authority of presumptions depends in effect that the conception of the social world they express must be identical or sufficiently close to that of the recipients of legal discourse. If these are not convinced of the probability of the solutions imposed to them, the judicial institution runs the risk of being thrown back to its own ideology, which litigants might then feel authorize to contest."[62] In a polyandrous society, for example, the classical presumption of paternity would have little basis.

The presumptions used to induce trust in digital signatures proceed from a slightly different logic, however, because they are not grounded in any empirical sociological truth. Indeed, as evidence law reform swept the planet in the late 1990s, no one had ever used digital signatures to secure a single e-commerce transaction, let alone gone to court over them.[63] The presumption of trustworthiness could be based only on the technocratic processes of evaluation of the conformance of technological devices with standardized requirements. Yet the path between such processes and a widespread perception of "trustworthy" transactions is far from obvious. The layers upon layers of bureaucratic approbation necessary for a signature mechanism to qualify for the presumption are no less opaque and require no less of an act of faith from litigants and judges than trust in cryptography itself. In a very real sense, then, like handwriting analysis, the efficacy of cryptography as a forensic technology could only be presumed to work, with little to no empirical evidence to show for it.

In fact, the "tried-and-trued" common sense that might form the basis of a presumption would tend to point in the opposite direction. Every media report on new breaches and threats to cryptographic systems—and they are a regular occurrence—also threatens the credibility of the presumption.[64] Hence, in using the Civil Code "to pilot the economy," legislators were asking the law to put at risk one of its most precious assets: the legitimacy that founds much of its authority. Is it any wonder then that French judges ultimately hesitated to tie their conviction to the putative trustworthiness of highly complex technical systems, whose large scale deployment remains—for both makers and users—uncharted territory?

All of which brings us back to Lessig, code, and regulation. Gutwirth, de Hert, and Sutter have pointed out that in Lessig's theory, "law, economy, technology and social norms must be assumed to be regulatory practices."[65] That is, in achieving an optimal mutual orientation toward regulatory goals, each must accommodate its own particular mode of existence to the superior cause of regulation. In the case of digital signatures, for example, the law should have accepted the potential sacrifice of some legitimacy in the service of the greater good of mass adoption of public-key technologies and the badly needed security these might have afforded the Information Society.

Indeed, Alder's historical account of the deficient forensics of handwriting analysis suggests that over time, the law might have come to accommodate the presumed trustworthiness of cryptographic signatures in spite of its uncertain qualities. But French law's reliance on written proof can be understood only on account of its overall reliability, as determined by hundreds of years of litigation, along with the resulting case law and scholarly debates—in other words, determined by the modes of deliberation and being in the world that uniquely define law as a social practice. To presume the reliability of cryptographic signatures a priori, without the benefits of these processes, is an altogether different proposition.

Is it thus not possible that Judge Easterbrook was not being flippant when he suggested that *doing nothing* is the precondition to the creative response of law to technology? That, as Gutwirth, de Hert, and Sutter further suggest, "It is only if we let technologies develop themselves to the point where they become actually problematic that lawyers can intervene and add their own appreciation to the picture"?[66] Indeed, it is a remarkable characteristic of the reform described in this chapter that it occurred prior to any actual litigation over digital signatures. One consequence of such an a priori process and of Lessig's approach in general is that it "does not give a chance to the unexpected possibilities that can emerge from the development of the new technologies that he wants to regulate. Neither does he give a chance to the unexpected creativity of the other practices that will come to grips with these technologies."[67] The next chapter is thus concerned with tracing the path of digital signatures as various professional groups—notaries, officers of civil status, land registry judges—sought to integrate them within their daily business routines, and indeed, came to grips with their constraints and possibilities in creative and unexpected ways.

6 Paper and State

On the way to Senate floor, the French bill on electronic signatures was augmented with a terse one-sentence amendment. It stated that "authentic acts can be established on electronic media if drafted and preserved under conditions established by decree from the *Conseil d'État.*" In fewer than two dozen words, the amendment linked a documentary practice dating back to the Romans with the brave new world of electronic networks. The practice is simple: it consists of granting higher evidential value to documents produced by *professional scribes* vested with various degrees of authority by the state. Created following specific rules of form and preserved under appropriate conditions, these documents enjoy a *presumption of authenticity*, providing potential litigants with a higher grade of evidentiary ammunition than that offered by private acts.

Under their various titles—scribe, chancellor, referendary, keeper of the seals, royal notaries—the professionals entrusted with these tasks highlight the essential role of written documents in the organization of the state and the exercise of its power.[1] In *Seeing like a State*, James C. Scott has tied the emergence of the modern state to its ability to develop methods that could reliably associate individuals and space with administrative writings, such as identity papers and mapping surveys. By increasing the "legibility" of citizens and space to a degree of granularity previously unknown, such writings provided the state with new ways to fulfill its traditional objectives of conscription, taxation, and prevention of rebellion.[2] For written documents to provide the technological means necessary to the pursuit of these goals, centuries of cultural, legal, institutional, and technological evolution were necessary. As Clanchy notes,

> Documents did not immediately inspire trust. As with other innovations in technology, there was a long and complex period of evolution . . . before methods of

production were developed which proved acceptable to both traditionalists and to experts in literacy. There was no straight and simple line of progress from memory to written record. People had to persuade—and it was difficult to do—that documentary proof was a sufficient improvement over existing methods to merit the extra expense and mastery of novel techniques which it demanded.[3]

Indeed, the history of written evidence can be understood only in its relationship to the technology it supplanted: witness testimony. In Roman law, writing functioned merely as a memorandum of testimony and as record of the witnesses' presence at the scene of contract; in the Early and High Middle Ages, writing stood subordinate to the oral contract, a material sign whose evidential value remains dependent on its recognition by witnesses. Even then, "the expression of a grant in writing was often less important to the parties than the performance of ceremonial acts of which the charter itself makes no record. The writing was of secondary importance, and was hedged about with repetitious clauses, because less confidence was placed in it than in the oaths and public ceremonies which had traditionally sanctioned conveyances."[4] In France, it is only between the fourteenth and the sixteenth centuries that writing severed that dependence and testified in and of itself under the condition that it be produced and preserved following specific rules.[5] Separate rules evolved for two important categories of written documents: private acts and registers.

In the French southern legal tradition, several kinds of scribes, empowered by various authorities, were able to confer a presumption of authenticity to their written acts: at first by a simple attestation that the acts were written of their own hand; later by the apposition of a registered personal mark; and still later by the fact that notaries signed as delegates of public authority.[6] In the North, authentication of private acts evolved from Germanic and Carolingian traditions of declarations by parties in front of a public tribunal, so as to later benefit from the testimony of privileged witnesses (i.e., professional judges). Such declarations were gradually shifted to representatives of public and moral authorities—for example, municipal, royal, or ecclesiastic.

A broad range of material and institutional technologies were leveraged in the service of authentication: acts in multiple copies, chirographs, deposits in trusted repositories, registration with authorities, transcription in special registers, and many combinations of these. With the 1554 Fontainebleau ordinance, Henri II established the notary's signature as the essential requirement of reliable written evidence: "From today on, all contracts and obligations, receipts and private acts, be, in addition to the notaries' signatures, signed by the consenting parties when they know how to sign, or if they do not know how, at their request, by an honest party know to them."[7] Citing the need to reduce litigation and unburden courts, Louis the XIV's 1667 civil ordinance further declares that henceforth, no witness testimony would be allowed to oppose such notarized documents with respect to their contents or anything that might have been said before, during, or since the signing.

The evidential value of registers developed through the practical needs for reliable identification—in much narrower form than what the concept conveys today. When, in the early sixteenth century, the Bishop of Nantes requires his priests to establish parish registers documenting baptisms, it is solely to prevent marriages forbidden by "spiritual relationships" (e.g., godsons and godmothers). Royal authorities soon discover the usefulness of such registers for combating fraud in the administration of ecclesiastical benefits. With the aim of establishing an individual's date of majority, the 1539 *Ordonnance de Villers-Cotterêts* requires priests to hold "registers as proof of baptisms, including the day and hour of birth" and declares the power of such documents to testify to that effect. In spite of the material and organizational difficulties met in implementing such requirements, the 1579 *Ordonnance de Blois* further demands that priests uphold registers of baptisms, marriages, and death. In order to "avoid proof by testimony often required in court regarding birth, marriage, death, and burials," the *Ordonnance* requires that priests deposit their register yearly at the regional *greffe des jurisdictions*.

Louis XIV's *Ordonnance civile de 1667* significantly extends the role of the registers by requiring they serve to testify to the *status* of persons: that is, in addition to their date of birth, registers must record their filiation and matrimonial status. The *Ordonnance* further specifies a number of form requirements: inscriptions must be written down within days of the event, without any blank space between them; registers must be held in double originals, with the second copy (the *grosse*) to be deposited at the *greffe des jurisdictions* within the first six weeks of the new year, where it will be initialed at the beginning and end by the judge. These new requirements are supported by an enhanced evidential status: parish registers will constitute the default mode of proof of civil status in court, while testimony will be allowed solely in cases of lost or inexistent registers.[8] Given their now essential role as evidence in litigation, the *Ordonnance* requires registers' custodians to deliver copies of inscriptions ("extracts") to interested parties, against a fee fixed by the state. Throughout the seventeenth and eighteenth centuries, a steady stream of rules further specifies the correct maintenance of registers, the data they record, and their corresponding power to testify on an expanded range of issues relative to individuals' civil status. In 1787, the difficulty for protestants to establish their status finally leads to the separation of the role of the priest as church official and as *officier d'état civil*, officer of civil status, representative of royal power.

The 1804 Napoleonic Civil Code would bring together the various professionals empowered to create reliable written evidence under the umbrella of a single legal category: *authenticity*.[9] In its elegant aphoristic style, the Code simply defines authentic acts as those produced according to required rules of forms ("*solenités*") by a public officer vested with the authority of the state. Beyond notarized contracts and registers of civil status, a broad range of documents would eventually fall under the umbrella of authenticity: land registers, court decisions and their copies, official testimonies from bailiffs, and so on. For such documents, the system brings much convenience: authentic acts testify in and of themselves, not only beyond testimony, but beyond all other written evidence. Firmly seated at the top of the evidential hierarchy, they can be contested only through a complex procedure whose failure exposes to damages. Conversely, public officers face prison and heavy fines for committing the serious crime of forgery—*faux en écriture publique*.[10]

Although the Code provides the overarching definition of authenticity, the formal requirements specific to each type of public officers are specified in application decrees (*décrets d'application*), regularly updated as the tasks and circumstances of each professional group evolve. Yet as one of France's most eminent scholars of authenticity, Pierre Catala, noted, "Article 1317, which defines authentic acts, has resisted electricity, wireless communications, the telegraph, the telephone, the telex, and radio transmissions. Not a single letter which constitutes it has been modified since 1804."[11] That is, not until the 2000 evidence law reform. The Senate's bold declaration that authentic acts could be established on electronic media thus constituted a significant leap for all concerned parties, especially as it left all specifics to future decrees.

The drafting of those decrees would require thorough examination of a form of evidence whose material qualities could be understood only within the institutions and practices that ensured its production, preservation, and evaluation. This examination would not proceed from a blank slate. Many of the professions involved had already invested significant efforts and capital to experiment with the potential of networking technologies to modernize their workflow—and perhaps, along the way, their professional image as well. To various degrees, all of them were already producing, transmitting, storing, and even authenticating electronic authentic acts.

In this chapter, I examine three of these institutional responses to the new paradigm of electronic authenticity: the deployment of a profession-wide public-key infrastructure by the *Conseil supérieur du notariat* (CSN); the development of an electronic signature solution by the *Service central d'état civil* (SCEC) in Nantes; and the transcription of 2 million entries of the Alsace-Moselle's land registers into a database. Each response was driven by different sets of motivations, organizational issues, and historical trajectories of documentary practices. Notaries were primarily concerned with the role of the privileged witness in the context of real estate contracts concluded over computer networks; officers of civil status, with leveraging the benefits of digitization in the context of identity documents exclusively delivered in print; and the land registry, with the creation of a database whose contents could be relied on with the same degree of confidence the paper registers had previously enjoyed.[12]

What might we learn from such studies? As noted in chapter 4, cryptographers have tended to assume that the properties of cryptographic objects will translate transparently into the complex social and institutional settings they are deployed in. That is, all stakeholders—consumers, service providers, legal professionals, regulators, and so on—are assumed to understand and interact with cryptographic technologies exactly as intended by their designers. Through descriptions of actual contexts in which digital signatures are being deployed, this chapter argues that this is not an effective social theory of technology. Instead, as the case studies will demonstrate, the integration of digital signatures within work practices, institutional settings, legal traditions, and user's cognitive models requires significant transformations to the original cryptographic model. Such case studies then might provide useful feedback for examining the adequacy of the model, inform its possible revision, or inspire altogether new designs to emerge.

The case studies also provide evidence of the depth of our historical engagement with paper. In *The Myth of the Paperless Office*, Abigail Sellen and Richard Harper, two human-computer interaction researchers, provide an extensive argument for why this relationship matters. In a series of ethnographic studies of office tasks, they demonstrate how "paper and work practices have coevolved over the years, and changing these long-standing work patterns with existing social, technological, and cultural infrastructures is difficult."[13] There is thus something highly problematic about the portrayal of the digital sublime as freedom from the tyranny of paper.[14] Such a conceptualization effectively prevents us from devising adequate strategies for managing this massive transition in how we go about accomplishing administrative tasks, materially and cognitively. As Sellen and Harper note, "There need to be clear-cut reasons for making changes, based on a good understanding of the existing social, physical, and technological infrastructure already in place in any given work setting. Change for the sake of change is hugely problematic. Going paperless for the sake of 'out with the old, in with the new' is destined to end in failure."[15]

The three case studies that follow, each showcasing a different approach to managing technological change, suggest that there is indeed much wisdom in these remarks.

Dematerialized Notaries

In the fall of 1999, the Conseil supérieur du notariat, the governing body of the French notarial profession, announced the grand opening of its secure interface to cyberspace, the *Réseau Electronique NotariAL*, or REAL. The timing of the official opening of the REAL network was not fortuitous but came rather at the precise moment when the draft bill on electronic signatures entered its first reading at the Senate. A full-fledged notarial public-key infrastructure, REAL would provide incontrovertible proof of the ability of the profession to reinvent itself and shed its medieval instruments of pen and paper for the modern smart card—in short, to enter a new age of electronic notarial authenticity (see figures 6.1 and 6.2). The bringing about of such a new age would involve profound changes within

Figure 6.1
"The notarial profession, guarantor of authenticity." 1997 cover, *Notaires Vie Professionelle*, the professional magazine published by the Conseil supérieur du notariat. Image courtesy of the Conseil supérieur du notariat.

Figure 6.2
"The card of the notarial electronic network." 1999 cover, *Notaires Vie Professionelle*. The smart card containing the cryptographic keys was eventually replaced with a USB key. Image courtesy of the Conseil supérieur du notariat.

the profession, both at the material level, through the deployment of the notarial PKI, and at more conceptual levels, through the development of a new legal concept of electronic authenticity.

Notaries could deploy considerable resources in the service of these objectives. The modern French notarial profession is wealthy and well organized.[16] The basis of that wealth is a monopoly granted by the state, whereby real estate contracts—buying, selling, exchanging, dividing, bequeathing, mortgaging—must be manufactured by a notary. A number of other acts are often formalized by notaries, even though the law does not formally require it. Wills, for example, are legally valid as long as they are written and signed in the hand of the testator, but often benefit from notarial authenticity, which testifies to the free and informed consent of the individual in stating his last wishes. About half of the individuals who enter notarial offices do so for matters related to real estate; a quarter do so for donations, wills, and marriage contracts. Notarial business is thus firmly established on its lucrative monopolistic base, with a global revenue half that of lawyers, a profession that counts ten times as many practitioners.

In addition to France, the notarial system is established in sixty-one different nations across four continents—among others, Italy, Spain, Germany, Russia, most of the former African and Asian colonies of France, and almost all of South and Central America. China adopted the notarial system in the late 1980s, as part of the reform of its justice system (although not as a liberal profession). Absent from this list are countries of common-law tradition, in which notaries perform a much simpler procedure of certification of documents and signatures.[17] Notaries thus perceive the hegemonic potential of common-law institutions through globalization processes such as those enabled by the EU and UNCITRAL as the single most important threat to their existence. The International Union of Latin Law Notaries (UINL) represents the profession at these bodies and others, including the World Trade Organization and the European Parliament.

The electronic signature bill, the most significant update to French evidence rules since the enactment of the Civil Code, represented a unique occasion to demonstrate the profession's continued relevance. Notaries were in a particularly good position to argue their case: Alain Lambert, past president of the Conseil supérieur and a driving force behind the development of new technologies within the profession, held a seat at the Senate.

On February 8, 2000, he exhorted the High Assembly to forge ahead with the reform:

> The supremacy of writing with regard to evidence law should not be diminished. The situation is different with regard to the question of media. A confusion has established itself over the years between writing and its traditional media, paper, but I implore you, do not remain fixated on this confusion. In my opinion, writing must be legally defined as independent of media, so as to stand a better chance of surviving in the future. I formally pronounce myself in favor of a perfect equality between electronic media and paper. Any intermediary solution would marginalize the French proof system.[18]

Minister of Justice and Guardian of the Seals Élisabeth Guigou felt more wary of the move, underlining the importance of maintaining public confidence in legal authenticity:

> Authentic acts draw a particular strength from the intervention of a third party invested with a mission of public interest. This third party is a privileged witness of the operation attested by the act, and of the respect of form requirements. By the trust they inspire, authentic acts constitute the best guarantee of legal security. We must thus be particularly careful that their dematerialization not bring into question the guarantees of authenticity which they bear. We must find, for authentic acts, a new electronic formalism which could be substituted to the actual requirements attached to the paper medium.

Guigou also expressed serious concern with the looming problem of ensuring the long-term preservation of signed authentic acts:

> Contrary to private acts, which must only be preserved for a maximal duration of thirty years, authentic acts must be preserved for an unlimited duration. Technological solutions must thus guarantee the long-term preservation of the acts. But current electronic technologies can only guarantee preservation of information for a limited period, due to their rapid obsolescence. . . . I say it very clearly, the technical conditions for the dematerialization of authentic acts are not there yet.[19]

Guigou's hesitations with respect to reforming the system of civil law authenticity were well founded. The first issue, the definition of a new formalism for authenticity, touched directly on the problem of the physical presence of the trusted witness. Although handwritten signatures had in the past enabled documents to testify "in and of themselves," authentic acts could not do away with the impartial third party who alone vests them with special evidential powers. If anything, public-key technologies seemed to significantly weaken the legal guarantees of civil law authenticity: although cryptographic signatures used over the Internet made possible a distributed contractual scene, with parties potentially sitting thousands of miles away from each other, the model could neither ensure party's consent to their obligations, nor guarantee that parties controlled their private key. The second issue, the long-term preservation of signed acts, seemed even more intractable. French law requires notaries to preserve the acts under their care for one hundred years, typically in their offices, after which the acts are turned over to departmental archives. Preserving the evidential qualities of signed electronic documents over such periods seemed not only beyond the capabilities of individual notaries, but, as Guigou pointed out, beyond the capabilities of technology itself. On both counts, the notarial profession would need to come up with innovative solutions with significant implications for the original cryptographic signature model.

Authentic Formalism

To address these issues, the Ministry of Justice convened in March 2000 a working group composed of eminent jurists, technical specialists, and representatives from the various legal professions. The working group was presented with the charge of researching the conditions for a new electronic formalism which could be substituted to the actual requirements associated with the paper media. Given the complexity of these questions and their high symbolic charge, the group was to be vested with a double mission: first, after investigation of the particularities of each type of authentic acts (courts decisions, records of civil status, notarized acts, etc.), submit concrete propositions for the drafting of profession-specific application decrees; second, reflect critically on a comprehensive framework for electronic authenticity, to be implemented in a general application decree. The framework would provide answers to the following questions:

1. How can the deep guarantees of authenticity (counsel of the parties, control of the expression of their consent, etc.) be preserved in the electronic context?

2. Under which conditions and following which forms can the electronic signature of the public officer and of the parties be affixed to authentic acts?

3. How can the unlimited preservation of electronic authentic acts be insured?

The first plenary meeting of the working group underlined the difficulties ahead. The thirty or so people appointed by the Ministry of Justice included no less than eight eminent law professors (six from Paris), several notaries, bailiffs, judges, court clerks, commercial court clerks, officers of civil status, archivists, and other lesser deities of the colorful and esoteric French judicial pantheon. Behind the Civil Code's succinct definition of authenticity laid a staggering heterogeneity of professions, practices, materials, and purposes, with so little in common that one member predicted no overarching concept of electronic authenticity could emerge from such a diverse and conflicted collection of professional interests. Discussions over notarial acts held particular import. Though the heterogeneity of the working group made clear that no single profession was "typical" of authenticity, in the eyes of the public, notaries in effect symbolized the civilist tradition of the trusted witness and its ability to confer high evidential value to significant documents. As the professional group whose existence depended entirely on its monopoly to grant authenticity over real estate transactions, no definition of electronic authenticity could emerge which did not meet its criteria.

The most fundamental question facing the notarial profession hinged on the requirement for parties to physically appear in front of the notary so that he may verify their understanding and free consent to their contractual obligations. As Pierre Catala explains, "The heart of the problem lies in the *writing* of the authentic title proper. The title draws its entire strength from the simultaneous presence of the parties and of the public officer . . . so that the solemnities required by texts can be simultaneously accomplished. Authenticity cannot be accomplished without the physical presence of the contracting parties before the special witness habilitated to receive the act."[20]

Yet for notaries, the appeal of a "dematerialized" authentic act hinged precisely on the possibility of concluding a real estate transaction without requiring all parties to physically meet. Given European integration and the gradual removal of obstacles to trade among member states, this notion was widely perceived as the service that would make or break the future of the profession.[21] Such a new contractual scene, involving some yet-to-be-determined configuration of parties, notaries, and documents, interacting through networked devices, would bear little resemblance to what the profession had known before. The problem was how to design it without losing the very soul of the profession—the trusted witness and its guarantee of the special evidential value of authenticity.[22]

Alain Lambert, in an early meeting of the notarial subcommittee, stated the official position of the profession: "The physical presence of the notary is essential to the authentic act; thus, the consent of the parties cannot be witnessed at a distance. If this principle must be modified to adapt the authentic act to the electronic medium, such a modification must then also apply to the paper media, since the concept of authenticity cannot be different according to the underlying media of the *instrumentum*."

The biggest problem such an argument faced was the fact that the notarial profession had already sought to—and indeed, succeeded in—breaching this principle. In the early 1970s, it had lobbied the government, requesting the notarial contractual scene be divided in two discrete moments, to be performed by two distinct parties. Because witnessing the consent of the parties to the act is a lengthy process—the act must be read to them, they must initialize each page, and so on—the profession argued that it could be entrusted to a specially authorized notarial clerk (*clerc habilité*), and the final signature on the act would remain the notary's privilege, to be affixed at a later, more convenient time.

The move profoundly shocked one of France's most eminent scholars of notarial law, Jacques Flour, who vehemently critiqued the decree. Flour argued that "when it comes to solemn acts, there is no distinction between *instrumentum* and *negotium*."[23] That is, the manufacturing of the *instrumentum* (the record of contractual agreement) in accordance with the rules dictating the appropriate forms, is itself the *negotium*, that is, a performance with the legal consequence of binding the parties to the obligations contained in the contract. And, as Flour sternly remarked, the party responsible for the proper manufacturing of the *instrumentum* is—must be—the notary, under penalty of authentic acts losing their special evidential value: "The requirement of the presence of the notary has never been considered as the vain manifestation of some mystical kind of formalism. . . . [The authentic act]'s evidential force is explained by the fact that one can—and one must—trust the affirmations of a public officer. The notary, as is classically defined, is a 'privileged witness.' If he does not witness the affixing of the signatures, he is not a witness; the act can thus not be an authentic one."[24]

Throughout the year, the sub-committee debated the possible parameters of the new contractual mise en scène—including the use of multiple distributed notaries, procurations for transmission of a single party's consent, and even the use of video technologies and high-bandwidth electronic links. All proposals suffered from the same fundamental lack of elegance, desperately clunky in comparison with the *ancient régime* elegance of the traditional scenario, or with the modern design of disembodied Alice and Bob happily contracting in cyberspace. Even as the Conseil supérieur boasted it fully met the framework required by the March 13 law, the expensive public-key infrastructure put in place by the profession seemed to offer little in the way of a concrete model of electronic authenticity. Yet, the President of the Conseil ensured, notaries had the technological upper hand in the Information Age:

[The evidence law reform] introduces in the virtual world comparable dispositions to those which we have known for a long time in the traditional universe of contract law. Moreover, the explicit reference to authentic acts, desired by a unanimous parliament, strengthen the role of the notary, promoter of legal security, by widening this eminent mission to computerized transactions. One must see here a kind of recognition of the efforts of the profession, notably through its REAL network, to rapidly adapt to the information technology revolution. The door of the future is open; let's begin walking on the new paths with confidence.[25]

The reality was somewhat murkier. Although the notarial profession had acquired what was by all accounts a promising (and expensive) piece of cyberspace real estate, it was entirely unclear what it could used for. What would a rank-and-file notary gain by undergoing the laborious and costly process of subscribing to the network, acquiring the signature card, and installing all necessary hardware and software? The Conseil supérieur could only offer vague promises: "Electronic messaging and related services will give us . . . gains in productivity. These exchanges will be fully secure."[26] Yet no market for electronic notarial authenticity seemed likely to emerge in the immediate to near future. The network's main selling point lay in the future provision of strong authentication for real-time access to sensitive online information resources, such as the cadastral database of the *Fichiers des hypothèques*. As a sales pitch, however, access control lacked the rhetorical appeal of digital signatures.

Additional uncertainties seemed to further undermine the applicability of cryptographic signatures to civil law authenticity. As a member of the working group, I submitted in April 2001 a memo outlining significant concerns with the long-term preservation of signed electronic authentic acts. The memo noted that the cryptographic signature model failed to distinguish between two distinct contexts for verification: the first one, when Bob initially receives the document, and the second one, during litigation, when the document is presented to the judge as evidence. This later verification may occur years after signature creation—in fact, potentially as many years as specified by retention requirements for the document in question. Given this possibility, litigation also requires solutions to the long-term *legibility* of electronic documents in the face of constant hardware and software obsolescence.

This issue of *digital preservation* has emerged in recent years as one of the most significant and troubling challenges posed by computerization. Although there is at this stage little experience or theoretical discussion of its implications, a widespread strategy relies on periodic migrations of documents' encoding formats. In order to fight off technological obsolescence, one might choose to convert a document encoded in a proprietary word processing format (say, Word 5.1) to either a more manageable open standard (say, PDF) or a more recent version of the format (say, Word 6).[27]

This is problematic: given cryptographic signature verification fails if a single bit of the signed message is modified, the verification cannot distinguish between those modifications motivated by malicious intervention and those motivated by archival preservation procedures. For signature verification to perform its forensic truth in the course of litigation, the signed document must thus be frozen in its original state. In other words, one can preserve the ability to verify the original signature or one can ensure the document remains legible over time, but *one cannot do both at the same time*.[28] Given the requirements for *unlimited* archiving of authentic acts, this presented a serious hurdle. Even if such issues could be resolved, it seemed likely that the long-term preservation of electronic authentic acts would require means beyond the ability of individual professionals, and that more centralized forms of archiving would need to emerge.

Toward the First Electronic Authentic Act

The working group's final report was submitted to the Ministry of Justice in the fall of 2001. By then, the blaze that had been the New Economy was already smoldering, and the impetus for rapid and radical adaptation of French evidence law to information technologies had lost much of its symbolic charge. The pressure to publish the second application decree had eased off, and even the notarial profession—which had led the charge into this uncertain territory— seemed ready for a pause. Thus, as a baseline principle, the report could suggest that each profession (notaries, officers of civil status, court clerks, etc.) be left to organize the computerization of authentic acts at the pace best appropriate to its needs and resources.

The report avoided any metaphysical confrontation over the meaning of physical presence, simply stating that "whatever the new possibilities which the electronic media offers with regard to witnessing consent at a distance, to modify the actual principle of the physical presence of the public officer would imply a questioning of the principle of authenticity which the legislator has not sought."[29] If the French state wanted to make the physical presence of the notary optional, it would have to get rid of authenticity as currently defined. With regard to the signature of the public officer, it remained resolutely neutral, requiring only that it be affixed by a physically present public officer. In particular, it did not specifically endorse the "secure electronic signatures" framework of the first application decree, underlining that the issues raised relative to their long-term preservation raised substantive challenges.

The suggestion displeased the Ministry of Justice, which noted with some impatience that "the report manifests a certain hesitation with regard to the asymmetric signature mechanism. . . . In the case that such a method, even with additional requirements, cannot be used for authentic acts, it would be interesting that the report suggest which other technologies it intends to propose." The Ministry promptly convened a second working group with the hope of conjuring more immediate solutions. It would nevertheless take another three years before an application decree could be published in August 2005, finally setting the rules for the signature, preservation, and distributed creation of electronic notarial acts.[30] To date, no general decree applicable to all the professions has been published.

The 2005 decree takes a decisive stance with respect to the conditions for electronic notarized contracts. First, notaries will henceforth be required to use cryptographic signatures, as defined in the 2001 application decree and implemented in the profession's public-key infrastructure. However, parties and witnesses to the act must be able to affix their signature through a system that simply displays the image of their handwritten signatures on the screen. The image of the notary's seal must also be visible on all copies of the act.

Second, in order to ensure their long-term integrity and legibility, electronic notarial acts, along with all relevant and necessary metadata, will be preserved in a central institutional repository. The decree takes stock of the practical requirements of digital preservation, stating in article 28 that "the series of operations required for the preservation of an act, *in particular, format migrations*, are without effect on its status as original."[31] No guidance was provided however with respect to the impact of these operations on the original signature of the notary and on the resulting evidential power of the act. In effect, the decree implicitly recognized that the notary's original signature on a document would eventually function as another (if essential) piece of metadata, rather than as the sole locus of its authenticity.

Finally, the solution to the notarial mise en scène for "distance acts" would rely on two notaries, one for each party. The procedure was staged for the first time in 2004 at the 100th Annual Meeting of the profession. In front of hundreds of their colleagues, the notaries used web cameras and collaborative software to simultaneously edit the act. *Notaires Vie Professionnelle*, the newsletter of the Conseil supérieur, provided a play-by-play of the event: "Rapidly, the video link is established and Me Reynis and his client appear on the screen, both perfectly clear and smiling. . . . As if they were sitting face to face in the same office, the two notaries, visibly enchanted with the experience, cordially salute each other before beginning the procedure."[32] The two notaries confirmed to each other the consent of their respective clients, helped them apply their signatures using graphical pads, and finally, applied their individual cryptographic signatures to the act (see figure 6.3). A standing ovation saluted the completion of the performance, perhaps to celebrate this "great professional premiere," or perhaps because the technology had, on the occasion of this very public demonstration, mercifully collaborated without a glitch.

In spite of these successes, another four years of technological and institutional fine tuning would elapse before a full-blown ceremony could officially signal the start of the electronic notarial age. On October 28, 2008, Rachida Dati, Minister of Justice and Keeper of the Seals, used a graphical pad to apply her handwritten signature to the first official

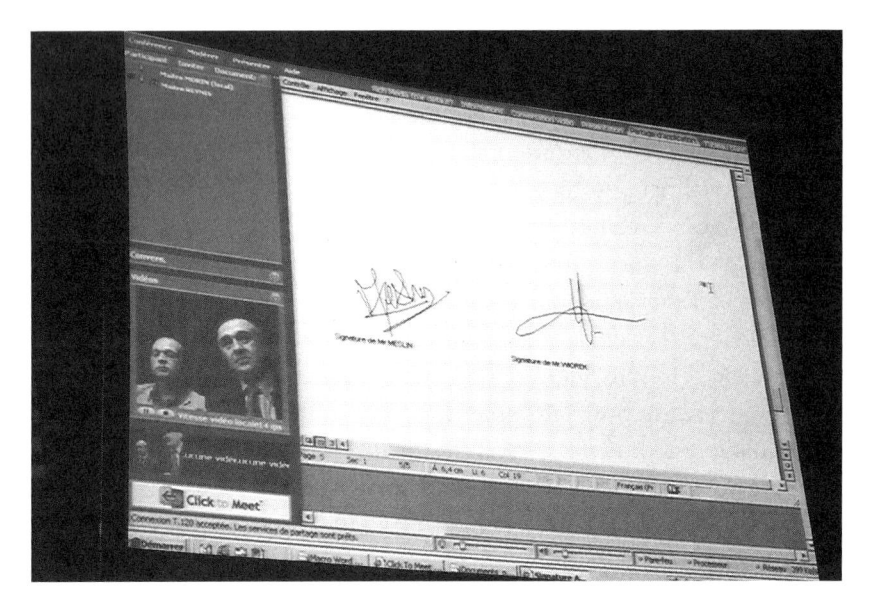

Figure 6.3
Simulation of the new notarial contractual scene, staged and projected on a screen at the 2004 Annual Meeting of the profession. On the lower left-hand corner of the screen, parties and their notaries can witness their mutual consent through a video link. The new rules for electronic authentic acts mandate the continuing inclusion of handwritten signatures as well as the application of the cryptographic signatures of the notaries. Photograph courtesy of the Conseil supérieur du notariat.

electronic authentic act (see figure 6.4). After the president of the Conseil supérieur followed suit with his cryptographic signature, the deed was finally done. There was no doubt, however, that the scene of theses signatures differed in fundamental respects from the one initially envisioned by cryptographers in figure 4.2.

Records of Civil Status

Scattered on my desk, a selection of administrative dispatches from various corners of the French bureaucratic empire: the records of civil status of French nationals born in France's former colonial empire, including Algeria, the protectorates of Tunisia and Morocco, Indochina, and other former African, Asian, and Indian Ocean colonies (see figure 6.5). I collected them during a visit at the *Service central d'état civil*, an administrative unit of the

Figure 6.4
Rachida Dati, Minister of Justice and Keeper of the Seals, in 2008 signs the first electronic authentic act using a graphical pad. Photograph by Luc Pérénom, courtesy of the Conseil supérieur du notariat.

French Ministry of Foreign Affairs located in the outskirts of Nantes. The inheritor of the administrative apparatus deployed by the French state in its former colonies, the SCEC is competent for all events relative to the civil status of French citizens having occurred outside of the French territory, including birth, marriage, divorce, adoption, and the like. Behind this bland legal attribution lies a fascinating administrative history and a formidable evidentiary machine: every year, the SCEC delivers about a million and a half authentic copies of the 15 million records it holds so that citizens may fulfill bureaucratic demands for identification.[33]

To increase the productivity of the public officers who deliver these copies, the SCEC has developed systems and procedures to partially automate their workflow. Developed outside of the cryptographic framework, the design of these systems draws on different assumptions with respect to the function of signatures, the physical presence of the parties, and the evidentiary requirements to be met by records produced electronically. These assumptions are informed by the long tradition of material and semiotics techniques developed over centuries of experience with the

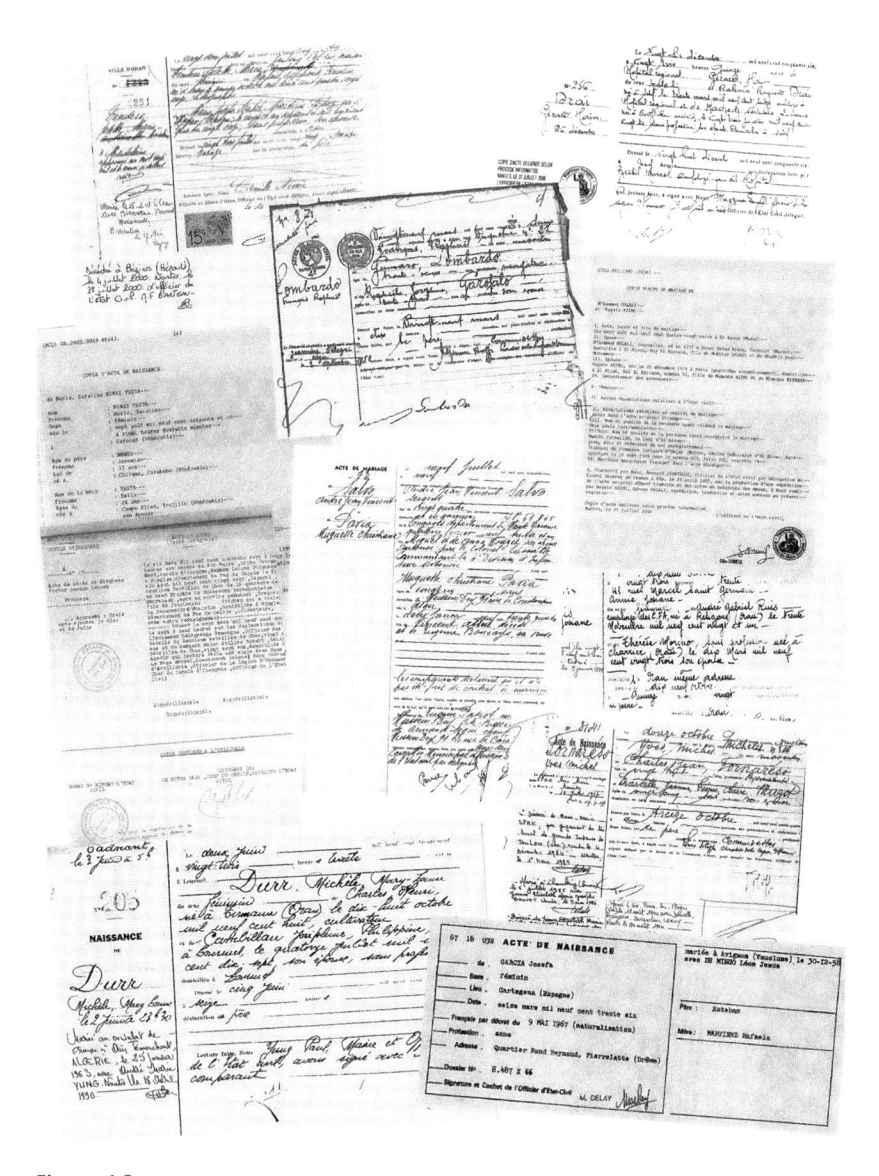

Figure 6.5
A selection of records of civil status from consular offices and former French colonies. Images courtesy of the Service central d'état civil.

production of documentary evidence. Given their convenience and their operational deployment in the production of millions of identification records, the systems developed by the SCEC would eventually constitute a serious conceptual challenge to those, such as notaries, who sought to ground the reform of civil law authenticity in cryptographic technologies.

On one level, records of civil status can be read as pure concentrates of administrative rationality, tersely listing major data points of an individual life—birth, marriage, adoption, divorce, death:

Birth Certificate, Sabrina, Mona CHAÏBI—On December ninth, nineteen sixty six, at five hours and thirty minutes pm, was born, at AIN TAYA (Alger), Sabrina, Mona, female, of Saïd CHAÏBI, born in EL HARRACH (Alger–10th arrondissement), on July thirteen nineteen forty, a shopkeeper, and of Gisèle, Marie-Thérèse JEAN, born in LOOMARIAQUER (Morbihan), on April fifth, nineteen forty three, no occupation, his wife, both residing in ALGER-PLAGE (Alger).[34]

The birth certificate serves as the master record, in the margin of which events modifying the civil status of a French national—such as adoption, marriage, naturalization, divorce, death, and so on—must be transcribed, further tracing the life trajectory of the individual: "Married in CARACAS (Venezuela), June 5th 1993, with Edouard, Christian, Laurent, RUELLOT." And finally, "Deceased in BÉZIERS (Hérault), July 4th 2000."

In this way, although individual records exist for each event (e.g., marriage or death certificate), the birth certificate provides the fullest description of an individual's administrative identity at any moment. This identity is uniquely defined at the intersection of multiple coordinates—time and date, birthplace, filiation, profession, residence. For the state, identity is not an essence, but an intricate web of signs.[35] The document performs more than a mere listing of data points however, as its creation requires parties and the public officer to read and confirm their declarations by affixing their signature. It is the enactment of a ritual "where the public order is committed, where the officer, the witnesses, and even the parties fulfill a civic duty which makes them liable to committing forgery."[36]

The documents held by the SCEC were produced under colonial rule in a broad range of conditions and recorded on media of varied quality, size, and shapes, from school notebooks to bound registers, microfilms, electronic text files, and scanned digital images. Although the photocopies I am working from have flattened the material diversity of the originals into a single contemporary technological form, most of the last hundred years of office technologies have been enrolled at some point or another in the service of producing these documents: handwriting, typewriting, word processing (both freestyle and on printed forms), microfilming, digital scans of paper documents, transcriptions of paper documents into database software, and—of course—photocopying. In part, this diversity results from the complex rules governing the production of copies, as codified in the *Instruction générale relative à l'état civil* (IGREC), a document providing a unique window on the documentary practices of the French state. The IGREC specifies copies must faithfully reproduce, without adaptation, indications included in the original (e.g., geographic names or calendar). However, they must not reproduce indications no longer considered acceptable, including any that would reveal race, religion, foreign nationality, or cause of death. Such tasks are complicated by poor condition of the originals, poor indexing, or altogether missing records—only 60 percent of the civil status records created in Algeria during colonial rule were microfilmed, for example—often requiring that records be reconstituted from whatever information is available. Copies then are often altogether new records, rather than mere mechanical reproductions.

Regardless of the technologies that produced them, the documents display their data points in a rich array of visual forms—seals, stamps, signatures, marginal annotations, alternation of printed and handwritten characters, uppercase and lowercase, printed frames, and so on. Each must be decoded in the context of its individual semiotic logic, but also according to the (implicit) rules governing their spatial relationships: for example, signatures authenticate what is written *above* them, and the vertical ordering of annotations indicates chronology.

Beyond the obvious signatures and seals, the documents also exhibit a great diversity of authentication technologies. More than outright fraud, it is the noise of sign systems that constantly threatens the document's integrity. A simple misspelling or the inversion of first name and surname weakens or even nullifies the record's power to identify. Rules for manufacture of originals and copies thus rely extensively on simple techniques to combat this noise, provoke the attention of the trusted witness, enhance the visual legibility of documents, and prevent obvious forms of fraud:

1. Names are always listed in first name, last name order; both last names and town names are written in capitals to facilitate rapid scanning of the document.

2. Dates are written in longhand; numbers are padded with dashes to prevent addition of numerals; white spaces at the end of lines are filled with dashes. The number of words crossed out must be declared and signed on the records. In addition to their signatures, parties and officers are identified by their full names.

3. Pages are numbered "1 of . . . ." For multiple-page records, the top-left corner of each page is folded on several levels, stamped with the seal, and then stapled, so that each page carries the image of part of the seal.

4. Records are printed on security paper, containing dimensional information, watermarks, and other features.

In the production of reliable records, language, typography, visual design, and the material features of paper thus freely mingle in mutually supportive ways. Evaluating the evidential qualities of such documents is then a process of interpretation that apprehends content, visual form, and media holistically, rather than as necessarily distinct systems of meaning.[37]

It is in this context that the SCEC has over the last two decades undertaken various computerization projects aimed at simplifying the records production process. First to be targeted were the records created by the consular offices—about 200,000 records yearly. An in-house software package lets officers create the records as plain-text ASCII files, with numbered sections establishing the structure of act. The most conspicuous difference between traditional records and such electronic ones is the absence of handwritten signatures from either the consular officer having established the act or the officers having established the marginal notes (the authentic paper copy delivered by the SCEC does bear the stamp and signature of the delivering officer).

In 1999, the SCEC awarded an eighteenth-month contract to an outside contractor for the digitization of 3 million consular and colonial records, with the hope of eventually servicing electronically 80 percent of requests for copies. The mass digitization effort brought the total of electronic records managed by the SCEC to 5 million (3.5 as images and 1.5 as text files). Under the name of SAGA, a series of software applications were developed by the computer division of the SCEC to enable officers to clean up and annotate the records. Similar to the tool found in off-the-shelf "paint" computer programs, the cleanup tool provides for clipping a region of the record, moving it around, rotating it, and erasing smudges and other residue of the scanning process. Officers found it useful to move annotations around in order to increase the visual legibility of records. The tool provides standardized versions of the most often used annotations—the IGREC lists more than fifty different core categories, with many variations. After their fields are filled out, the annotations are visually positioned on the page and merged *as images* with the existing image of the record.

In a second development phase, a third tool enabled the officers to gain yet more time in producing copies and extracts. Although each such copy and extract requires the officers to affix her seal, date, and signature, the date and seal were not technically part of the officer's signature and could just as well be integrated within the computer system itself. The SCEC thus designed a digital seal composed of a text which read: "CERTIFIED COPY, NANTES, [*date*], THE OFFICER OF CIVIL STATUS, [*first name, last name*]" along with the seal of the Republic. The only thing left for the officer to manually inscribe was the handwritten signature itself.

The SCEC dreamt of a completely automated production process—from online requesting of documents (first Minitel, then Internet) to computerized production of electronic copies (mostly accomplished) and the sorting, folding, and filling out of the envelopes to be sent out through an automated mail robot. The only remaining obstacle to the process was the need for the handwritten signature of public officer. The IGREC was explicit: it could be only manual: "Copies and extracts must be signed by the officer. By signature, one must understand the handwritten apposition of the officer's name on the act. It is this signature that confers to the act its authentic character."[38]

Yet the temptation was great. Officers had already begun using the seal tool and were thus getting gradually accustomed to affixing the validating signs electronically. Integrating a scanned image of each officer's signature into the seal tool would be a simple job, now that the required software had been developed. In meetings with the SCEC, the Ministry of Justice expressed deep reservations with regard to the legal validity of any such electronic signature, arguing that the necessity for the officer to *manually sign* authentic copies had been well established both by legislation and case law.

Paper and State 147

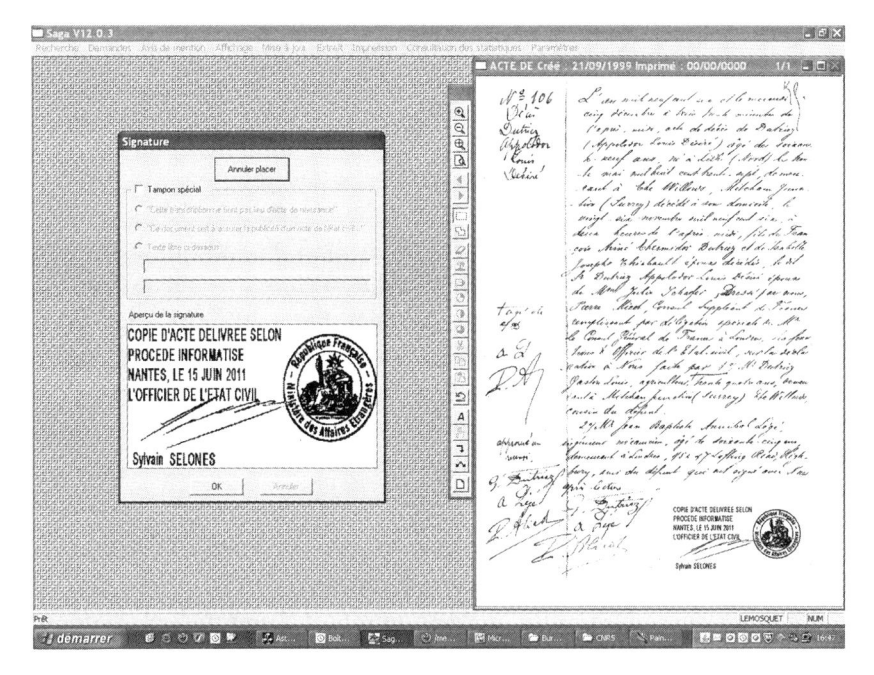

Figure 6.6
The SAGA tool for the signature of scanned copies of records of civil status at the Service central d'état civil. Copies are then printed and delivered on security paper. Screenshot courtesy of the Service central d'état civil.

The SCEC's legal counsel argued that the computer was just another writing implement: officers at the SCEC were simply abandoning one tool, the pen, to replace it with another, the digitized signature, but in both cases remained fully in control of the signing process. In both cases, they were simply *manually affixing* their signature, in full compliance with the rules of the IGREC. In the end, the Ministry of Justice did not oppose the move, in spite of a legal ambiguity somewhat at odds with the solemn character of authentic acts. Officers of civil status at the SCEC stopped using their handwritten signatures and switched to the new system, which almost entirely eliminated any physical interaction with the paper document (see figure 6.6). The system was eventually endorsed by the first working group on electronic authenticity, much to the consternation of the Ministry of Justice, which noted:

The report defines as an "electronic signature" the scanned image of handwritten signature as used by the SCEC. It would be preferable that such a statement with regard to the qualification of this process as an electronic signature not be part of the report. Indeed, such a scanned signature constitutes in fact a copy of a handwritten signature, which does not seem to meet, for security specialists, the definition of an electronic signature, notably because of the lack of a definite link between the document and the signing action.

The status of the signature process of the SCEC was to remain unsettled: handwritten signature, as defined by the IGREC, or electronic signature, as defined by the Civil Code? It is therefore telling that more than ten years after the promulgation of the *Loi du 13 mars 2000*, no application decrees have been published relative to the computerization of records of civil status.

The Land Registry of Alsace-Moselle

Scott has described how the emergence of the "all-seeing" modern state required innovative combinations of documentary technologies, professional practices, and legal rules into sophisticated information systems. Cadastral maps and property registers, for example, ensured a manageable form of land taxation by providing an reliable survey of all landholdings and their owners.[39] This section describes the computerization of one such property register, the land registry of Alsace-Moselle.[40] Operated by 36 judges and 150 clerks distributed among 46 sites, the registry provides access to the essential facts regarding land parcels and the rights and obligations attached to these parcels. At the heart of this formidable system lie 40,000 bound registers containing more than 2.5 million sheets and growing by 175,000 new inscriptions annually. Real estate professionals—including notaries, bankers, and bailiffs—continuously access the register to, respectively, prepare contracts, authorize loans, and recover property for more than 2 million land owners and 4.5 million parcels of land. Created in 1891 under German jurisdiction, the registry was recognized by French law in 1924, under the limited sovereignty (*juridiction gracieuse*) that the French state grants to the region.

The registry functions as an openly accessible database, providing interested parties with convenient and synthetic access to the essential legal facts of properties and land owners. Like notarized contracts and records of civil status, the registry relies on the signature of neutral third parties—specialized judges—to ensure the evidential power of these legal facts.

Because open access results in increased risks of fraud, however, the judges' signature grants inscriptions in the registry only a mere presumption of trustworthiness, rather than the full force of authenticity. Hence, the challenge of computerization laid in providing a system that could continue to deliver a similar blend of convenience and legal certainty. As in the case of the notarial profession, fulfilling these needs would require creative adaption of the cryptographic signature model to documentary practices dating back several centuries.

The land registry system is organized following a mixture of French civil law principles and German procedures and institutions. It fulfills the legal requirements for *publicité foncière*, which secures third-party rights (mortgage, liens, etc.) on real estate. The date of an application for inscription in the registry fixes the legal effect of the rights, establishing a set order by which the third-party rights on a property are recognized in case of default. Because inscription in the registry finalizes real estate transactions, a request for inscription must be verified by an officer of the state, a land registry judge (*juge du livre foncier*).

The paper-based land registry system is centered around two principal types of documents, the *ordonnance* and the *feuillet*, a two-page-wide form bound into A2-size (16.5 × 23.4 inches) registers (see figure 6.7). The

Figure 6.7
A few of the 40,000 A2-size bound registers of the Alsace-Moselle land registry. Photograph by the author.

ordonnance results from a request for inscription, typically by a notary acting on behalf of a client who has purchased property. The judge is responsible for establishing the validity of documents provided by the notary (real estate contract, records of civil status of the parties, etc.) and for verifying the validity of the request with respect to the property (characteristics of the land parcels, mortgage, liens, etc.). By signing the *ordonnance*, the judge engages his personal responsibility that the information is correct. Once signed, the *ordonnance* is transcribed by a specialized clerk into the appropriate *feuillet* along with the date the request for inscription was received. The judge further attests that the information has been correctly transcribed into the paper registers by signing each inscription.

The top of the *feuillets* identify the land owner (card indexes for both land owners and land parcels provide direct access to the relevant *feuillets* of the registers) (see figure 6.8). The body of the *feuillet* is divided vertically in three main sections: the first records the cadaster reference of the property, address, type (e.g., land, housing), reference to the previous owner's *feuillet*, reference to the *ordonnance* that transferred the property to the present owner, and the nature of the transfer (e.g., sale, donation); for each property listed in the first section, charges and encumbrances may be listed in the second section (e.g., right of passage, *usufruit*), and the third section is used for mortgages and liens. Each individual entry in a section of a *feuillet* is the result of a separate *ordonnance* by a judge and associated by a reference number with a physical (paper) file, the annex. The annex contains the *ordonnance* itself and all other related documents the judge may have consulted and verified in the process of creating the *ordonnance*—copies of contracts, cadastre surveys, identity papers of the parties, and any others.

The large size of registers, the careful visual design of the pages, and the organization in columns and rows are designed to provide relevant professionals with a synthetic visualization of the essential information relative to real estate transactions—for example, the entire set of mortgages and liens associated with a particular parcel. The registers are public records, however, open for consultation to anyone with a demonstrable interest in a transaction, and thus vulnerable to falsification, forgery, and so on. A request for inscription thus results in the production of two distinct kinds of records organized in a two-tiered evidential system: signed by the judge, the *ordonnance d'inscription* has the evidential force of authentic acts; also

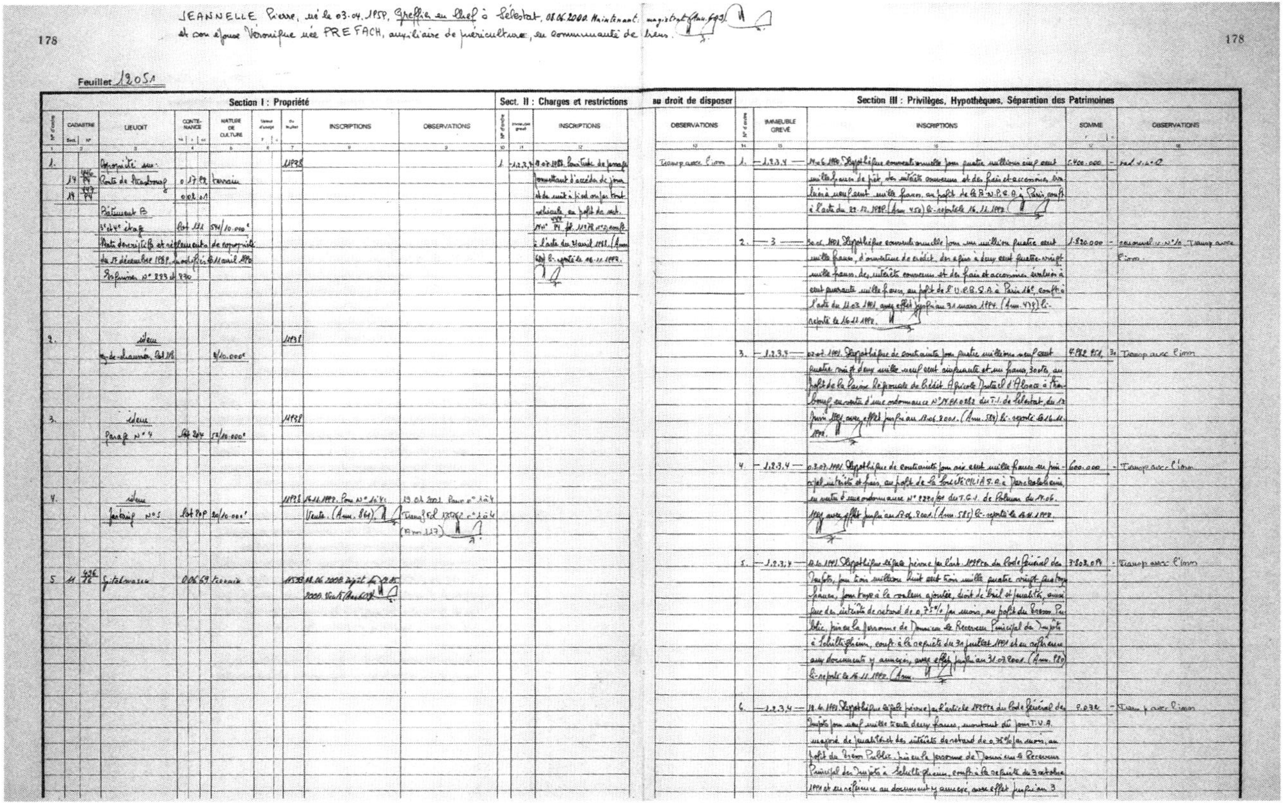

Figure 6.8

Facsimile of a *feuillet*. The top left of the *feuillet* identifies the owner of the properties listed in the *feuillet*. Section I identifies the properties and references the cadastral maps, section II lists the charges and encumbrances, and section III lists mortgages and liens. The second columns of section II and III indicate the priority order for third-party rights on the property. Each individual entry is signed by the land registry judge. Expired entries are deleted by underlining them in red. Image courtesy of Pierre Jeanelle.

signed by the judge, the inscription itself is presumed valid only until proof of the contrary. Thus, although parties rely primarily on the contents of the registers during the ordinary course of business, it is the *ordonnance* that serves as evidence in case of conflict.

For all its qualities, the system showed increasing signs of strain in the context of the increased complexity of urban real estate and rapid rates at which property is nowadays exchanged. Electronic tools seemed obvious candidates to overcome both the physical limitations of the *feuillets* and the slow and tedious process of transcription. Discussed since the 1980s, the computerization of the registry began in earnest in 1994 with the creation of a specifically dedicated administrative body, the *Groupement pour l'Informatisation du Livre Foncier d'Alsace-Moselle* (GILFAM). Its charter specifies that the goal of computerization of the land registry is to "facilitate and speed up the process of requests for new inscriptions, automate information exchange between the registry and the cadastre, optimize information storage and enable remote consultation of the register." Funded by a special tax levied on all real estate transactions, in 2002 the GILFAM awarded IBM and a consulting firm a €60 million contract to oversee and implement the computerization of the registry. The project was a flagship one for IBM, featured in its 2003 annual report as an example of "the integration of technology and law in effective e-government." Noting that business process reengineering, technology development, and legislative adaptation had proceeded hand in hand, the report noted that "the model can apply to governments everywhere as they transform themselves to become on demand."[41]

Computerized Version

The computerization began in earnest with the transcription of the contents of 40,000 registers into structured data, a considerable technical and organizational challenge. After preprocessing all registers to increase their legibility, all 2.5 million *feuillets* were digitized using a custom high-speed page-turning scanning apparatus. The resulting TIFF files were transferred to Madagascar for transcription, a three-year process requiring a team of one hundred data entry operators—for quality-control purposes, two data-entry operators transcribed each page of the register. Because of the cost, only active entries were transcribed, with inactive entries remaining available through the scanned images of the register.

The database's data model was closely mapped to the organization of a single *feuillet*. To each section of the *feuillet* corresponds a base table: land owners, land parcels, restrictions, mortgages. Although—in contrast to the paper registers—it is now possible to query the database based on any and all criteria, the two most important views remain the ownership history of a given land parcel and the set of land parcels owned by a particular individual. The individual registry offices now exist to provide public points of access, and the central database is under the responsibility of the GILFAM. Two copies of the database operate simultaneously, synchronized at the end of each day: one, read-only, for consultation by authorized users; the other for modification by land registry personnel.

The process of preparing an *ordonnance d'inscription* is considerably simplified. Using web-based software, the data fields relative to individuals and parcels are retrieved directly from the database, eliminating the need for repeated retranscription of complex real estate information by users and clerks alike. Judges perform the same verifications as before, using software that provides them with a "before" and "after" view of the changes the inscription will effect in the database. A region-wide public-key infrastructure links together the registry offices and the central database. After securing control of a private key through triple authentication procedures (password, biometric, and hardware token), the judge may sign the *ordonnance*. There is no longer a need for its transcription into the register: at the moment of signature, in a single step, the *ordonnance* is created as a signed XML document stored in the database, and the relevant fields of the database are updated.

As in the past, the *ordonnance* enjoys the evidential force of authenticity. However, in contrast to the paper-based system, there are no longer inscriptions to be signed by the judge, as these now consist of discrete data items stored in various tables of the database. In the computerized system, the presumption of trustworthiness that was previously granted to the inscriptions must thus be inferred from other authentication procedures, including role-based access privileges and the general soundness of the software architecture. In addition, land registry systems designers have implemented additional mechanisms to ensure the contents of the database remain faithful to the signed *ordonnance*s, the procedural and legal origin of the inscription process. At regular intervals, a software procedure traverses sequentially all stored *ordonnance*s, verifies their digital signatures, and compares their data fields to the corresponding database records. Whether caused by malice, human error, or system failure, discrepancies between the signed *ordonnance*s and the database can thus be detected early. The approach is an innovative twist on the original cryptographic signature model: rather than solely expecting digital signatures to perform as evidence in a court of law, the land registry uses them to provide continuous authentication services, that is, regularly performed declarations of the integrity and origin of the data. Users are thus insured that the contents of the database reflect as faithfully as possible the *ordonnance*s signed by the judge.

In March 2002, the Alsace-Moselle registry law was amended in order to recognize the legal value of the land register held on data-processing media and its conformance with the new articles of the Civil Code relative to electronic signatures. It also appointed the GILFAM as a permanent public body, with the responsibility of ensuring the long-term maintenance of the computing infrastructure necessary to the operation of the land registry.

Conclusion

The case studies offered in this chapter have considerable implications for our understanding of the role of signatures in the production of reliable written evidence. The working group's investigations and the practical issues faced by public officers in the production of electronically signed documents tested both the possibilities and limitations of the cryptographic signature model. By far, the most significant adaptation to the model relates to the technical conditions necessary for the long-term legibility of electronic documents. As the notarial application decree recognized, these conditions will involve periodic migration of a document's encoding format. The consequences of this are important: the cryptographic demonstration of integrity resulting from the performance of signature verification over a self-identical string of bits cannot be sustained over the long term. Thus for all but the shortest legal retention requirements, the *event* of signature verification will have to be merely documented, rather than preserved for eventual litigation.[42]

This is also the conclusion reached by the U.S. National Archives and Records Administration (NARA), the federal agency responsible for the preservation of all governmental records. Its official 2005 policy for cryptographically signed records of transactions provides the record-keeping requirements "for establishing or supporting the trustworthiness of the transaction and meeting evidentiary requirements in any legal proceeding relating to the transaction."[43] The policy bluntly states that "for digitally signed records that have been scheduled and appraised as permanent, NARA currently has no intention of using the digital signature's re-validation capabilities to establish authenticity of the record or of maintaining that capability into the future."[44] Because it does not have the resources to maintain the complex and expensive infrastructure required for the performance of signature verification, NARA will rely on the transferring agency for attesting "to the authenticity and integrity of the record at the time of transfer of legal custody of the materials to NARA."[45] For nonpermanent records under the responsibility of the original agency, NARA suggests that digitally signed records be supplemented with a "textual, easily understood 'summary trust record' . . . that should collect, at a minimum, the fact that the PKI digital signature is valid, the date/time validated, and the transaction ID."[46] Thus, the event of signature verification, the visible and provable demonstration of authenticity with the power to compel a judge's assent, is supplemented or altogether replaced by a simple attestation that the event took place at some earlier point in time.

Lynch and colleagues describe a similar situation in criminal law with respect to DNA profiling. Although the technology was initially granted a status of irrefutable proof of identification, it met with a surprising defeat during the course of O. J. Simpson's murder trial in 1995. As they noted,

By following the samples from the crime scene to the laboratory, and then from the laboratory to the tribunal, one realizes that the genetic fingerprint may only serve its role of competent witness *if and only if* the succession of transactions during sampling, transport, preservation, digitization, and analysis of the sample is itself testified to by witnesses, certified and duly registered by responsible authorities. To be considered as such, the truth contained in the automatic signature (the genetic bar code) must be accompanied, surrounded by a whole series of bureaucratic traces: handwritten signatures on standard forms, actual bar-codes affixed on bags containing the samples, etc."[47]

Rather than the DNA sample, it is those bureaucratic traces that were successfully contested during the Simpson trial. The requirements for the long-term preservation of authentic acts follow a similar logic: in order to perform as the "competent witness" of a commitment, electronic writing must be fortified by recorded traces of all the manipulations it is susceptible to incur: creation, modifications, annotations, signature, conversion, transmission, and so on. Likewise, digital signatures are unable to testify *in and of themselves* of the identity and integrity of a document. Their effectiveness depends on the numerous traces that testify to their own identity and integrity as evidence: handwritten authorization forms, public-key certificates, access logs, and the like. Although the signature holds a special rank among those traces, in many respects, it is also *just another piece of metadata*.

This lack of self-intelligibility of the signature is indeed a central dynamic of all three case studies in this chapter. The power of the signature as a forensic object can be understood only in relationship to its *institutionalized performance,* a dynamic present from the very beginnings of civil law authenticity. As Fraenkel explains, signed documents provided a more portable form of evidence than one founded on the availability of the original witnesses to the contract:

> To be able to forego witnesses to confirm a commitment means that the document which states such a commitment is no longer dependent on the physical existence of the contracting parties. It is sufficient that they have been present once, at the moment of its creation. . . . The legal effect of the document is no longer tied to the length of their lives. . . . The legal instrument is even more independent of the formal circumstances surrounding a ceremony where statements, gestures, and manipulation of objects were all necessary to establish the legal effects of the contract. The scene of the modern contract is entirely different: it is writing which holds the central role, surrounded by the notary and the parties. And it is the affixing of autograph signatures which subsumes the gestuality of bodies.[48]

Yet although written documents and their signatures make possible the virtualization of the contractual scene, their capacity to testify continues to flow from a set of formal circumstances whose correct performance is ensured by the trusted witness, the public officer. The signature's power as a forensic trace cannot be reduced to its mere ability to identify parties or provide for the integrity of the document. Nor can it be understood outside of the institutional contexts of its creation and verification.

This power is further exemplified by the SCEC, whose system—to the dismay of the French Ministry of Justice—merely provides a mechanical reproduction of the public officer's signature. Yet the SCEC's electronic signature enabled significant gains in productivity while keeping stable the main parameters of the system: the practical necessity of delivering paper records, the legal requirements for "handwritten" signatures, and—crucially—the solemn character of the public officer's signature. By preserving the visual environment of the act, seal, and handwritten signature, the system provides cognitive continuity, a new yet familiar context for the public officers to signify their commitment to the contents of the record, their most important professional responsibility.[49]

Familiarity and continuity may even breed innovation. The computerization of the land registry takes place in the context of a trend that cuts across the three case studies: the data fields of notarial contracts, records of civil status, and *ordonnances d'inscription* are populated directly from the personal and institutional databases of notaries, town halls, and administrative agencies. Rather than the production and authentication of these documents, it is instead the ability to repurpose, centralize, or exchange this data through shared document ontologies and communication protocols that is driving the development of administrative information systems. Indeed, both the notarial and land registry application decrees included specific requirements for interoperability with respect to both data exchange and authentication. In such a context, the institutional mechanisms deployed to guarantee data quality and appropriate access control become particularly significant. The solutions developed by the GILFAM to ensure the presumption of authenticity of its online register are thus particularly intriguing. The use of the judge's signature as a trigger to committing data to the system, as well as the periodic verifications of the conformity of the database with the signed *ordonnances d'inscription*, presents new and unforeseen applications of cryptographic signatures in the context of emerging documentary practices.

Indeed, these various adaptations of the digital signature model to the practical constraints of real-world institutional settings outlined in this chapter suggest the potential for a different approach to the design of cryptographic analogues. As Sellen and Harper's ethnographic investigations of office life demonstrate, paying close attention to paper and its material affordances provides a powerful entry point into the complex ecologies of tools, procedures, and moral codes that constitute administrative work. Designers might then develop technologies that "allow people to leverage the skills they already possess and to draw on the everyday knowledge they already have."[50] Instead of merely emphasizing the putative sublimity of the digital, designers might instead focus on creating tools that have "clear value for people in the activities they already carry out." In either case, the integration of such technologies in the workplace is likely to proceed more smoothly. But there might be even more significant payoffs to such an engagement with materiality: "in our experience, taking inspiration from the way people currently do things has typically allowed us . . . to find new inspiration and develop highly original concepts. . . . To look at paper use as a design resource, therefore, clearly does not mean doing design through mimicking paper."[51]

In the next chapter, I broadly apply this insight to the design of cryptographic analogues in general and offer examples of how the material world might serve as a resource in the fulfillment of cryptographic design goals.

7   The Cryptographic Imagination

The laboratory setup displayed in figure 7.1 captures an intriguing dimension of modern cryptography. Hovering just above the surface of a computer chip, a simple homemade sensor measures the electromagnetic leakage that occurs as the chip performs the steps of a cryptographic algorithm. Various statistical treatments are then applied to these measurements in order to estimate the bits of the secret key and thus break the algorithm. Such *side-channel* cryptanalysis was pioneered by Paul Kocher in 1999, when he realized that the mathematics of a cryptosystem could be subverted by adopting a completely different route than that envisioned by its designers:

> Integrated circuits are built out of individual transistors, which act as voltage-controlled switches. Current flows across the transistor substrate when charge is applied to (or removed from) the gate. This current then delivers charge to the gates of other transistors, interconnect wires, and other circuit loads. The motion of electric charge consumes power and produces electromagnetic radiation, both of which are externally detectable. Therefore, *individual transistors produce externally observable electrical behavior.*[1]

In an announcement that rocked the cryptography world, Kocher demonstrated that both public- and secret-key cryptosystems were vulnerable to such attacks and that although it is possible to defend against them, the necessary countermeasures involve some significant cost or efficiency trade-offs: either the physical devices must be shielded, or algorithms must be fortified by "introducing noise into measurements, decorrelating internal variables from secret parameters, and temporally decorrelating cryptographic operations." Thus, just like the Enigma machine operators in World War II (see "Electromechanical Devices" in chapter 2), chips must

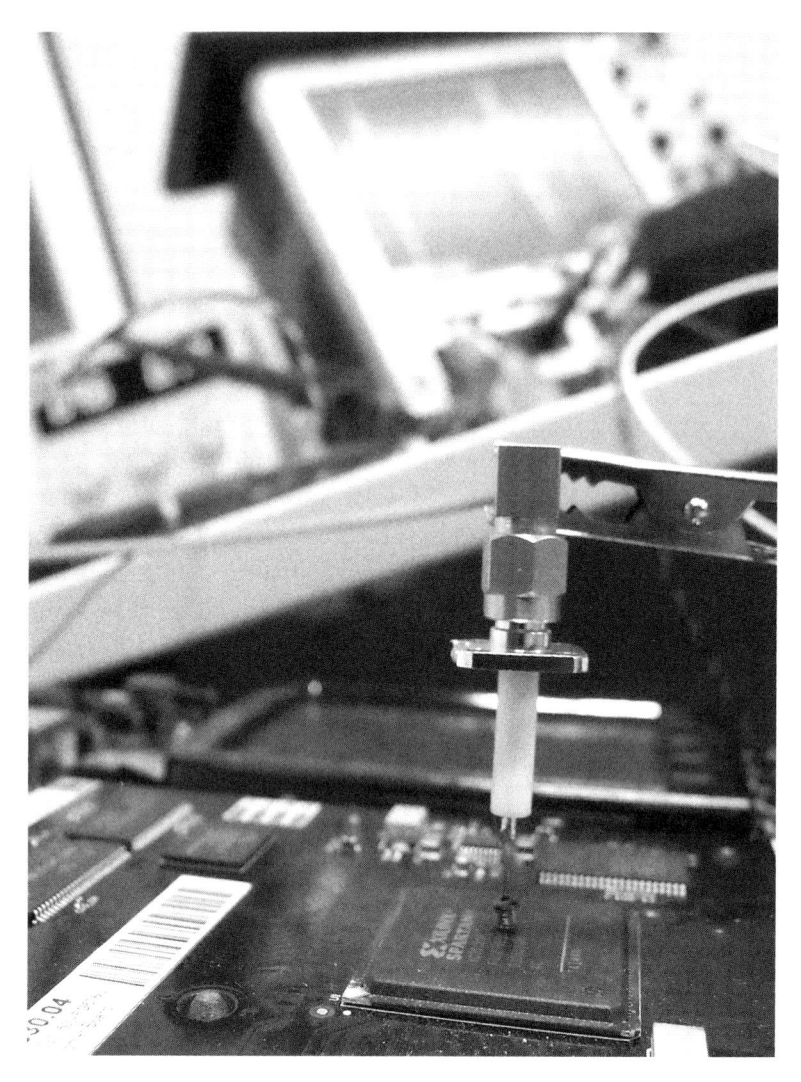

Figure 7.1
Measuring electromagnetic radiation emanating from a chip as it performs a cryptographic hash algorithm. Image courtesy of Olivier Benoît and Thomas Peyrin.

be protected against their own predictable routine behavior and what that behavior may reveal to an interested observer.

The sensing contraption was built to measure the electromagnetic leakage of a specific type of cryptographic algorithms: hash functions.[2] A fundamental element of the modern cryptographer's toolbox, cryptographic hash functions are essential to the efficiency and security of RSA digital signatures (see "The Early History" in chapter 4) but are also used in software protection, version control systems, and identification protocols. Because of the very high speed such constructions can achieve, the most widespread hash functions are built according to principles similar to those of DES, using repeated rounds of basic "bit shaking" operations of confusion and diffusion.

The efficiency benefits of such functions come with a significant disadvantage however. In contrast to public-key algorithms, "It is difficult to say something concrete about the security of a hash function such as MD4 since it is not 'based' on a well-studied problem such as factoring or the Discrete Log problem. So, as is the case with DES, confidence in the security of the system can only be attained over time, as the system is studied and (one hopes) not found to be insecure."[3] Indeed, although hash functions based on number-theoretic problems would be much more amenable to the mathematical formalization necessary for analysis under the provable security framework, efforts in that direction have to date mostly resulted in "an embarrassing history of insecure proposals."[4]

The sensing apparatus depicted in figure 7.1 thus points to what are perhaps surprising dimensions of the relationship between mathematics and computing. On the one hand, although mathematical theorems do not consume energy or leak radiation, their embodiment as algorithms performed on computers do. On the other hand, there are computer algorithms that have no (elegant and interesting) mathematical representations and, consequently, about which little can be proven. Thus, though common references to computers as "universal Turing machines" suggest they are intimately, fundamentally, mathematical objects, the relationship is considerably more complex and open-ended than it might appear at first glance.[5]

In this chapter, I explore some of the ways in which the relationship has been realized in cryptographic models. I begin this exploration with an account of a controversy familiar to researchers in the field, that surrounding the epistemological implications of the "Random Oracle Model." Because the controversy has grown increasingly acrimonious in recent years, I will tread very lightly, with the modest goal of arguing two related points: first, that in contrast with the rest of the cryptographic signature model, the controversy represents an engagement of the cryptographic research community with the question of what constitute acceptable abstractions in mathematical modeling; second, that the community pragmatically recognizes that "provable security" obtains under a broad range of assumptions about the physical world.[6]

The Random Oracle Model

Yet another dimension of the revolution prophesied by Diffie and Hellman in "New Directions" concerned methods for certification of the soundness of cryptographic systems. At the time, such certification came with a large disclaimer: after surviving sustained cryptanalytic examination by the community, a cryptosystem such as DES would be certified as "free of weaknesses, *as far as the community is aware*." The caveat underlined the recognition that the research community could not guarantee that, on the one hand, such cryptosystems would not fall in the future to yet undiscovered attacks, and on the other hand, that such methods had not already been discovered but undisclosed (e.g., by the intelligence establishment). The only exception to the rule concerned the Vernam one-time pad, proven absolutely secure under Shannon's information-theoretic framework, at the cost of an equally absolute impracticality.

In "New Directions," Diffie and Hellman claimed that two emerging mathematical disciplines, computational complexity and algorithmics, would offer an alternative. Less haphazard than conviction obtained through practical experience and community consensus, more practical than information theory, *provable security* would provide the surest method of certification:

Judging the worth of new systems has always been a central concern of cryptographers. During the sixteenth and seventeenth centuries, mathematical arguments were often invoked to argue the strength of cryptographic methods, usually relying on counting methods which showed the astronomical number of possible keys. . . . As systems whose strength had been so argued were repeatedly broken, the notion of giving mathematical proofs for the security of systems fell into disrepute and was replaced by certification by cryptanalytic assault. . . . Although some general rules have been developed, which aid the designer in avoiding obvious weaknesses, the ultimate test is an assault on the system by skilled cryptanalysts under the most favorable conditions (e.g., a chosen plaintext attack). The development of computer has led for the first time to a mathematical theory of algorithms which can begin to approach the difficult problem of estimating the computational difficulty of breaking a cryptographic system. The position of mathematical proof may thus come full circle and be reestablished as the best method of certification.[7]

Yet the realization of this aspect of Diffie and Hellman's program has encountered surprisingly tenacious difficulties. The mathematical successes flowing from the framing of cryptography within computational complexity and algorithmics are undisputed. A broad range of number-theoretic primitives (e.g., encryption, digital signatures, pseudorandom generators) have been defined and analyzed by cryptographers working within the computational complexity framework. These primitives have been further assembled into protocols that enable parties communicating over networks to realize remarkable communication feats—e.g., flip coins or exchange cash anonymously—with the certainty of mathematical proof. However, the practical payoffs have been less spectacular. The impact of provable security on fielded cryptographic systems has been disappointingly small, "in the sense that these ideas were reflected almost not at all in protocols used in practice."[8]

Mihir Bellare and Philip Rogaway have suggested that the cryptographic theory/practice divide is due to the fact that "theoretical work often seems to gain provable security only at the cost of efficiency."[9] Block ciphers, such as DES, have remained the most popular atomic primitive, as they are much more efficient than number-theoretic primitives such as RSA encryption. Indeed, "DES is generally at least 100 times as fast in software and between 1,000 and 10,000 times as fast in hardware, depending on the implementation."[10] Yet the provable security line of work has relied exclusively on number-theoretic primitives as the foundation for protocol design because they are characterized by well-defined mathematical problems.

The problem is compounded by the fact that, over the last thirty-five years, very few new, possibly faster, number-theoretic problems have emerged that have withstood the test of time: "Good atomic primitives are rare, as are people who understand their workings . . . The reason is that the design (or discovery) of good atomic primitives is more an art than a science."[11] Furthermore, cryptography deals with a problem significantly different than the ordinary fare of computational complexity, that of defining secure protocols, that is, "distributed algorithms defined by a sequence of steps precisely specifying the actions required of the two or more entities to achieve a specific security objective."[12] However, there has been no straightforward path between good atomic primitives and good protocols.[13] As Bellare points out, "the problem with protocol design is that a poorly designed protocol can be insecure *even though the underlying atomic primitive is good.*"[14] A significant component of the contemporary cryptographic research program has thus sought to lay down well-defined principles to guide designers in building provably secure, protocols, using atomic primitives with precise mathematical properties.

Overall, this endeavor has failed to convince practitioners. As Phil Rogaway recounts, cryptographic system designers have been "alienated by the language of asymptotic complexity, the high level statements of results that fell under it, and the algorithmic inefficiency that seemed endemic to early work. There emerged a pronounced culture gap between cryptographic theory and practice. Theorists and practitioners ignored one another, attending disjoint conferences. Neither group regarded the other as having anything much to say."[15]

One highly controversial proposal for restarting the conversation is Bellare and Rogaway's program for "Practice-Oriented Provable Security," based on the Random Oracle Model (ROM). Bellare and Rogaway were motivated by the persistent issues encountered in proving the security of RSA signatures. As described in "The Early History" in chapter 4, RSA signatures use a "hash-then-decrypt" approach: messages are first hashed and then signed ("decrypted") with the signer's private key. Proving the security of RSA signatures thus requires taking into account the security properties of the hash function. But, as noted previously by Stinson, none of the efficient hash functions used in practice (such as SHA-1 or MD5) are founded on the kind number-theoretic problems that would enable their analysis under the complexity theory framework. The security of RSA signatures thus relies on a combination of computational assumptions and on assumptions relative to the community's faith in the lack of known attacks. Given the appeal of digital signatures as "non-repudiable" forensic objects, this is an uncomfortable state of affairs. As Bellare and Rogaway note, "We stress that we don't know of any *attack* on this scheme. But we prefer, for such important primitives, to have some proof of security rather than just an absence of known attacks."[16]

The ROM is an attempt to solve this lingering problem. The principle is simple: if a cryptographic function truly fulfills its properties of collision resistance, it is not possible to find the message m that corresponds to the output $h(m)$ of the function. That is, for all intents and purposes, the output of a cryptographic hash function appears perfectly random to all participants in the signature protocol. The ROM provides a methodology that simply assumes this ideal state of affair to be the case: "Provide all parties—good and bad alike—with access to a (public) function h; prove correct a protocol assuming h is truly random, i.e. a random oracle; later, in practice, set h to some specific function derived in some way from a standard cryptographic hash function like SHA-1 or RIPEMD-160."[17]

The ROM is thus a framework in which perfect mathematical idealizations (random oracles) of a troublesome real world cryptographic object (hash functions) are assumed to exist for the purpose of proving the overall correctness of the protocol. "Later, in practice," after the idealized protocol has been proven correct, designers should simply replace the idealization with the real-world object. The issue for the cryptographic research community has been to ascertain the relationship, if any, between the idealized protocol proved under the ROM and the one relying on the real-world function.[18]

Given that no real-world deterministic hash function produces truly random outputs, Bellare and Rogaway have emphasized from the beginning that proofs under the ROM should not enjoy the same status as "ordinary" proofs: "We stress that the proof is in the random oracle model and the last step is heuristic in nature. It is a thesis of this paper that significant assurance benefits nonetheless remain."[19] Determining the precise nature of those benefits has, however, proven highly controversial. At the very least, Bellare argued, proof under ROM is better than no proof at all: "In comparison with totally ad hoc design, a proof in the random oracle model has the benefit of viewing the scheme with regard to its meeting a strong and formal notion of security, even if this is assuming some underlying primitive is very strong. This is better than not formally modeling the security of the scheme in any way. This explains why the random oracle model is viewed as a bridge between theory and practice."[20]

Worried that proofs under ROM would become standard issue in the cryptographic toolbox, three prominent theoreticians vehemently disagreed: "Although the random oracle methodology seems to be useful in practice, it is unclear how to put this methodology on firm grounds."[21] In interviews with me, cryptographers voiced various degrees of discomfort with the model. Birgit Pfitzmann, for example, was concerned that more work was needed before the epistemological status of proofs under ROM could be ascertained: "The random oracle model is not an assumption, it is an abstraction. An assumption, like 'factoring is hard' can be proven true or false, eventually. But to say that a hash function is as good as a random oracle is not an assumption—it is a simple abstraction, which cannot be proved or disproved. And because, at the moment, there is no formalization of that abstraction, all we can do is hope that it does not abstract from anything important. But we don't know yet."

Pointcheval and Stern have sought to resolve the tension between the two camps by suggesting the model does not indeed provide proofs, but rather, *arguments*.[22] Although they do not formally clarify the relationship of such arguments to provable security, they suggest these provide "quite strong indication that the overall design . . . is presumably correct." Thus, cryptographers should accept proofs under ROM as useful adjuncts to either the heuristic measure provided by cryptanalysis or the provable security provided by complexity theory. However well-intentioned an interpretation, Rogaway disagreed with its implications: "To some people, proofs in the Random Oracle model are effectively not proofs. One well-known researcher calls them *heuristic arguments*. That isn't right. A proof in the Random Oracle model is still a proof, it's just a proof in a model of computation that some people don't find worthwhile."[23] Goldreich disagreed in no uncertain terms: "The ROM has caused more harm than good, because many people confuse it for the 'real thing' (while it is merely an extremely idealized sanity check). . . . Given the sour state of affairs, it seems good to us to abolish the ROM. At the very minimum, one should issue a fierce warning that *security in the ROM does not provide any indication towards security in the standard model.*"[24]

Regardless of its epistemological validity, the best argument for using the ROM might just be that it brings under the framework of provable security objects that would otherwise remain outside of it, namely signatures: "All things being equal, a proof of security in the random oracle model is not as good as a proof of security in the 'real world,' but is much better than no proof at all. Anyway, it does not seem unreasonable to use the random oracle model, *since that is the only way we know of to justify the security of ordinary RSA signatures.*"[25] That such *realpolitik* of mathematical proof has become has become more or less the norm is attested to by the significant proportion of conference papers that today justify their results under the ROM framework.[26]

The discussion within the community over the epistemological status of the ROM implies that the move to frame cryptography within computational complexity is not without its own paradoxes and problems. Cryptographic theory and practice remain populated by highly useful objects eluding mathematical characterization, whose certification is simply a function of the collective experience of the community. Even within the provable security framework, proof is a variegated affair: primitives may be based on the assumption of the computational intractability of several number-theoretic problems, including integer factorization, RSA, quadratic residuosity, discrete logarithms over finite groups or elliptic curves, Diffie-Hellman, and so on.[27] Yet, as Bellare points out, "in the bulk of cases, we do not know how to compare the assumptions underlying various proofs of security."[28] Thus, instead of neatly falling under the single, all-encompassing model of analytical proof suggested by the "provable security" label, cryptography exhibits a wide range of modes of persuasion that cannot be easily ranked. I argue that such a state of affairs does not testify to some disciplinary methodological shortcomings but rather is inevitable given the breadth of cryptography's intellectual ambitions and the wide range of real-world artifacts, protocols, and sign systems it seeks to engage with.

Indeed, I even suggest the controversy has had beneficial consequences, insofar as it has provided the occasion for the community's first sustained discussion of the models that inform its mathematical practices. In fact, until then, the community had not even recognized its reliance on models, as articulated by Rogaway:

> When you are working within the Random Oracle model, you are working within a specific model, and a not-so-realistic one at that. What is often not recognized is that when you are working within the standard model, you are *also* working within a specific model, and a not-so-realistic one. The standard model *also* abstracts away key aspects of the real world—like the fact that real computation takes time, uses power, and leaks radiation. There *is* a big gap between the Random Oracle model and reality (hash functions *aren't* like random oracles) —and there is *also* a big gap between the standard model and reality.[29]

It is significant that Rogaway refers to radiation leakage and the side-channels attacks discussed at the beginning of this chapter. Like the ROM, the attacks discovered by Kocher and colleagues have brought to the surface the abstractions that underline the "standard model," with far-reaching implications for the community of theory-oriented cryptographers. Famed theoretician Silvio Micali and his colleague Leonid Reyzin put it plainly: "Such 'physical observation attacks' *bypass* the impressive barrier of mathematical security erected so far, and successfully break mathematically impregnable systems. The great practicality and the inherent availability of physical attacks threaten the very relevance of complexity-theoretic security."[30]

In response to this threat, a new paradigm of *physical security* has emerged as an alternative to the traditional assumptions built into the provable security paradigm. In this model, in addition to their usual computational abstractions, cryptographers integrate explicit assumptions about the physicality of computing devices, relative to their power consumption, their electromagnetic leakage, the availability of countermeasures (such as tamper-proofing and physical shielding), and the various levels of access adversaries enjoy to the device. For example, Goldwasser proposes "one-time programs" whose security properties are dependent on "one-time memories," a secure hardware device, with the following characteristics: "memory locations that are *never accessed* by the device are *never leaked* via a side channel . . . and the device has a *single* tamper-proof bit . . . the device is very inexpensive, low energy, and disposable, much like RFID tags used in clothing."[31] Goldwasser is able to perform a traditional mathematical analysis of the security of one-time programs given their implementation using devices with the required physical properties.

Inevitably, the same issues creep up again and researchers find themselves questioning the *fitness* of the model relative to its environment: "when moving to a physical setting, we need to determine what are the physical limits of the adversary. Therefore, the question arises of how relevant the physical models are and to which extent they capture the engineering experience."[32] It is thus not surprising that, in the spirit of the ROM, Standaert, Malkin, and Yung have already felt the need for a "practice-oriented" version of the physical security model. This new model will aim to "reduce the gap between the previously introduced theoretical notions of physical security and the actual attacks performed and understood by cryptographic engineers," with the hope of trading "some theoretical generality for more applicability to various applications and designs."[33] Such proposals are symptoms of a healthy scientific process: given that theory and practice are both constantly evolving, the fitness of models is a question that must necessarily remain open and subject to permanent negotiation.

In the remainder of this chapter, I want to explore some of the possibilities suggested by the ROM controversy and the emergence of the physical security model. If cryptographic practice already integrates a broad diversity of modes of persuasion, and if the "standard model" can be extended to incorporate the unruly materiality of the computer, what research avenues might this open up? Here, I explore some strands of research that draw on other materialities as *design resources*: those of human bodies, for example, and their capacity for memory, perception, cognition, and those of the material world—for example, paper and sealed envelopes. Just like that of the computer, these materialities have largely remained outside the purview of the "standard model," as their formalization results in proofs which perhaps no longer feel as clean and rigorous as those obtained within purely abstract models.

Memory

Memory constitutes one of the most widespread elements of security technology design, as exemplified by the challenge-and-response protocols (login, password) that today secure access to most electronic services and devices. In theory, access control based on textual passwords should offer adequate security, because, for eight-character passwords of digits and mixed-case letters, the total numbers of choices, the *password space*, is about 2×10^{14}, or about 2 hundred trillion possible passwords. However, users understandably choose easy-to-remember passwords, combinations of letters and numbers that have some meaning attached to them.[34] Thus, given the constraints of human memory, a password scheme's security is more appropriately defined by the size of its *memorable* password space than that of its full password space.[35] Instead of undertaking an exhaustive key search, attackers can draw guesses from dictionaries with just a few million words to effectively capture a significant portion of that much-reduced memorable password space.

To help thwart such *dictionary attacks*, systems typically implement rules that coerce users in selecting passwords more evenly spread across the total password space of the scheme—for example, mixing letters and typographical characters, using passphrases, or enforcing frequent replacement.[36] However, users often respond to such measures with even worse security strategies, for example, writing down their passwords under their mouse pads. As Smith quips, classical password selection rules imply that the best passwords "must be impossible to remember and never written down."[37]

One interesting response to this seemingly intractable conundrum has been to take advantage of the dual linguistic and graphical dimensions of textual passwords.[38] That is, passwords are memorized, but also input into computers as *written* signs. This approach leads to possible strategies for enhancing the memorability of passwords by coupling together visual and linguistic mnemonic techniques. Such approaches are interesting on two levels: on the one hand, they might effectively increase the *memorable* password space without additionally burdening the user's memory; on the other hand, to measure this effectiveness, researchers must somehow integrate into their mathematical models the empirical insights provided by experimental psychologists working in the field of memory and cognition.

Input Orderings

A first strategy stems from the realization that computer software and input devices impose a specific temporal order on the way users enter their passwords: first letter first, second letter second . . . last letter last. Yet using a graphical input device, it is possible to *decouple* the elements of the input from their temporal order. That is, the various characters of a password can be entered according to different ordering strategies—for example, by starting with the last character, from the outside in, or any other input strategy (see figure 7.2).

This decoupling immediately leads to a sizable increase of the password space: for a password of k characters where $k = 8$, the new password space exceeds the conventional one by a factor of $k! = 40320$. Obviously, not all ordering strategies are equally memorable, and it is not clear how one might quantify the increase in the memory password space other than by empirical trials. Nevertheless, the scheme provides a first entry point into

The Cryptographic Imagination 171

```
0. _ _ _ _ _ _ _ _        0. _ _ _ _ _ _ _ _
1. t _ _ _ _ _ _ _        1. _ _ _ _ _ _ _ t
2. t o _ _ _ _ _ _        2. o _ _ _ _ _ _ t
3. t o m _ _ _ _ _        3. o m _ _ _ _ _ t
4. t o m a _ _ _ _        4. o m a _ _ _ _ t
5. t o m a t _ _ _        5. o m a t _ _ _ t
6. t o m a t o _ _        6. o m a t o _ _ t
```
    (a) Left-to-right   (b) Rotated left

```
0. _ _ _ _ _ _ _ _        0. _ _ _ _ _ _ _ _
1. t _ _ _ _ _ _ _        1. _ _ _ _ _ _ _ t
2. t _ _ _ _ o _ _        2. _ _ _ _ o _ t
3. t m _ _ _ o _ _        3. m _ _ _ o _ t
4. t m _ _ a o _ _        4. m _ _ a o _ _ t
5. t m t _ a o _ _        5. m t _ a o _ _ t
6. t m t o a o _ _        6. m t o a o _ _ t
```
    (c) Outside-in   (d) A more complex example

Figure 7.2
Variations on inputting the "tomato" password, from Ian Jermyn, Alain Mayer, Fabian Monrose, Michael K. Reiter, and Aviel D. Rubin, "The Design and Analysis of Graphical Passwords," in *Proceedings of the 8th USENIX Security Symposium* (Berkeley: USENIX Association, 1999). Used by permission.

strategies that take advantage of the dual graphical/linguistic nature of passwords.

Graphical Passwords

A second strategy relies on the *picture effect*, "the substantial improvement of performance in recall and recognition with pictorial representations of to-be-remembered material over verbal representations."[39] The most accepted explanation for the picture effect is currently provided by *dual-code theory*, which proposes that knowledge is encoded and processed in two functionally distinct memory systems—one verbal, for linguistic information, one nonverbal, for perceptual information. Dual-code theory hypothesizes that "pictures automatically engage multiple representations and associations with other knowledge about the world, thus encouraging a more elaborate encoding than occurs with words."[40]

The idea behind graphical passwords is simple: the password is a drawing on a grid (say, 4 × 4), such as can be implemented on the screen of a smartphone (see figure 7.3). Each cell on the grid is denoted by (x, y)

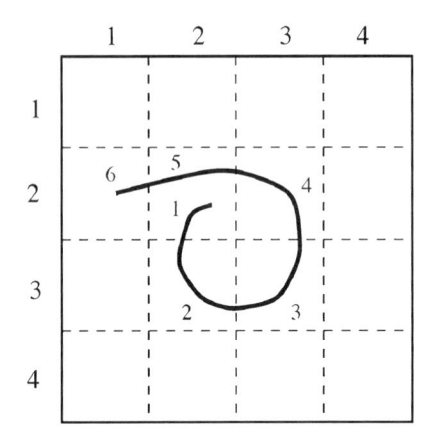

Figure 7.3
Input of a graphical password on a 4 × 4 grid, from Ian Jermyn, Alain Mayer, Fabian Monrose, Michael K. Reiter, and Aviel D. Rubin, "The Design and Analysis of Graphical Passwords," in *Proceedings of the 8th USENIX Security Symposium* (Berkeley: USENIX Association, 1999). Used by permission.

coordinates and the drawing is mapped to a sequence of coordinate pairs by listing in order the cells through which the drawing passes. In this case, the drawing corresponds to the sequence (2,2), (3,2), (3,3), (2,3), (2,2), (2,1), (5,5), where the distinguished coordinate (5,5) indicates a "pen-up" event. Authentication is successful when a user enters a drawing that follows the same sequence of coordinates as that entered in the device when choosing the password.

If the principle of the "Draw-A-Secret" (DAS) scheme is itself simple, its security analysis presents some considerable challenges. As Jermyn and colleagues point out, "Due to the dependence of the security of a scheme on the passwords that users choose in practice, a new password scheme cannot be *proven* better than an old scheme."[41] That is, it is not possible to determine the size of the set of *memorable* DAS passwords other than through empirical studies.

Yet one might still try and show that the set of memorable DAS passwords is greater than that of textual passwords. This is difficult, however. Dictionary attacks are effective not only because users do not choose their passwords uniformly across the entire password space, but also because attackers have knowledge of that distribution. For textual passwords, this includes "information about specific peaks in distribution (users often choose passwords based on their own name), and information about gross properties (words in the English dictionary are likely to be chosen)." What is crucial is that "without knowledge of the distribution, an attacker would be not better off than if users were in fact choosing uniformly."[42]

Given this fact, a measure of security of DAS may be derived from the investigation of the scheme's "weak password subspaces," classes of images more likely to be chosen by users because of their memorability.[43] The distribution of graphical passwords induced by such classes might inform the "graphical dictionaries" necessary for a brute force attack on the scheme. Although such distributions may not be determined with an empirical certainty conducive to precise "formal" proof, Jermyn and colleagues suggest that they can nevertheless be estimated by modeling users' choices. These estimates can then be used to construct "plausibility arguments" for the security of graphical password schemes. For example, they investigate the size of the memorable password space consisting solely of rectangles, four connected strokes at right angles, that may be placed anywhere on the grid. Even with such a limited model, they calculate the space to be equivalent to some of the dictionaries used against textual passwords.

Drawing from empirical findings in experimental psychology, Thorpe and van Oorschot conjecture that two principles may drive user choices of graphical passwords; on the one hand, because "people are more likely to recall symmetric images and patterns, and people perceive mirror symmetry as having a special status, a significant subset of users are likely to choose mirror symmetric patterns"; on the other hand, people are more likely to recall drawings with low number of *components*, that is, visually distinct parts of an image.[44] Based on these conjectures, they build two distinct graphical dictionaries and provide an extensive analysis of the attacks they might yield on graphical password schemes.[45]

Perception

The perceptual system has always played a central role in the evaluation of paper-and-ink security artifacts. From the visual examination of handwritten signatures to the feel of a banknote's paper and the semiotics of official documents, the security properties of such artifacts is evaluated, with various degrees of formal expertise, through their tactile, visual, auditory, and olfactory characteristics, as registered and compared through the perceptual system.[46] Though perception may appear to introduce a hopelessly subjective dimension into the mathematical proof process, several proposals have sought to enroll it as an element of cryptographic design, including hash visualization functions and visual cryptography.

Hash Visualization Functions

The distribution of public keys through certificates does not in itself solve the key distribution problem, but merely displaces it (see "Security Services" in chapter 4). In order to verify digital signatures, users still need to acquire the authentic public key of the certification authority. However, securely obtaining the key through an electronic network would require users to have a public key in the first place. For this reason, web browsers are provided with preinstalled "root" public-key certificates, which users must simply trust to have remained authentic and uncorrupted.

Because such blind trust puts the entire signature verification process on a shaky foundation, Anderson and colleagues have advocated the distribution of confirmatory information through offline means. For example, a telephone book–like register might contain a "fingerprint" (the hash) of the certification authority's public key. Users can then compare the fingerprints of public keys embedded in their web browsers with those in the register and thus "ground the trust required for electronic commerce and other online applications in the trust that has been built up over the years in the world of print publishing."[47] For example, an entry in Anderson's 1988 *Global Trust Register* reads as follows:

Verisign Inc.

1390. Shorebird Way, Mountain View, CA 94043, USA

Tel: +1 650 961 7500

Fax: +1 650 961 7300

practices@verisign.com

http://www.verisign.com

VeriSign Class 1 Primary CA

00　EC 35 D1 : 64 A0 B9 24 :: 16 79 C0 64 : C1 06 48 84

Perrig and Song have pointed out that even this process can be cumbersome and prone to error, as users need to laboriously compare the sixteen hexadecimal digits of the fingerprints. They propose that *hash visualization*

The Cryptographic Imagination

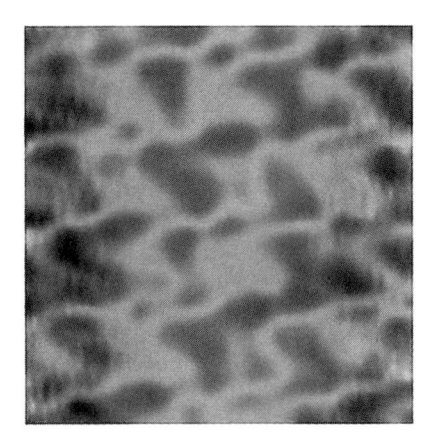

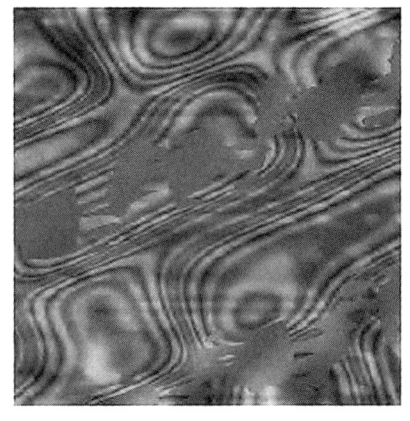

Figure 7.4
Two hash visualizations of public key fingerprints. The first hash is for fingerprint 51 86 E8 4E : 46 D7 B5 4E :: 29 D2 35 F4 : 41 89 5F 20; the second is for 51 86 E8 1F : BC B1 C3 71 :: B5 18 10 DB : 5F DC F6 20. From Adrian Perrig and Dawn Song, "Hash Visualization: A New Technique to Improve Real-World Security," in *International Workshop on Cryptographic Techniques and E-Commerce (CrypTEC'99)* (1999). Used by permission.

functions—blending metrics from cryptography and image processing—can provide a more usable method for comparing public key fingerprints.[48] Hash visualization functions build on the traditional requirements for cryptographic hashing: *compression*, that is, a function *h* maps an input bitstring *x* of arbitrary length to an output $y = h(x)$, a bitstring of fixed length; *efficiency*, that is, $h(x)$ must be easy to compute; *collision resistance*, the idea that it is not possible to invert the function, that is, given a bitstring *y*, it is computationally infeasible to find the input *x* that corresponds to $h(x) = y$.

Instead of outputting bitstrings, Perrig and Song suggest that hash functions could just as well output images (see figure 7.4). With the help of such a function, users could simply compare the hash visualization of their browser's public key with the one published in a register to determine if the key is authentic. The problem then becomes one of defining an appropriate metric of image equality and inequality. The authors propose a measure of *nearness*: two images I_1 and I_2 are *near* (noted $I_1 \approx I_2$) if they are *perceptually indistinguishable*. Given such a metric, they can rewrite the traditional definition of cryptographically hash functions as follows:

1. *Image generation*   A cryptographic hash visualization function h maps an input x of arbitrary length to an output image $y = h(x)$ of fixed size.
2. *Efficiency*   Given h and an input x, $h(x)$ is easy to compute.
3. *Collision resistance*   For any output y, it is computationally infeasible to find the input x such that $h(x) \approx y$.

Additional methods for exchanging hashes over insecure channels include a scheme based on the comparison of glyphs and also Phil Zimmerman's *biometric word lists*.[49] Developed for the PGP free encryption software, it is meant "to convey binary information in an authenticated manner over a voice channel, such as a telephone, via biometric signatures. The human voice that speaks the words, if recognized by the listener, serves as a means of biometric authentication of the data carried by the words."[50] The system is patterned along the lines of the alphabet used in the military to unambiguously transmit letters over noisy channels. The PGP biometric word list contains 256 words chosen for their linguistic distance, each representing the 256 bytes values of 0 to 255. A public key fingerprint of, for example, hexadecimal values E582: 94F2: E9A2: 2748: 6E8B:: 061B: 31CC: 528F: D7FA: 3F19 would be spoken as "topmost Istanbul: Pluto vagabond: treadmill Pacific: brackish dictator: goldfish Medusa:: afflict bravado: chatter revolver: Dupont midsummer: stopwatch whimsical: cowbell bottomless."

Visual Cryptography

Introduced in 1994 by Moni Naor and Adi Shamir, visual cryptography offers a new type of cryptographic scheme whereby the encrypted material is "decoded directly by the human visual system."[51] The system conceals the plaintext picture by splitting it into two distinct layers: a ciphertext, printed on paper, and a secret key, printed on a transparency. Taken individually, each layer looks like random noise, but overlaying them one over the other reveals the plaintext (see figure 7.5). Like Vernam's one-time pad, the system is perfectly secure in the information theoretic sense. That is, even after having intercepted the ciphertext, an attacker can do no better than flip a coin to guess the value of each pixel of the plaintext.

The shares are constructed by substituting each pixel of the plaintext with blocks of four subpixels, following the rules in figure 7.6: for each

The Cryptographic Imagination

Plaintext   *Ciphertext (layer #1)*

Secret key (layer #2)   *Revealed plaintext (#3)*

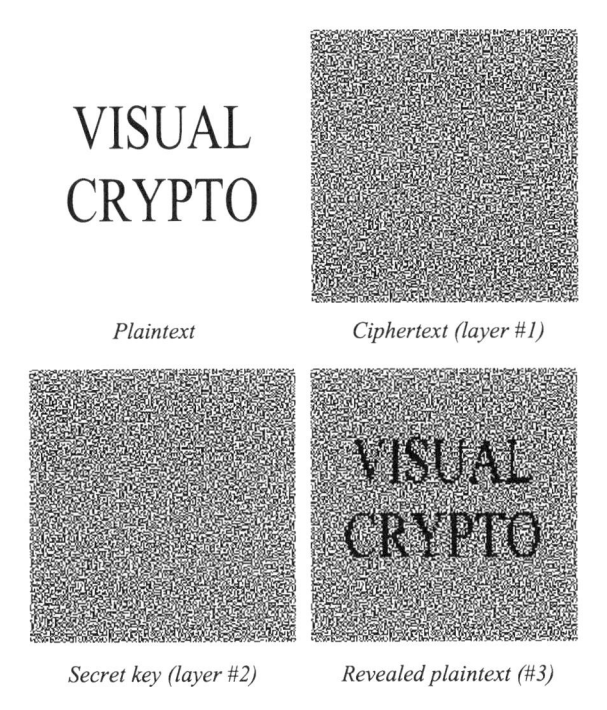

Figure 7.5
Visual cryptography: superposing the ciphertext (layer #1) with the secret key (layer #2) reveals the encrypted plaintext (#3). Image by the author.

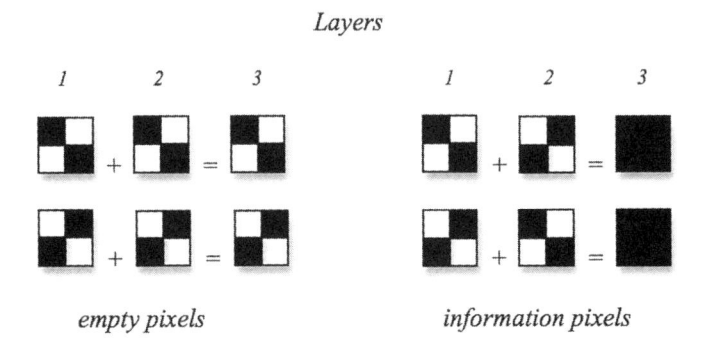

Layers

empty pixels   *information pixels*

Figure 7.6
How to construct the ciphertext and the secret key, based on each pixel of the plaintext. Image by the author.

white pixel of the original image, choose at random either ▨ or ▨, assign it to the ciphertext layer (#1), and assign the complementary empty pixel to the secret key layer (#2). For each black pixel, pick at random either ▨ or ▨, assign it to the ciphertext layer, and assign the complementary information pixel to the secret key layer. Overlaying the two layers will display layer #3, with empty pixels displaying as gray, and information pixels as black. Intuitively, one can see that even if the two layers are constructed together from the plaintext, taken separately they reveal no information whatsoever to an attacker.

Beyond its reliance on the visual system for decryption, the scheme has interesting advantages: once printed out, the ciphertext can be faxed, photocopied, scanned, and in general can survive multiple translations between the digital and the physical domain. Visual cryptography has been generalized to include grayscale, halftone, and color images, and researchers have explored its potential applications to watermarking, secure printing, and voting.[52]

Naor and Pinkas have extended the original concept to the problem of authentication and identification. Remarkably, the resulting protocols do not depend on any number-theoretic computational assumptions but rather on assumptions regarding the visual capabilities of human participants. Indeed, one of the authors' stated goals is to develop a framework that provides for rigorous security proofs of "protocols in which humans take an active part." Such analysis presents new challenges:

It is hard to rigorously analyze processes which involve humans since there is no easy mathematical model of human behavior. In order to prove the security of such protocols the human part in the protocol should be explicitly defined. Then it is possible to isolate the capabilities required from the human participant (e.g., the ability to verify that a certain image is totally black). The security of the protocol must be reduced to the assumption that a "normal" person has these capabilities. This assumption can then be verified through empirical tests.[53]

By varying these assumptions, the authors provide proofs for protocols that rely on "sharp-eyed" and "not so sharp-eyed" humans, and a taxonomy organized according to design trade-offs between security and the visual capabilities required of human participants. Although, on the surface, the resulting proofs resemble the standard fare of the computational complexity framework, they represent a surprising irruption of human bodies into the usually immaterial world of cryptographic protocols.

Material Objects

In visual cryptography, assumptions regarding the relative difficulty of number-theoretic problems are traded for assumptions regarding the capabilities of the human visual system. This exchange leads to a series of schemes categorized according to trade-offs between protocol security and other design constraints. Pursuing an intriguing path, Moran and Naor have argued that it is also possible to further extend the "standard model" by including the capabilities of some of the traditional paper-and-ink objects that have provided security in the physical world—for example, sealed envelopes and scratch-cards (such as those used for instant lotteries). They model such objects as "tamper-evident seals," defined as "a cryptographic primitive that captures the properties of a sealed envelope: while the envelope is sealed, it is impossible to tell what's inside, but if the seal is broken the envelope cannot be resealed (so any tampering is evident)."[54] Not only are the protocols designed to be implemented using actual physical envelopes, but Moran and Naor place explicit upper bounds on the number of rounds and envelopes that can be used so that the protocols remain practical for humans, rather than mere theoretical constructs. Just like the visual authentication schemes, the security of the resulting protocols does not rely on any computational assumptions but rather on the (physical) tamper-evident properties of the envelopes.[55]

These tamper-evident seals are introduced in the context of an information security problem with important implications: survey-based methodologies encounter elevated bias when investigating socially desirable or undesirable behaviors (e.g., voting preferences or immigration status), as survey respondents tend to lie. One solution is to use a "randomized response" technique, first proposed by Warner in 1965.[56] In its simplest version, the respondent privately flips a coin before answering the question. Heads, he answers truthfully, tails, he lies. Given that only half the population surveyed will have answered truthfully, the researcher merely doubles the observed response to obtain the true proportion. Yet individual respondents are shielded by the uncertainty generated by the coin toss, as each is equally likely to have lied—that is, the protocol provides them with *plausible deniability.*

As befits the work of cryptographers, Moran and Naor's protocols are designed to address the issue whereby a respondent maliciously deviates from the protocol so as to influence the outcome of the survey, perhaps for political reasons. Equally problematic, however, is getting honest respondents to perform the protocol correctly: randomized response methodologies can become rapidly cumbersome, requiring respondents "to perform complex randomization tasks for which interviewers must provide seemingly 'mindboggling' explanations; the result can be respondent suspicion, confusion, and uncertainty as to the level of disclosure that a truthful answer entails."[57]

Moran and Naor's "human-centric protocols" thus bring additional benefits to the table. Because the security properties of scratch-cards or sealed envelopes are well understood, respondents are more likely to believe that the protocols perform as advertised than if they were implemented using computers. As they note, "the computers and operating system actually implementing the protocol may not be trusted (even though the protocol itself is). . . . Even for an expert, it is very difficult to verify that a computer implementation of a complex protocol is correct."[58] Basing cryptographic primitives on familiar technologies with a long social history may thus provide a way to develop collective trust in modern cryptographic protocols while maintaining the rigorous mathematical analysis characteristic of the provable security framework.

Cognition

Developing such collective trust may require not only transparency of technical means but also the ability for users to understand how the protocols themselves perform their often mysterious feats. In fact, the security proofs of Moran and Naor's human-centric protocols depend on the ability of honest parties to follow instructions correctly, something they recognize is difficult to either guarantee or model mathematically. Perhaps, then, the development of something akin to *cryptographic literacy* is just as necessary to information security as that of impregnable mathematical protocols.

Researchers tackling this issue have tended to adopt one of two distinct approaches.[59] The first one frames the issue in terms of "public understanding of science"; that is, the cryptographic literacy problem lies in getting the general public to understand the capabilities of modern cryptographic protocols for ensuring security and privacy over networks. Cryptographic literacy allows the public to "cultivate a higher level of trust for systems that use sophisticated protocols to protect information. Just as an understanding of biology goes a long way towards making informed decisions on environmental issues, understanding the technical issues involved in cryptography enables informed decisions on privacy issues." Indeed, the confounding lack of uptake of cryptographic technologies in the marketplace may be attributed to the public's inability to grasp their potential: "If more people knew about such things, they would lobby for their adoption to better protect privacy in everyday transactions."[60]

Such research thus focuses on the design of effective pedagogical tools for explaining cryptographic capabilities to lay publics as might be found in schools, universities, popular science television programs, and the like. Encryption and key distribution, for example, might be demonstrated using a chain and padlock, and the intrinsic cryptographic properties of playing cards can be used to develop "simple and meaningful visual metaphors" for many protocols.[61] Given their familiarity and inherent dramatic structure, even children's folk tales may prove helpful: Quisquater and colleagues leverage the story of Ali Baba and the Forty Thieves in the service of explaining zero-knowledge protocols to children—even including advanced theoretical concepts such as simulation and parallel executions.[62]

Although also concerned with the popularization of cryptographic concepts, the second approach to cryptographic literacy conceives of this objective as one that may drive cryptographic research itself.[63] In this vein, Fellows and Koblitz have proposed the development of a "Kid Krypto" subdiscipline, where the *accessibility* of protocols is a design goal in its own right: "As in the case of the more traditional criteria—efficiency and security—the search for cryptosystems that meet the accessibility standard naturally leads to interesting theoretical and practical questions. It is a new challenge to determine how much can be really be done with minimal mathematical knowledge, and to find ways to present cryptographic ideas at a completely naïve level."[64] Kid Krypto is also unplugged, "crayon-technology" cryptography. It is not exposure to computers that leads to cryptographic literacy, but rather, "wide-ranging experience working in a creative and exciting way with algorithms, problem-solving techniques and logical modes of thought."[65]

In "Comparing Information Without Leaking It," Fagin, Naor, and Winkler join the cognitive criterion of accessibility and the material criterion of "unplugged cryptography" into the single design objective of *simplicity*: cryptographic protocols should exhibit both ease of implementation and understanding, and parties to them "should be required to expend only a small amount of time, energy, and money to learn, use, and be confident in the protocol."[66] The paper was motivated by a real-life situation: during a conversation, two managers at a company realize they both have received confidential complaints about the same sensitive matter. In confiding to each other, they face a dilemma: if the complaints originate from two different individuals, their privacy will have been compromised.

Cryptographers have developed sophisticated protocols for this problem of "secret function evaluation."[67] Such protocols would allow the managers to carry this type of conversation over electronic networks, without relying on any trusted third parties, with mathematical guarantees that their conversation will not leak any information whatsoever. Such guarantees come at a cost however: the protocols "are complex schemes that only certain experts can be expected to understand. Thus, blind trust is given to the system designer. An additional point is that these solutions are not yet genuinely practical, even if implemented with the best possible care. Our goal in this article is to provide some schemes whose implementation is so transparent that no expertise is needed to verify correctness. We hope that some of these schemes will provide not only practical solutions to our problem, but also insight into the subtleties of communication and information."[68]

Fagin, Naor, and Winkler eventually come up with fourteen different solutions for the managers' problem, with different trade-offs between design criteria.[69] The last solution is provided by the first author's thirteen-year-old son, who wonders why the managers can't simply inquire directly to the complaining parties. Indeed, in the end, this will be the solution that the managers adopt to resolve their conundrum.

Conclusion

The controversies and research projects outlined in this chapter point to an intriguing dynamic. Although modern cryptography sought to ground its practices in abstract mathematical worlds of binary information, number theory, and computational complexity, several material phenomena made a claim for their relevance to these practices. Hash functions, electromagnetic radiation, the human perceptual system, sealed envelopes, and the cognitive capabilities of users requested—with varying degrees of urgency—that they be included in the deliberations. In response, the standard model that has informed much cryptographic work in the Diffie-Hellman era has been extended to include random oracles, the physical leakage of power, users' visual acuity, and the security properties of scratch-cards.

Engaging with the inescapable materiality of information does not signify some kind of demotion or regression. Instead, it suggests that what perhaps best characterizes cryptographic practice is not an inevitable ascension to mathematics, but rather ingenuity, playfulness, and pragmatism in its devotion to achieving (and defeating) counterintuitive communication goals. Over the course of history, this ingenuity has consistently taken advantage of the material properties of physical media, of the logical properties of information encoding, and of their mutual interactions in the service of these goals.

I propose an engagement with the material world offers in fact important benefits. Taking advantage of the embodied capabilities of human beings (memory, perception, cognition) and of the cultural and institutional familiarity of pen-and-paper technologies (books, paper, envelopes) may provide multiple pathways to broader social acceptance of cryptographic design goals. Not only does embracing the material world offer rich sources of inspiration for design, but it also enables more complex strategies of technology adoption than the "build it and they will come" philosophy that has so far implicitly driven the efforts of the community. Rather than emphasizing its radical discontinuity with the paper-and-ink world, cryptographic design can draw from existing cultural practices and technological infrastructures as *resources*. Such an approach would directly enhance the abilities of cryptographic technologies to suture themselves into the existing social fabric, on multiple levels—cognitively, materially, institutionally.

In *The Languages of Edison's Light*, Charles Bazerman argued that a key to Edison's commercial successes laid precisely in his skill at negotiating the boundaries of tradition and invention: "Despite the great changes that came in the wake of the new technology, incandescent light and power had first to be built on historical continuities of meaning and value. It had to take a place within the discourse and the representational meaning systems of the time before it could transform them. Electrical light had to find representational terms that could be comprehended before it could create its own new world of experience and meaning."[70] By embracing embodiment and institutions, cryptographers gain access to multiple registers of such "representational terms." Rather than being stuck with the limited rhetorical range afforded by technological determinism, cryptographers would enjoy a much broader range of narratives, arguments, and practical experiences from which to articulate the new configurations of privacy, anonymity, proof, and accountability that cryptographic protocols make possible.

These benefits will come at certain costs. Insofar as they are based on assumptions that can only be verified empirically, the proofs flowing from this extended model provide for a different kind of mathematical certainty than those based on number theory. Yet this is nothing particularly new. As Reuben Hersh has suggested, "our inherited notion of 'rigorous proof' is not carved in marble. People will modify that notion, will allow machine computation, numerical evidence, probabilistic algorithms, if they find it advantageous to do so."[71] Indeed, from interactive proof systems to DNA computation and probabilistic algorithms, cryptography itself has powerfully motivated researchers to push the boundaries of what counts as mathematical proof.[72]

The controversies surrounding the ROM and physical security framework demonstrate that the models that inform cryptographic theory do evolve and adapt—indeed, even coexist. Sandra Mitchell, a philosopher of science, has proposed scientists embrace multiple explanatory models as a form of *pluralism* that "recognizes the diversity of causal structures that populate our world." The choice between coarse- and fine-grained abstractions need not be fought on theoretical grounds, as "they are both 'true' and 'accurate' ways to capture features of the world we want to represent. This is the crucial point: what determines the level of abstraction or granularity is pragmatic and *can be answered only with reference to the particular context and scientific objective*. Different representations will be better for solving different problems."[73]

This chapter presented a series of arguments suggesting that working from a plurality of models would in fact allow for a different engagement with the material world and perhaps for renewed creativity and greater social relevance. Such an engagement will also require the reimagination of cryptographers' role as designers of the security protocols that will mediate relationships over networks. In a material world, resources—material, perceptual, cognitive—are unevenly distributed. Different models will integrate different abstractions of these resources, different assumptions about their distributions. As a design goal, "security" might then hold different meanings for different people, meanings that could no longer be understood as self-evident but instead as themselves worthy of inquiry and debate. To conclude this book, then, I retrace some of our steps to bring us back to a debate where the terms of an important security protocol—voting—were contested and scrutinized for the entire world to see.

8 Epilogue

In August 2010, a CNN poll revealed that only 42 percent of Americans believed that Barack Obama was "definitively born in the U.S."[1] It would not be until the release of the original (paper) birth certificate in April 2011 that the nagging doubts over his eligibility to hold the world's most prestigious office would finally subside. The presidency of Obama's predecessor, George W. Bush, had been tainted by similar questions over the authenticity of a mundane paper artifact, the voting ballot. Indeed, the inability of voting ballots to deliver, even under intense scrutiny, conclusive evidence of voters' intention threatened to derail the legitimacy of the American electoral process.

The material failure of the technology to deliver an unambiguous verdict had significant consequences, not the least of which was the Supreme Court's direct intervention in settling the election's outcome. It also revealed that the political process of the most technologically advanced nation on earth and flag-bearer of democracy depended on antiquated technologies, rigged up through a patchwork of local regulations that no comprehensive federal law had ever tamed. More than any other election before it, *Bush v. Gore* powerfully drove the point that "to vote is not simply to form and to express a political opinion. It is, inseparably, to participate in a technological process."[2]

Indeed, in yet another manifestation of the intimate relationship of paper and political power, democracy itself seems indissociable from the technology of the secret ballot. Combined with the voting booth, it functions as democracy's most powerful symbol, its correct implementation the litmus test for the *bona fides* of new converts. The 2000 election was thus a massive catastrophe, one that launched multiple initiatives for legislative and technical reform seeking to restore the process to acceptable levels of integrity. The combination of computer networks and cryptography should have offered, as it promised with other paper-based protocols, previously unmatched levels of mathematical security. Indeed, David Chaum identified voting as a cryptographic problem as early as 1981, and subsequent research formalized it as a prime example of multiparty computation, wherein n parties wish to calculate a function $f(n)$ of their inputs (the majority vote) while ensuring that each participant learns nothing beyond her own vote and that a coalition of cheaters cannot corrupt the computation of $f(n)$.[3]

Yet initial reports on computer-based voting revealed fundamental problems, with potential for damage vastly exceeding that of hanging chads. The CalTech/MIT Voting Technology Project—a multidisciplinary panel of political and computer scientists—noted that with respect to the crucial issue of "residual votes"—that is, ballots that for whatever reasons end up uncounted, unmarked, or spoiled—it appeared that "machine voting, on the whole, has performed significantly worse than the paper systems."[4] As an infrastructure for voting, the Internet itself appeared far from ready for prime time, with experts concluding that "Internet voting . . . cannot be made secure for use in real elections for the foreseeable future."[5] The leading computer-based market solution, direct-recording electronic (DRE) voting machines, elicited even greater concerns: although such machines exhibited broad and pervasive susceptibility to fraud, they operated as impenetrable "black boxes," utterly opaque to inspection by either voters or auditors. The overall and somewhat surprising conclusion of these investigations was that "the best solutions are voting systems having a 'voter-verifiable audit trail,' where a computerized voting system prints a paper ballot that can be read and verified by the voter."[6]

Today, interest in voter-verifiable systems has unleashed a cryptographic renaissance of sorts. The deployment of elections implementing *end-to-end voting* (E2E), the ability for voters to verify their votes have been correctly counted, has become crypto's newest social cause. It combines a practical real-world issue with an interesting mathematical problem: how can one issue a verifiable ballot to voters without providing them with the necessary proof to sell their vote? A classic cryptographic conundrum, it has generated a small research boom complete with conferences, books, field trials, and a multitude of proposals for concrete systems.[7] Perhaps the most potent symbol of this renewed disciplinary vigor is the return of David Chaum. More than any other member of the cryptographic community, he personified the social and entrepreneurial ambitions of the discipline in the 1980s and 1990s but retreated from the front lines in the aftermath of the market demise of DigiCash, the business venture that implemented his anonymous payment mechanism.

Yet thirty-five years after "New Directions," there are few signs that the design methodology that drives these endeavors has been updated. The business of cryptography still begins with Goldreich's "definitional activity," in which "the functionality underlying a natural security concern is identified, and an adequate cryptographic problem is defined."[8] Using the case of digital signatures, this book has proposed and provided evidence that this approach suffers from blind spots that generate significant and recurring difficulties for the social ambitions of cryptography.

The first blind spot stems from the idea that "natural security concerns" exist as timeless entities, independent of the cryptographer's own social and historical world, and that their "underlying functionality" can be readily identified.[9] Yet even the requirement for secrecy that seems today utterly indissociable from the voting process was once a radical innovation subject to considerable controversy: "It was generally believed that to be seen to vote, and to be accountable for one's choice, were necessary components of citizenship. Conversely, as John Stuart Mill put it very explicitly, secrecy has something to do with selfishness. 'The spirit of vote by ballot—the interpretation likely to be put on it in the mind of an elector—is that the suffrage is given to him for himself; for his particular use and benefit, and not as a trust for the public.'"[10] Similarly, our needs and desire for privacy, anonymity, and authentication vary according to time, place, and purpose, and cryptographers should remain wary of claims to their self-evident character as "natural security concerns."

The second issue, abundantly illustrated in this book, is that the cryptographic modeling of security protocols is not itself a neutral intervention. The design goal of "end-to-end voting," for example, is a classic cryptographic move—eliminating trust in (corruptible) voting authorities in favor of trust in (incorruptible) mathematics. Such moves inevitably lead to infinite regress, however, given the mathematics of cryptography must be certified by cryptographers, themselves authorized through their training and degrees, themselves accredited through other social institutions.

A voter-verifiable ballot will continue to require considerable faith in the correct functioning and goodwill of a host of social institutions.

The third issue is that the methodology does not account for the creative dimension of cryptographic designs. Though Simmons defined the research program of contemporary cryptography as the design of mathematical equivalents to paper-based security protocols, a considerable proportion of cryptographic protocols have no clear equivalents in the real world. The use of cryptographic primitives as building blocks allows for the design of innovative protocols, with previously unheard of functionalities such as undeniable or ring signatures (see "Mutations" in chapter 4). Such protocols realize new configurations of accountability, trust, and power among participants but can hardly be accounted for in terms of "natural security concerns."

After the New Directions that proudly claimed cryptography's independence from military control, these are then perhaps times for forging New Alliances. These alliances would take advantage of the interests and creative resources of other parties interested the new world of electronic security—users, legal professionals, social scientists, and others.[11] They would relate to the world of paper as a deep and broad source of inspiration, rather than as a historical accident to be overcome. They would even embrace cryptography's own creative process without requiring its designs be justified under "real-world" scenarios. Crafting such alliances will require cryptographers to articulate new arguments, beyond the mere authority of mathematics, for why their work matters. It will also likely open new doors to social relevance and renew the creative engagement with the material world that has always been the hallmark of the field.

Acknowledgments

I gratefully acknowledge the generous help of the many who have supported this project at the following institutions: the *Laboratoire d'informatique théorique et quantique* and the *Centre de recherche en droit public* at the University of Montreal; the Department of Science and Technology Studies at Rensselaer Polytechnic Institute; in France, the *Centre d'études sur la coopération juridique internationale* at the CNRS, the *Mission de recherche Droit et Justice*, the *Conseil supérieur du notariat*, the archives service at the Ministry of Justice, the *Service central de l'état civil* in Nantes, and the *Groupement pour l'informatisation du livre foncier d'Alsace-Moselle* in Strasbourg; the Inter-PARES project at the University of British Columbia and the Graduate School of Education and Information Studies at UCLA. The library and support staff at these institutions provided invaluable assistance.

I am also grateful for the financial support of the following institutions: the Global Legal Studies at the National Science Foundation, the Natural Sciences and Engineering Research Council and the Social Science and Humanities Research Council of Canada, the *Centre national de la recherche scientifique*, the Quebec Ministry of International Relations, the French Ministry of Foreign Affairs, Quebec's *Fonds pour la formation de chercheurs et l'aide à la recherche,* and the UCLA's Office of Faculty Diversity and Development.

For their help and kind permission to reproduce visual materials, I am indebted to Dr. Warwick Ford, Adam Back, the *Conseil supérieur du notariat*, the *Service central d'état civil*, Pierre Jeannelle, Phillippe Strosser, Olivier Benoît, Adrian Perrig, Ian Jermyn, Alain Mayer, Fabian Monrose, Michael K. Reiter, and Aviel D. Rubin.

For their moral, material, intellectual, and emotional support, I owe thanks to the advising team *extraordinaire* of Kim and Mike Fortun, to

Isabelle de Lamberterie, Normand and Monique Lapointe, Danièle Bourque, Ariane Lazaridès, Luce Des Marais, Johanna Drucker, and to Sandra Harding for her untiring mentoring. Without them, this project would have been truly impossible. Finally, I am thankful to Marguerite Avery, Kathleen Caruso, and Katie Persons at the MIT Press for their guidance through the editorial process.

After almost a decade of residence in the United States, it seems fitting to end this work with a homage to that most American of literary forms, the disclaimer: I am of course solely responsible for any and all omissions, mistakes, and opinions.

Notes

1 Introduction

1. In effect, a short-form certificate is a statement from the record custodian that she holds the original document. The long-form certificate is available only to persons who can demonstrate "tangible interest" in the document—for example, heirs.

2. See, for example, William J. Mitchell, *The Reconfigured Eye: Visual Truth in the Post-Photographic Era* (Cambridge, MA: MIT Press, 1994); Pablo J. Boczkowski, *Digitizing the News: Innovation in Online Newspapers* (Cambridge, MA: MIT Press, 2004); Christine L. Borgman, *Scholarship in the Digital Age: Information, Infrastructure, and the Internet* (Cambridge, MA: MIT Press, 2007); Kathryn Henderson, *On Line and on Paper: Visual Representations, Visual Culture, and Computer Graphics in Design Engineering* (Cambridge, MA: MIT Press, 1999).

3. Bruno Latour, "Drawing Things Together," in *Representation in Scientific Practice*, ed. Michael Lynch and Steve Woolgar (Cambridge, MA: MIT Press, 1990), 55.

4. One public-key technology, the Secure Socket Layer (SSL), did succeed in achieving widespread infrastructural deployment as the cryptographic protocol (represented as the padlock icon) embedded in all browsers to authenticate servers. Its success prompted famed cryptographer Ron Rivest to testify to a congressional committee that "codes I have developed are used daily to secure millions of on-line Internet transactions." (See http://people.csail.mit.edu/rivest/rivest-may-24-01-testimony.txt.) Yet the effectiveness of SSL is much debated: security expert Bruce Schneier argues that "SSL does encrypt credit card transactions on the Internet, but it is not the source of security for the participants. That security comes from credit card company procedures, allowing a consumer to repudiate any line item charge before paying the bill. . . . As it is used, with the average user not bothering to verify the certificates exchanged and no revocation mechanisms, SSL is just simply (very slow) Diffie-Hellman key-exchange method. Digital certificates provide no actual security for electronic commerce; it's a complete sham." Bruce Schneier, *Secrets and Lies: Digital Security in a Networked World* (New York: Wiley, 2000), 238–239.

5. An eloquent articulation of this line of thought is provided by Michael Benedikt: "Cyberspace: The realm of pure information, filling like a lake, siphoning the jangle of messages transfiguring the physical world, decontaminating the natural and urban landscapes, redeeming them, saving them from the chain-dragging bulldozers of the paper industry, from the diesel smoke of courier and post office trucks, from jet fuel fumes and clogged airports, from billboards, trashy and pretentious architecture, hour-long freeway commutes, ticket lines and choked subways . . . from all the inefficiencies, pollutions (chemical and informational), and corruptions attendant to the process of moving information attached to *things*—from paper to brains—across, over, and under the vast and bumpy surface of the earth rather than letting it fly free in the soft hail of electrons that is cyberspace." Michael Benedikt, *Cyberspace: First Steps* (Cambridge, MA: MIT Press, 1991), 3. For a discussion of the immateriality trope in computing, see Jean-François Blanchette, "A Material History of Bits," *Journal of the American Association for Information Science and Technology* 62, no. 6 (2011): 1042–1057.

6. John Perry Barlow, "A Declaration of the Independence of Cyberspace," *The Humanist* 56, no. 3 (1996): 18–19.

7. Nicholas Negroponte, *Being Digital* (New York: Vintage Books, 1996), 61.

8. George L. Paul, *Foundations of Digital Evidence* (Chicago: American Bar Association, 2008), 19.

9. Alfred J. Menezes, Paul C. van Oorschot, and Scott A. Vanstone, *Handbook of Applied Cryptography* (Boca Raton: CRC Press, 1997), 3.

10. Abigail J. Sellen and Richard H. R. Harper, *The Myth of the Paperless Office* (Cambridge, MA: MIT Press, 2002), 196.

11. Ibid., 187.

12. Phil Agre, *Computation and Human Experience* (Cambridge: Cambridge University Press, 1997), 57–58. See also Lucille Alice Suchman, *Human–Machine Reconfigurations: Plans and Situated Actions* (Cambridge: Cambridge University Press, 2007); John Seely Brown and Paul Duguid, *The Social Life of Information* (Boston: Harvard Business School Press, 2000); and Paul Dourish, *Where the Action Is: The Foundations of Embodied Interaction* (Cambridge, MA: MIT Press, 2001).

13. Claudio Ciborra, *The Labyrinths of Information: Challenging the Wisdom of Systems* (Oxford: Oxford University Press, 2002), 21.

14. Sellen and Harper, *The Myth of the Paperless Office*, 198.

15. Whitfield Diffie and Martin E. Hellman, "New Directions in Cryptography," *IEEE Transactions on Information Theory* 22, no. 6 (1976): 644–654.

16. See Susan Landau, "Find Me a Hash," *Notices of the American Mathematical Society* 53, no. 3 (March 2006): 330–332.

17. Ian Hacking, *The Taming of Chance* (Cambridge: Cambridge University Press, 1990), 3.

18. Theodore Porter, *Trust in Numbers: The Pursuit of Objectivity in Science and Public Life* (Princeton: Princeton University Press, 1995), 45.

19. Brian Rotman has argued extensively for loosening mathematics' fixation on analytical proof, arguing that "mathematics, contrary to its self-promotion as a purely theoretical science of necessary truth, is now—courtesy of the digital computer—also an experimental practice." Brian Rotman, *Ad Infinitum—The Ghost in Turing's Machine: Taking God Out of Mathematics and Putting the Body Back In: An Essay in Corporeal Semiotics* (Stanford: Stanford University Press, 1993), 101.

20. Given the prevalence of modeling in scientific practice, there is a remarkable dearth of literature on the topic in science studies—exceptions include Mary B. Hesse, *Models and Analogies in Science* (Notre Dame: University of Notre Dame Press, 1966); Ronald N. Giere, *Science Without Laws* (Chicago: University of Chicago Press, 1999); Mary S. Morgan and Margaret Morrison, *Models as Mediators: Perspectives on Natural and Social Sciences* (Cambridge: Cambridge University Press, 1999); and Bas C. van Fraassen, *Scientific Representation: Paradoxes of Perspective* (Oxford: Clarendon Press, 2008).

21. Davis and Hersch's analysis of seven different formulations of the Chinese remainder theorem is a simple and powerful reminder that the drive toward formalization and abstraction is itself an historical trend. They note that "computer science in its theoretical formulation is dominated by a spirit of abstraction which defers to no other branch of mathematics in its zealotry." Philip J. Davis and Reuben Hersh, *The Mathematical Experience* (Boston: Houghton Mifflin, 1981), 194.

22. As Ross Anderson has pointed out, "a trusted component or system is one which you can insure," that is, one in which the specific liability can be evaluated and transferred to a third party, rather than prevented at all cost. See Ross Anderson, "Why Cryptosystems Fail," *Communications of the ACM* 37, no. 11 (1994): 32–40, and, in general, Ross Anderson, *Security Engineering: A Guide to Building Dependable Distributed Systems*, 2nd ed. (New York: Wiley, 2008).

23. As Sheila Jasanoff notes, "Litigation becomes an avenue for working out, often at an early stage, the compromises necessary for securing the social acceptance of a new technology, for example, by making it more responsive to well-articulated social needs, without capitulating to more radical critiques." Sheila Jasanoff, *Science at the Bar: Law, Science, and Technology in America* (Cambridge, MA: Harvard University Press, 1995), 140.

24. Ibid., 207.

25. See, for example, Simon Cole, *Suspect Identities: A History of Fingerprinting and Criminal Identification* (Cambridge, MA: Harvard University Press, 2002); Jay D.

Aronson, *Genetic Witness: Science, Law, and Controversy in the Making of DNA Profiling* (New Brunswick: Rutgers University Press, 2007); Michael Lynch, Simon A. Cole, Ruth McNally, and Kathleen Jordan, *Truth Machine: The Contentious History of DNA Fingerprinting* (Chicago: University of Chicago Press, 2008); Henri Levy-Bruhl, *La preuve judiciaire* (Paris: Librairie Marcel Rivière et Cie, 1964); Xavier Lagarde, *Réflexion critique sur le droit de la preuve* (Paris: Librairie générale de droit et de jurisprudence, 1994); Michael T. Clanchy, *From Memory to Written Record, England, 1066–1307*, 2nd ed. (Oxford: Blackwell, 1993).

26. Lawrence Lessig, *Code and Other Laws of Cyberspace* (New York: Basic Books, 1999).

27. Rosemary J. Coombe, *The Cultural Life of Intellectual Properties: Authorship, Appropriation, and the Law* (Durham: Duke University Press, 1998), 9.

28. Isabelle Stengers, *La vierge et le neutrino: Les scientifiques dans la tourmente* (Paris: Les empêcheurs de penser en rond, 2006), 35–36.

29. For example: "A good security design has not secrets in its details. . . . The antithesis is *security by obscurity* . . . if a system is designed with security by obscurity, then that security is delicate." Schneier, *Secrets and Lies*, 344. My argument is precisely echoed by Koblitz and Menezes when they suggest that "a lot of people in industry, government, and academia would like to truly understand to what extent they can have confidence in the systems they use to protect, encrypt, and authenticate data. . . . Cryptography is more an art than a science. Its fruits, and even its inner working, should be accessible to a broad public." Neal Koblitz and Alfred J. Menezes, "Another Look at 'Provable Security,'" *Journal of Cryptology* 20, no. 1 (2007): 3–37.

30. The title is borrowed from Ron Rivest's characterization that "cryptography is about *communication in the presence of adversaries*." Ron Rivest, "Cryptology," in *Handbook of Theoretical Computer Science*, ed. Jan van Leeuwen (New York: Elsevier, 1990), 717; emphasis in original.

31. Frank H. Easterbrook, "Cyberspace and the Law of the Horse," *Chicago Legal Forum* (1996): 207–216; Lawrence Lessig, "The Law of the Horse: What Cyberlaw Might Teach," *Harvard Law Review* 113, no. 2 (1999): 501–549.

32. I owe this title to Shawn J. Rosenheim's insightful book *The Cryptographic Imagination: Secret Writing from Poe to the Internet* (Baltimore: Johns Hopkins University Press, 1995).

2 Communication in the Presence of Adversaries

1. Simon Singh, *The Code Book: The Science of Secrecy from Ancient Egypt to Quantum Cryptography* (New York: Anchor, 2000), 345.

Notes

2. Steven Levy, *Crypto: How the Code Rebels Beat the Government, Saving Privacy in the Digital Age* (New York: Viking, 2001).

3. Jim L. Massey, "An Introduction to Contemporary Cryptography," *Proceedings of the IEEE* 76, no. 5 (1988), 535. Other examples include: "Since the turn of the century, many mathematicians have attempted to find objective criteria to measure the security of cryptographic systems, transforming an ancient art into an exact science," Gilles Brassard, *Cryptologie contemporaine* (Paris: Masson, 1992), 2; "Cryptography, over the ages, has been an art practiced by many who have devised ad hoc techniques to meet some of the information security requirements. The last twenty years have been a period of transition as the discipline moved from an art to a science," Menezes, van Oorschot, and Vanstone, *Handbook of Applied Cryptography*, 6; and "We emphasize two aspects of the transition from classical to modern cryptography: . . . (2) the move from an engineering-art which strives on ad-hoc tricks to a scientific discipline based on rigorous approaches and techniques," Oded Goldreich, *Modern Cryptography, Probabilistic Proofs, and Pseudorandomness* (Berlin: Springer, 1999), vii.

4. Jacques Stern, *La science du secret* (Paris: Editions Odile Jacob, 1998), 10.

5. David Kahn, *The Codebreakers: The Story of Secret Writing* (New York: Macmillan, 1967).

6. Ibid., 109–110.

7. Statistical methods still apply to some degree because identical elements in the plaintext encrypted by the same portion of the key result in identical ciphertext elements. See Douglas R. Stinson, *Cryptography: Theory and Practice* (Boca Raton: CRC Press, 1995), 31–36, and Kahn, *The Codebreakers*, 208–213.

8. Kahn, *The Codebreakers*, 150–151, 192.

9. "Several factors suggest that codes may be more difficult to break than ciphers: the key (code-book) is vastly larger than typical cipher keys; codes may result in data compression; and statistical analysis is complicated by the large plaintext unit block size." Menezes, van Oorschot, and Vanstone, *Handbook of Applied Cryptography*, 241.

10. Kahn, *The Codebreakers*, 174.

11. Ibid., 192.

12. Auguste Kerckhoffs, "La cryptographie militaire," *Journal des Sciences Militaires* 9 (1883): 6–7. Similarly, "Although modern cryptographic techniques started to develop during the Renaissance, we find in 1641 that John Wilkins still preferred hiding over ciphering because it arouses less suspicion." Fabien Petitcolas, Ross Anderson, and Markus Kuhn, "Information Hiding—A Survey," *Proceedings of the IEEE* 87, no. 7 (1999): 1062–1078.

13. Kerckhoffs, "La cryptographie militaire," 5 (my translation).

14. *The Handbook of Applied Cryptography*, the most important reference of the field, explains in an opening note, "This book only considers cryptography as it applies to information in digital form," providing references to encryption of analog signals, physical security, and steganography, all security methods it considers to lie outside modern cryptography proper. See Menezes, van Oorschot, and Vanstone, *Handbook of Applied Cryptography*, 45–46. Neither Stinson's *Cryptography*, Brassard's *Cryptologie contemporaine*, nor Simmons's *Contemporary Cryptology* mention it. This does not mean that research on information hiding has not thrived—an international conference on the topic has taken place annually since 1996—but rather, that it has been difficult to situate the contributions of the field within the dominant framework of contemporary cryptography.

15. Fascination with computer-based information technologies has tended to induce a global amnesia with regard to prior communication revolutions. In *The Cryptographic Imagination*, Shawn Rosenheim suggests that in fact, the advent of the telegraph (whose cultural legacy has remained underexamined) should be taken as *the* crucial historical departure from which to examine the development of postmodern identities. He argues all communication technologies created since—including the transatlantic cable, the telephone, radio, television, and even the digital computer—can be simply viewed as further elaborations of the telegraph's initial premises. As the first electric telecommunications device, Morse's telegraph is the significant point of rupture, severing the link between transportation and communication, separating bodies and information, and ushering an era where "the Newtonian unities of being are replaced by the prosthetic extension of the self over a network of wires." Rosenheim, *The Cryptographic Imagination*, 91. In a similar vein, Laura Otis remarks that "what is new about networking is very little." Laura Otis, *Networking: Communicating with Bodies and Machines in the Nineteenth Century* (Ann Arbor: University of Michigan Press, 2001), 221.

16. Kahn, *The Codebreakers*, 189.

17. Ibid., 190.

18. Tom Standage, *The Victorian Internet: The Remarkable Story of the Telegraph and the Nineteenth Century's On-Line Pioneers* (New York: Walker and Co., 1998), chapter 7.

19. Kahn, *The Codebreakers*, 190.

20. Ibid., 191.

21. Kerckhoffs, "La cryptographie militaire," 12 (my translation).

22. He wrote with more than a tinge of exasperation: "I am astonished to see our experts and professors teach and recommend for use in warfare, systems to which

Notes

a cryptanalyst with even a modicum of experience would find the key in less than an hour." Ibid., 10 (my translation).

23. Ibid., 9 (my translation).

24. Kahn, *The Codebreakers*, 299.

25. Ibid., 300. This kind of basic traffic analysis was still entirely relevant in the Vietnam war: "On January 25 [1968], NSA issued another alert, 'Coordinated Vietnamese Communist Offensive Evidenced.' The SIGINT report gave clear evidence that a major attack was about to take place, citing an "almost unprecedented volume of urgent messages . . . passing among major [enemy] commands." James Bamford, *Body of Secrets: Anatomy of the Ultra-Secret National Security Agency: From the Cold War through the Dawn of a New Century* (New York: Doubleday, 2001), 333. And later, "That night, David Parks noticed something very unusual. 'At twelve midnight, the enemy went on total radio silence,' he said. 'It was just as if someone had switched off a light—'Nil More Heard' on any frequency. . . . Military units go on radio silence for only one reason: they're up to something.'" Ibid., 334.

26. Kahn, *The Codebreakers*, 349.

27. As with much cryptographic security, proper procedure was everything. Kahn tells the story of the German takeover of a number of Dutch underground emitting stations: "Eventually the GiskesSchreider combine was running fourteen funkspiels. . . . Hitler himself was regularly reading reports on it that gave the texts of many of the messages; these were submitted by Himmler. The all-important security check continued to be omitted from many of the transmissions. . . . S.O.E [Special Operations Executive, the British organization that managed underground activities in Europe] actually bestirred itself a few times to wonder whether the Dutch operations had been penetrated and should therefore be terminated. Each time it decided to continue them because it felt that the security checks were 'inconclusive as a test.'" Ibid., 536. As a result, within a mere twenty months, fifty-four agents were captured in Holland, forty-seven of whom were shot without trial at the Mauthausen concentration camp.

28. Ibid., 32.

29. Ibid., 527–528.

30. I give here a simplified account of the operation of the Enigma. For a more technically detailed description, see Rebecca A. Ratcliff, *Delusions of Intelligence: Enigma, Ultra and the End of Secure Ciphers* (Cambridge: Cambridge University Press, 2006), 14–18. For the genesis of rotor machines, see Kahn, *The Codebreakers*, 410–434.

31. Ratcliff, *Delusions of Intelligence*, 24.

32. Ibid., 27.

33. For similar issues in breaking later German cryptosystems, see B. Jack Copeland, *Colossus: The Secrets of Bletchley Park's Code-breaking Computers* (Oxford: Oxford University Press, 2006), 195.

34. Alan Hodges, *Alan Turing: The Enigma* (London: Vintage, 1992), 224. Hodges notes the daunting practical and procedural aspects of the large-scale deployment of ciphering apparatus able to meet the needs of mobile warfare: "In fact, unless everything were spelled out in advance and in complete, rigid, detail, without any chance of ambiguity or error, there would have to be some form of indicator. . . . Good cryptography lay in the creation of an entire body of rules, not in this or that message. And serious cryptanalysis consisted of the work of recovering them; reconstructing the entire mechanical process which the cipher clerks performed, through an analysis of the entire mass of signals." Ibid., 164.

35. "The head of the German naval intelligence service at Naval High Command adhered to the opinion that it would be impossible for the enemy to have deciphered the signals. They continued to assume that that there was a spy network operating in their bases in occupied France, although nothing could have been further from the truth. And so their faith in machines and experts continued to be matched by distrust of men." Ibid., 244.

36. Ibid., 238.

37. The impact of the Enigma machine on world politics was to be felt long after the end of World War II. If the details of the Allied codebreaking successes were not revealed until 1974, it is quite simply because the Cold War and the demise of the old colonial empires brought about entirely new markets for military-strength ciphering machines, a market serviced in large part by Boris Hagelin: "The dozens of new nations that emerged from the ruins created a market for cipher machines far wider than any that had yet existed . . . to safeguard the communications of their little armies and of the diplomatic posts that they established all over the world." Kahn, *The Codebreakers*, 432. Obviously, none of the Cold War powers found any advantage in letting these newcomers to international politics know that their military and diplomatic communications were perhaps not as confidential as they might have expected them to be.

38. As if often the case with major scientific discoveries, the precise determination of who invented the one-time pad is problematic. In 2011, Steven Bellovin announced that a banker, Frank Miller, had discovered the principle and published it as part of a telegraphic codebook as early as 1882, but the system he devised seems to have never been used in practice. See Steven M. Bellovin, "Frank Miller: Inventor of the One-Time Pad," *Cryptologia* 35, no. 3 (2011): 203–222.

39. Kahn, *The Codebreakers*, 397.

40. Ibid., 402.

41. The system is "pseudorandom" insofar as it consists of a deterministic algorithm that outputs a sequence of numbers that appears random to the adversary. See Menezes, van Oorschot, and Vanstone, *Handbook of Applied Cryptography*, chapter 5.

42. A remarkable case of reverse engineering, as the codebreakers never set eyes on an actual Lorenz cipher until the end of the war. See Copeland, *Colossus*.

43. Claude E. Shannon, "Communication Theory of Secrecy Systems," *Bell System Technical Journal* 28, no. 4 (1949), 659. This companion paper to "A Mathematical Theory of Communication" was published but classified in 1946 and declassified in 1949. In an interview with Kahn, Shannon explained, "The work on both the mathematical theory of communications and the cryptology went forward concurrently from about 1941. I worked on both of them together and I had some of the ideas while working on the other. I wouldn't say one came before the other—they were so close together you couldn't separate them." Kahn, *The Codebreakers*, 744.

44. Gustavus J. Simmons, "Contemporary Cryptology: A Foreword," in *Contemporary Cryptology: The Science of Information Integrity*, ed. Gustavus J. Simmons (Piscataway, NJ: IEEE Press, 1992), 11.

45. Shannon, *Communication Theory of Secrecy Systems*, 656.

46. Kahn, *The Codebreakers*, 515.

47. Horst Feistel, "Cryptography and Computer Privacy," *Scientific American* 228, no. 5 (1973): 15–23.

48. Ibid., 2–3.

49. Shannon, *Communication Theory of Secrecy Systems*, 708–710.

50. Stinson, *Cryptography: Theory and Practice*, 83.

51. See James Bamford, *The Puzzle Palace: A Report on America's Most Secret Agency* (New York: Penguin Books, 1983), and Bamford, *Body of Secrets*, for a history and description of the NSA. To write about the NSA in the early 1980s, at a time when it was almost impossible to obtain any information about the agency (the NSA was exempt from FOIA requirements), Bamford had recourse to various investigative strategies, including traffic analysis in its most literal form: "Curious as to whether the cooperation [with British and Canadian intelligence agencies] was ongoing, Bamford took a drive through the parking lot outside of NSA headquarters, taking down the license plate numbers of cars that, based on their proximity to the buildings, were likely to belong to top officials. He noticed two vehicles with diplomatic plates. A trace revealed they belonged to an Englishman and a Canadian." Paul Constance, "How Jim Bamford Probed the NSA," *Cryptologia* 21, no. 1 (1997): 73.

52. The DES standardization process and the controversy that accompanied it have been extensively chronicled—see, for example, Miles E. Smid and Dennis K. Branstad, "The Data Encryption Standard: Past and Future," *Proceedings of IEEE* 76, no. 5 (1988):

550–599; Lance J. Hoffman, ed., *Building in Big Brother: The Cryptographic Policy Debate* (New York: Springer, 1995).

53. Menezes, van Oorschot, and Vanstone, *Handbook of Applied Cryptography*, 256.

54. Quoted in Smid and Branstad, "The Data Encryption Standard," 48.

55. Whitfield Diffie and Martin E. Hellman, "Exhaustive Cryptanalysis of the NBS Data Encryption Standard," *Computer* 10, no. 6 (June 1977), 74.

56. Menezes, van Oorschot, and Vanstone, *Handbook of Applied Cryptography*, 277.

57. Slavoj Žižek, *Iraq: The Borrowed Kettle* (London: Verso Books, 2005), 10.

58. See Philip E. Agre, "Toward a Critical Technical Practice: Lessons Learned in Trying to Reform AI," in *Social Science, Technical Systems, and Cooperative Work: Beyond the Great Divide*, ed. Geof Bowker, Les Gasser, Leigh Star, and Bill Turner (Hillsdale, NJ: Lawrence Erlbaum Associates, 1997), 131–157.

3 On the Brink of a Revolution

1. The history of Diffie and Hellman's invention has been extensively chronicled in the media and several journalistic accounts, such as Levy's *Crypto* and Singh's *The Code Book*. As often the case with scientific discovery, the concepts were somewhat "in the air," and other researchers have now been recognized as coinventors of public-key cryptography. Ralph Merkle first wrote about the concept in 1974 while an undergraduate at Berkeley; his work was repeatedly rejected until finally published in 1978—see Ralph C. Merkle, "Secure Communications over Insecure Channels," *Communications of the ACM* 21, no. 4 (1978): 294–299. A group of researchers at the British Government Communications Headquarters—James Ellis, Clifford Cocks, and Malcolm Williamson—also independently came up with the idea in 1969 and 1973, but their work remained classified and was recognized publicly only in 1997. Though Diffie has recognized the priority of their contribution, he commented, "In my view, the issue of how well they understood the significance of what they were doing remains open" (http://cryptome.org/ukpk-diffie.htm).

2. Diffie and Hellman, "New Directions in Cryptography," 644.

3. Among the numerous articles, reports, and books published on the topic, see: Susan Landau et al., "Crypto Policy Perspectives," *Communications of the ACM* 37, no. 8 (1994): 115–121; Lance J. Hoffman et al., "Cryptography Policy," *Communications of the ACM* 37, no. 9 (1994): 109–117; Hoffman, *Building in Big Brother*; Kenneth W. Dam and Herbert Lin, eds., *Cryptography's Role in Securing the Information Society (CRISIS)* (Washington, DC: National Academy Press, 1996); David Banisar, *Cryptography and Privacy Sourcebook* (Washington, DC: Electronic Privacy Information Center, 1996); David Banisar and Bruce Schneier, *The Electronic Privacy Papers: Documents on the Battle for Privacy in the Age of Surveillance* (New York: John Wiley and

Sons, 1997); and Whitfield Diffie and Susan Landau, *Privacy on the Line: The Politics of Wiretapping and Encryption* (Cambridge, MA: MIT Press, 1998).

4. Diffie and Hellman, "New Directions in Cryptography," 644.

5. Steven Levy, "The Cypherpunks vs. Uncle Sam," in *Building in Big Brother: The Cryptographic Policy Debate*, ed. Lance J. Hoffman (Berlin: Springer, 1995), 270.

6. Steven Levy, "Crypto: The Story of How a Group of Code Rebels Saved Your Privacy on the Internet," *Newsweek*, January 15, 2001, 42–52.

7. Levy, *Crypto*, 17.

8. See Menezes, van Oorschot, and Vanstone, *Handbook of Applied Cryptography*, 12.6.1.

9. Diffie and Hellman, "New Directions in Cryptography," 650.

10. Ibid., 652. The concept of trapdoors was also related to the recent debate over the actual security of the DES algorithm. Diffie and Hellman noted, "*Trap doors* have already been seen . . . in the form of *trap-door one way functions*, but other variations exist. A *trap-door cipher* is one which strongly resists cryptanalysis by anyone not in possession of *trap-door information* used in the design of the cipher. This allows the designer to break the system after he has sold it to a client and yet falsely to maintain his reputation as a builder of secure systems. . . . The situation is precisely analogous to a combination lock. Anyone who knows the combination can do in seconds what even a skilled locksmith would require hours to accomplish." Ibid., 652; emphasis in original.

11. Ron L. Rivest, Adi Shamir, and Leonard Adleman, "A Method for Obtaining Digital Signatures and Public-Key Cryptosystems," *Communications of the ACM* 21, no. 2 (1978): 120–126.

12. How does a known unknown become a bona fide mathematical conjecture? Jack Edmond explains, "The classes of problems which are respectively known and not known to have good algorithms are of great theoretical interest. . . . I conjecture that there is no good algorithm for the traveling salesman problem. My reasons are the same as for any mathematical conjecture: (1) It is a legitimate mathematical possibility, and (2) I do not know." Quoted in Christos H. Papadimitriou, *Computational Complexity* (Reading, MA: Addison-Wesley, 1994), 137.

13. For an overview, see Menezes, van Oorschot, and Vanstone, *Handbook of Applied Cryptography*, chapters 3, 4, and 14. Over time, this interest has waned. Shparlinski calls for the renewal of the special bonds between number theory and cryptography, noting that "over the years, the tight links and the mutual interest have somewhat diminished," as the cryptographic research community has become increasingly preoccupied with protocol design, a "not so mathematically rich part of cryptography." Igor E. Shparlinski, "Numbers at Work and Play," *Notices of the American Mathematical Society* 57, no. 3 (March 2010): 335.

14. Don Zagier, "The First 50 Million Prime Numbers," *The Mathematical Intelligencer* 1, no. 0 (1977): 8. Similar sentiments abound: "Number theory targets the most fundamental object of a human's mind: integer numbers. Its questions can be explained to high school students, while getting answers requires very deep and convoluted arguments. Its internal beauty has always been an irresistible attraction for mathematicians, computer scientists, engineers, and enthusiastic amateurs. Furthermore, its primal motivation has always been our natural intellectual curiosity rather than everyday practical needs." Shparlinski, "Numbers at Work and Play," 334. On the purity of number theory, G. H. Hardy famously wrote, "It is sometimes suggested that pure mathematicians glory in the uselessness of their work, and make it a boast that it has no practical applications. The imputation is usually based on an incautious saying attributed to Gauss, to the effect that, if mathematics is the queen of the sciences, then the theory of numbers is, because of its supreme uselessness, the queen of mathematics—I have never been able to find an exact quotation." G. H. Hardy, *A Mathematician's Apology* (Cambridge: Cambridge University Press, 1940), 120. Prime numbers have even inspired poetry: "None can foretell their coming. / Among the ordinal numbers / They do not reserve their seats, arrive unexpected. / Along the lines of cardinals / They rise like surprising pontiffs, / Each absolute, inscrutable, self-elected." Helen Spalding, "Let Us Now Praise Prime Numbers," in *Strange Attractors: Poems of Love and Mathematics*, ed. Sarah Glaz and JoAnne Growney (Wellesley: A. K. Peters, Ltd., 2008), 190.

15. Martin Gardner, *When You Were a Tadpole and I Was a Fish: And Other Speculations about This and That* (New York: Hill and Wang, 2009), 124.

16. Carl Pomerance, "Prime Numbers and the Search for Extraterrestrial Intelligence," in *Mathematical Adventures for Students and Amateurs*, ed. David F. Hayes and Tatiana Shubin (Washington, DC: The Mathematical Association of America, 2004), 2.

17. Gina Bari Kolata, "Cryptography: On the Brink of a Revolution?" *Science* 197, no. 4305 (1977): 747; Martin Gardner, "A New Kind of Cipher That Would Take Millions of Years to Break," *Scientific American* 237, no. 8 (1977): 120–124.

18. Derek Atkins, Michael Graff, Arjen Lenstra, and Paul Leyland, "The Magic Words Are Squeamish Ossifrage," in *Advances in Cryptology—ASIACRYPT '94*, ed. Josef Pieprzyk and Reihanah Safavi-Naini (Berlin: Springer, 1994), 261–277.

19. CRYPTO '83 became the first conference officially sponsored by the IACR, which now sponsors the annual CRYPTO, EUROCRYPT, and ASIACRYPT conferences, as well as the *Journal of Cryptology*. See http://www.iacr.org.

20. David Kahn's report on EUROCRYPT '83 notes that officials from governmental defense and cryptological agencies, including the NSA, were openly present. David Kahn, "EUROCRYPT 83: A Report," *Cryptologia* 7, no. 3 (1983): 254–256.

21. Susan Landau, "Primes, Codes and the National Security Agency," *Notices of the American Mathematical Society* 30, no. 1 (1983): 7–10.

22. Bamford, *The Puzzle Palace*, 456. Such restrictions were hardly without precedent. The most famous case occurred in the aftermath of the World War I. Stating, rather surprisingly, that "gentleman do not read each other's mail," U.S. Secretary of State Henry Stimson closed down in 1929 the main American cryptological operation. Unable to find work, its former head, Herbert Yardley, published a sensational tell-all, *The American Black Chamber*: a minor best-seller, it not only detailed the scope of American cryptological activities, but also documented the interception and decryption of Japanese diplomatic dispatches during the disarmament conference of November 1921. The ensuing Japanese fury prompted swift American reaction over Yardley's following literary project: the manuscript of *Japanese Diplomatic Secrets: 1919–1921* was seized and impounded by the U.S. government. Although neither Yardley nor his editors faced charges, Congress promptly passed into law the so-called Yardley Act, forbidding "the publication or sale of diplomatic codes obtained by virtue of one's employment by the United States." See David Kahn, *The Reader of Gentlemen's Mail: Herbert O. Yardley and the Birth of American Codebreaking* (New Haven: Yale University Press, 2004).

23. David Kahn, "The CRYPTO '82 Conference, Santa Barbara. A Report on a Conference," *Cryptologia* 7, no. 1 (1983): 1–5.

24. Susan Landau, "Zero Knowledge and the Department of Defense," *Notices of the American Mathematical Society* 35, no. 1 (1988): 5–12. See also Harold C. Relyea, ed., *Silencing Science: National Security Controls and Scientific Communication* (Norwood: Ablex Publishing Corporation, 1994).

25. As described by Kevin Kelly, then editor in chief of *Wired*, in a blurb for Steven Levy's *Crypto*.

26. For example, Ron Rivest wrote in *Scientific American*: "The widespread use of cryptography is a necessary consequence of the information revolution. With the coming of electronic communications on computer networks, people need a way to ensure that conversations and transactions remain confidential. Cryptography provides a solution to this problem, but it has spawned a heated policy debate. U.S. government wants to restrict the use of data encryption because they fear that criminals and spies may use the technology to their own advantage. . . . The ability to have private conversations is in my view an essential democratic right. Democracy depends on the ability of citizens to share their ideas freely, without fear of monitoring or reprisal; this principle should be upheld as much in cyberspace as it is in the real world. For the U.S. to restrict the right to use cryptography would be a setback for democracy—and a victory for Big Brother." Ron Rivest, "The Case Against Regulating Encryption Technology," *Scientific American* 279, no. 4 (1998): 116–117.

27. Tim May, "The Crypto Anarchist Manifesto," posting to the Cypherpunks electronic mailing list, November 22, 1992.

28. Peter Ludlow, *High Noon on the Electronic Frontier: Conceptual Issues in Cyberspace* (Cambridge, MA: MIT Press, 1996), xvii.

29. Philip R. Zimmermann, *PGP: Source Code and Internals* (Cambridge, MA: MIT Press, 1995).

30. Ronald L. Rivest, "Chaffing and Winnowing: Confidentiality without Encryption," *CryptoBytes* 4, no. 1 (1998): 12–17.

31. See, in general, Matt Curtin, *Brute Force: Cracking the Data Encryption Standard* (New York: Copernicus, 2005).

32. John Gilmore, *Cracking DES: Secrets of Encryption Research, Wiretap Politics and Chip Design* (Sebastopol, CA: O'Reilly Media, 1998), 18.

33. Global Internet Liberty Campaign, *Cryptography and Liberty: An International Survey of Encryption Policy* (February 1998), available at http://gilc.org/crypto/crypto-survey.html (accessed June 25, 2011).

34. Dorothy E. Denning, "The Future of Cryptography," in *The Governance of Cyberspace: Politics, Technology and Global Restructuring*, ed. Brian Loader (London: Routledge, 1997), 189. Within the cryptographic community, Denning was largely vilified for these positions—see Steven Levy, "Clipper Chick," *Wired* September 1996, 162.

35. Silvio Micali, "Fair Public-Key Cryptosystems," in *Advances in Cryptology—CRYPTO '92*, ed. Ernest F. Brickell (Berlin: Springer, 1992), 114.

36. Ibid., 116.

37. Ibid., 118.

38. Diffie and Landau, *Privacy on the Line*, 235.

39. Ibid., 238.

40. Ibid., 239.

41. Simmons, "A Foreword," vii–viii.

42. Ibid., viii.

43. Menezes, van Oorschot, and Vanstone, *Handbook of Applied Cryptography*, 4.

44. Ibid, 4.

45. Oded Goldreich, "On the Foundations of Modern Cryptography," in *Advances in Cryptology—CRYPTO'97*, ed. Burton S. Kalinski Jr. (Berlin: Springer, 1997), 46.

46. Ibid., 46.

47. The *Handbook of Applied Cryptography* relegates the issue to a footnote: "This book only considers cryptography as it applies to information in digital form. . . . Although in many cases physical means are employed to facilitate privacy, cryptography plays the major role. Physical means of providing privacy include fiber optic communication links, spread spectrum technology, TEMPEST techniques, and

tamper-resistant hardware. *Steganography* is that branch of information privacy which attempts to obscure the existence of data through such devices as invisible inks, secret compartments, the use of subliminal channels, and the like." Menezes, van Oorschot, and Vanstone, *Handbook of Applied Cryptography*, 45–46, n1.2.

48. Manuel Blum, "Coin Flipping by Telephone: A Protocol for Solving Impossible Problems," *ACM SIGACT News* 15, no. 1 (1983): 23.

49. Gustavus J. Simmons, "How to Insure That Data Acquired to Verify Treaty Compliance Are Trustworthy," in *Contemporary Cryptology: The Science of Information Integrity*, ed. Gustavus J. Simmons (Piscataway, NJ: IEEE Press, 1992): 615–630.

50. Gustavus J. Simmons, "The Prisoners' Problem and the Subliminal Channel," in *Advances in Cryptology, Proceedings of CRYPTO '83*, ed. David Chaum (New York: Plenum Press, 1984): 51–67. Gustavus J. Simmons, "The Subliminal Channel and Digital Signatures," in *Advances in Cryptology, Proceedings of EUROCRYPT '84*, ed. Thomas Beth, Norbert Cot, and Ingemar Ingemarsson (Berlin: Springer, 1985), 364–378.

51. Gustavus J. Simmons, "The History of Subliminal Channels," *IEEE Journal on Selected Areas in Communications* 16, no. 4 (2002): 452–462. The paper presents a fascinating account of the discovery of subliminal channels during the Cold War, when the two mutually distrusting superpowers sought to slowly diffuse their ability to annihilate each other. Another fascinating application of covert channels is described in Peter Winkler, "The Advent of Cryptology in the Game of Bridge," *Cryptologia* 7, no. 4 (1983): 327–332.

52. Adam Young and Moti Yung, "The Dark Side of 'Black-Box' Cryptography, or: Should We Trust Capstone?" in *Advances in Cryptology—CRYPTO '96*, ed. Neal Koblitz (Berlin: Springer, 1996), 89–103; Adam Young and Moti Yung, "Kleptography: Using Cryptography against Cryptography," in *Advances in Cryptology—EUROCRYPT '97*, ed. David Chaum, Christoph G. Günther, and Franz Picher (Berlin: Springer, 1997), 62–74; Adam Young and Moti Yung, *Malicious Cryptography: Exposing Cryptovirology* (New York: Wiley, 2004).

53. Young and Yung, "The Dark Side of 'Black-Box' Cryptography," 100.

54. David Chaum, "Untraceable Electronic Mail, Return Addresses, and Digital Pseudonyms," *Communications of the ACM* 24, no. 2 (February 1981): 84–90; David Chaum, "Security without Identification: Transaction Systems to Make Big Brother Obsolete," *Communications of the ACM* 28, no. 10 (October 1985): 1030–1044; David Chaum, "Achieving Electronic Privacy," *Scientific American* 267, no. 2 (August 1992): 96–101.

55. David Chaum, "Blind Signatures for Untraceable Payments," in *Advances in Cryptology Proceedings of CRYPTO '82*, ed. David Chaum, Ronald L. Rivest, and Alan T. Sherman (New York: Plenum, 1983), 199–203.

56. See Kevin Kelly, *Out of Control: The New Biology of Machines, Social Systems, and the Economic World* (Reading, MA: Addison-Wesley, 1994), chapter 12, and David Chaum, "FM Interviews: David Chaum," *First Monday* 4, no. 7 (1999).

57. Chaum's work has been continued notably by Stefan Brands, whose "U-Prove" technology was acquired by Microsoft in 2008. See Stefan Brands, *Rethinking Public Key Infrastructures and Digital Certificates: Building in Privacy* (Cambridge, MA: MIT Press, 2000).

58. Chaum, "Security Without Identification," 1044.

59. Chaum, "Digital Money," in *@Home, Doors of Perception 2* (1994), available at http://www.vanriet.com/doors/doors2/content.html (accessed June 24, 2011).

4 The Equivalent of a Written Signature

1. Diffie and Hellman, "New Directions in Cryptography," 649; emphasis added.

2. Béatrice Fraenkel, *La signature: Genèse d'un signe* (Paris: Gallimard, 1992), 78; my translation.

3. Latour, "Drawing Things Together," 54. A beautiful history of that most mundane of bureaucratic objects, the vertical file, is provided by JoAnne Yates, "From Press Book and Pigeonhole to Vertical Filing: Revolution in Storage and Access Systems for Correspondence," *Journal of Business Communication* 19, no. 3 (1982): 6–26. For a recent history of contemporary office technologies, see Delphine Gardey, *Écrire, calculer, classer: Comment une révolution de papier a transformé les sociétés contemporaines (1800–1940)* (Paris: La Découverte, 2008).

4. Levy, *Crypto*, 19.

5. Diffie and Hellman, "New Directions in Cryptography," 649.

6. Ibid., 645.

7. Ibid., 649.

8. Rivest, Shamir, and Adleman, "A Method for Obtaining Digital Signatures and Public-Key Cryptosystems," 121.

9. George Davida, *Chosen Signature Cryptanalysis of the RSA (MIT) Public Key Cryptosystem* (Department of Electrical and Computer Science, University of Wisconsin, 1982).

10. Dorothy E. Denning, "Digital Signatures with RSA and Other Public-Key Cryptosystems," *Communications of the ACM* 27, no. 4 (1984): 388–392.

11. This is a simplification of pre-image, second pre-image, and collision resistance—see Menezes, van Oorschot, and Vanstone, *Handbook of Applied Cryptography*, chapter 9.

12. See, for example, Burton Kaliski and Jessica Staddon, "Public-Key Cryptography Standards (PKCS) #1: RSA Cryptography Specifications Version 2.0" (RSA Laboratories, 1998).

13. Denning, "Digital Signatures with RSA and Other Public-Key Cryptosystems," 391.

14. Chris J. Mitchell, Fred Piper, and Peter R. Wild, "Digital Signatures," in *Contemporary Cryptology: The Science of Information Integrity*, ed. Gustavus J. Simmons (Piscataway, NJ: IEEE Press, 1992), 325–378.

15. Menezes, van Oorschot, and Vanstone, *Handbook of Applied Cryptography*, 361.

16. Richard E. Smith, *Authentication: From Passwords to Public Keys* (Boston: Addison-Wesley, 2002), 28–32.

17. Menezes, van Oorschot, and Vanstone, *Handbook of Applied Cryptography*, 361.

18. Feistel, "Cryptography and Computer Privacy," 17.

19. Menezes, van Oorschot, and Vanstone, *Handbook of Applied Cryptography*, 361.

20. Rivest, "Cryptology," 722.

21. Rivest, Shamir, and Adleman, "A Method for Obtaining Digital Signatures and Public-Key Cryptosystems," 121.

22. Rivest, Shamir, and Adleman, *Cryptographic Communications System and Method* (patent, September 1983), 2.39–2.43; emphasis added.

23. Rivest, "Cryptology," 739.

24. ISO, *Information Technology, Open Systems Interconnection, Security Frameworks for Open Systems, Part 4: Non-repudiation*, ISO/IEC 10181-4 (Geneva: ISO, 1996).

25. Jianying Zhou and Dieter Gollmann, "Evidence and Non-repudiation," *Journal of Network and Computer Applications* 20, no. 3 (1997): 268.

26. Menezes, van Oorschot, and Vanstone, *Handbook of Applied Cryptography*, 5.

27. Jane K. Winn, "The Emperor's New Clothes: The Shocking Truth about Digital Signatures and Internet Commerce," *Idaho Law Review* 37 (2001): 371n49. Within the cryptographic community, Michael Roe warned in a nuanced analysis that "evidence is not the same as mathematical proof." See Michael Roe, "Cryptography and Evidence," Ph.D. dissertation, University of Cambridge (1997). Roe has recently applied Austin's speech act theory and Derrida's critique of presence to the analysis of cryptographic protocols. See Michael Roe, "Non-repudiation and the Metaphysics of Presence," in *Proceedings of the 13th International Conference on Security Protocols*, ed. Bruce Christianson et al. (Berlin: Springer, 2007), 204–206.

28. Diffie and Hellman, "New Directions in Cryptography," 648.

29. Rivest, Shamir, and Adleman, "A Method for Obtaining Digital Signatures and Public-Key Cryptosystems," 122.

30. Loren M. Kohnfelder, "Towards a Practical Public-Key Cryptosystem," B.S. thesis, Massachusetts Institute of Technology, Electrical Engineering (1978), 40.

31. These trade-offs are similar to what the credit card industry has faced since its beginnings. In the 1980s, credit card providers would issue monthly reports of stolen cards to businesses while also requiring business owners to request authorization from a clearance center for transactions over a certain threshold. Today, the industry has largely moved to fully online authorization together with a broad range of fraud detection mechanisms to manage risk and liability. See Anderson, *Security Engineering*, section 10.5.

32. Datamonitor, *Public Key Infrastructure, 1999–2003* (n.p., 1999), 6.

33. Such a taxonomy is directly derived from those used to classify encryption systems—see Rivest, "Cryptology," 741, and Menezes, van Oorschot, and Vanstone, *Handbook of Applied Cryptography*, 41.

34. Rivest, "Cryptology," 741.

35. See Menezes, van Oorschot, and Vanstone, *Handbook of Applied Cryptography*, 4.4.2.

36. Burton Kaliski, "Emerging Standards for Public-Key Cryptography," in *Lectures on Data Security: Modern Cryptology in Theory and Practice*, ed. Ivan Damgård (Berlin: Springer, 1999), 98.

37. For example, "The security of RSA relies on the difficulty of factorizing n [the public key]. There are many algorithms for performing this operation, and in order to thwart the use of any currently known technique, the values p and q must be chosen carefully." ITU, *Recommendation X.509* (Geneva: International Telecommunications Union, 1997, C.6.2), available at http://www.itu.int/rec/T-REC-X.509 (accessed June 24, 2011).

38. Kaliski, "Emerging Standards for Public-Key Cryptography," 98.

39. Ibid., 98.

40. Hesse, *Models and Analogies in Science*, 1.

41. Leslie Lamport, "Constructing Digital Signatures from One-Way Function," Technical Report SRI-CSL-98, SRI International (October 1979).

42. David Chaum and Eugène Van Heyst, "Group Signatures," in *EUROCRYPT '91*, ed. Donald W. Davies (Berlin: Springer, 1991), 257–265.

43. Viktor Shoup, "Practical Threshold Signatures," in *Advances in Cryptology—EUROCRYPT 2000*, ed. Bart Preneel (Berlin: Springer, 2000), 207–220.

44. Ron Rivest, Adi Shamir, and Yael Tauman, "How to Leak a Secret," in *Advances in Cryptology—ASIACRYPT 2001*, ed. Colin Boyd (Berlin: Springer, 2001), 552–565.

45. Chaum, "Blind Signatures for Untraceable Payments."

46. Markus Stadler, Jean-Marc Piveteau, and Jan Camenisch, "Fair Blind Signatures," in *EUROCRYPT '95—Proceedings of the 14Th Annual International Conference on Theory and Application of Cryptographic Techniques*, ed. Louis C. Guillou and Jean-Jacques Quisquater (Berlin: Springer, 1995), 209–219.

47. Mihir Bellare and Sara Miner, "A Forward-Secure Digital Signature Scheme," in *Advances in Cryptology—CRYPTO '99*, ed. Michael Weiner (Berlin: Springer, 1999), 431–448.

48. David Chaum and Hans van Antwerpen, "Undeniable Signatures," in *Advances in Cryptology—CRYPTO '89 Proceedings*, ed. G. Brassard (Berlin: Springer-Verlag, 1990), 212–217.

49. Joan Boyar, David Chaum, Ivan Damgård, and Torben Pedersen, "Convertible Undeniable Signatures," *Advances in Cryptology—CRYPTO '90*, ed. Alfred J. Menezes and Scott A. Vanstone (Berlin: Springer, 1991), 189–205; David Chaum, "Designated Confirmer Signatures," in *Advances in Cryptology—EUROCRYPT '94*, ed. Alfredo De Santis (Berlin: Springer, 1995), 86–91.

50. Markus Jakobsson and Moti Yung, "Revokable and Versatile Electronic Money," in *Proceedings of the 3rd ACM Conference on Computer and Communications Security (CCS '96)* (New York: ACM Press, 1996), 76–87.

51. Birgit Pfitzmann, "Fail-Stop Signatures: Principles and Applications." In *Proceedings of Compsec '91, Eighth World Conference on Computer Security, Audit, and Control* (New York: Elsevier Science Publishers, 1991), 125–134.

52. Menezes, van Oorschot, and Vanstone, *Handbook of Applied Cryptography*, 488.

53. Pfitzmann, "Fail-Stop Signatures; Principles and Applications," 127–128.

54. Rivest, Shamir, and Tauman, "How to Leak a Secret," 554–555.

55. Andrey Nikolayevich Tikhonov, "Mathematical Models," in *Encyclopedia of Mathematics*, ed. Michiel Hazewinkel (Berlin: Springer-Verlag, 2002).

56. Morgan and Morrison, *Models as Mediators*, 12.

57. Ibid., 36.

58. Roman Frigg and Stephen Hartmann, "Models in Science," *Stanford Encyclopedia of Philosophy* (Summer 2009 ed.), ed. Edward N. Zalta, available at http://plato.stanford.edu/archives/sum2009/entries/models-science/ (accessed October 10, 2011).

59. Ian Hacking, *Representing and Intervening: Introductory Topics in the Philosophy of Natural Science* (Cambridge: Cambridge University Press, 1983), 216; Mary S. Morgan,

"Models, Stories, and the Economic World," *Journal of Economic Methodology* 8, no. 3 (2001): 361–384.

60. Sergio Sismondo, "Models, Simulations, and Their Objects," *Science in Context* 12, no. 2 (1999): 258.

61. Ibid., 247.

62. Tikhonov, "Mathematical Models." See the scientists interviewed in Daniela M. Bailer-Jones, "Scientists' Thoughts on Scientific Models," *Perspectives on Science* 10, no. 3 (2002): 275–301.

63. Giere, *Science Without Laws*, 93.

64. Ronald N. Giere, "How Models Are Used to Represent Reality," *Philosophy of Science* 71, no. 5 (2004): 747–748.

65. Paul N. Edwards, *A Vast Machine: Computer Models, Climate Data, and the Politics of Global Warming* (Cambridge, MA: MIT Press, 2010), xiii–xiv. See chapters 6–7 for a more specific discussion on climate modeling.

66. Donald A. MacKenzie, *An Engine, Not a Camera: How Financial Models Shape Markets* (Cambridge, MA: MIT Press, 2006), 11.

67. Donald A. MacKenzie, "An Equation and its Worlds," *Social Studies of Science* 33, no. 6 (2003): 831.

68. MacKenzie, *An Engine, Not a Camera*, 160.

69. Ibid., 256. MacKenzie does warn that this argument should not be taken to extremes. For example, "market practitioners' adoption of financial economics has not rendered fully performative economics' pervasive, often implicit, underlying assumption of rational egoism." MacKenzie, "An Equation and its Worlds," 831.

70. MacKenzie, *An Engine, Not a Camera*, 163.

71. Donald A. MacKenzie, *Material Markets: How Economic Agents Are Constructed* (Oxford: Oxford University Press, 2009), 15–16.

72. Herbert Mehrtens, "Mathematical Models," in *Models: The Third Dimension of Science*, ed. Soraya De Chadarevian and Nick Hopwood (Stanford: Stanford University Press, 2004), 276–306.

73. Ibid., 278. On the epistemological status of diagrams, see also Brian Rotman, "Thinking Dia-Grams: Mathematics, Writing, and Virtual Reality," *The South Atlantic Quarterly* 94, no. 2 (1995): 389–416; and Brian Rotman, *Mathematics as Sign: Writing, Imagining, Counting* (Stanford: Stanford University Press, 2000), especially chapter 2, "Making Marks on Paper."

74. Mehrtens, "Mathematical Models," 300. Gray narrates a similar process: "The modernist ideology in mathematics preached renunciation from the world, in the

sense that one did not do geometry or analysis—by taking as given what is presented by idealized common-sense. That tells you what a straight line is by accepting what is generally agreed and refining it into a definition. From the feeling that every rational person can recognize a straight line when they see one, the old argument moved to a belief that all such people share the concept, which if need be, can be articulated. The modernist argument preferred to define straight lines only as part of a system of definition for, as it might be, plane or higher-dimensional geometry, and it did this not by telling you what a straight line is, but by telling you what you could say about it. Whatever met the definition was a straight line, even if they might look very strange. There was no attempt to show that the new, implicit, definitions somehow captured the essence of the real object, because the real object was only incidentally what it was about." Jeremy Gray, "Modern Mathematics as a Cultural Phenomenon," in *The Architecture of Modern Mathematics*, ed. José Ferreirós and Jeremy Gray (Oxford: Oxford University Press, 2006), 390.

75. Goldreich, "On the Foundations of Modern Cryptography," 4; emphasis added.

76. Giovanni Di Crescenzo, "Foundations of Modern Cryptography," in *Contemporary Cryptology*, ed. Dario Catalano et al. (Basel: Birkhäuser Verlag, 2005), 89. In a beautifully ironic twist, Goldreich argues that handwritten signatures in fact *fail* to meet their own requirements, as modeled by cryptographers: "We note that the formulation of digital signatures also provides a clear statement of the essential ingredients of handwritten signatures. The ingredients are each person's ability to sign for him/herself, a universally agreed-upon verification procedure, and the belief (or assertion) that it is infeasible (or at least hard) to forge signatures in a manner that passes the verification procedure. It is not clear to what extent handwritten signatures do meet these requirements. In contrast, our treatment of digital-signature schemes provide precise statements concerning the extent to which digital signatures meet these requirements." Oded Goldreich, *Foundations of Cryptography: Basic Applications* (Cambridge: Cambridge University Press, 2004), 498.

77. Agre, *Computation and Human Experience*, 302.

5 Written Proof

1. The *Minitel* was an enormously successful videotex online service launched by France Telecom in 1980. It is still accessible and in use (http://www.minitel.fr); see Jack Kessler, "Networked Information in France, 1993: The Internet's Future," *Internet Research* 4, no. 1 (1994): 18–30.

2. Easterbrook, "Cyberspace and the Law of the Horse," 208.

3. Ibid., 208.

4. Lessig, *Code and Other Laws of Cyberspace*, 89.

5. Joel R. Reidenberg, "Lex Informatica: The Formulation of Information Policy Rules Through Technology," *Texas Law Review* 76, no. 3 (1998): 555.

6. Lessig, *Code and Other Laws of Cyberspace*, 35–36. The statement was removed from the second edition, Lawrence Lessig's *Code: Version 2.0* (New York: Basic Books, 2006), 53.

7. See, for example, A. Michael Froomkin, "The Metaphor Is the Key: Cryptography, the Clipper Chip, and the Constitution," *University of Pennsylvania Law Review* 709 (1995): 709–897; and Phillip R. Reitinger, "Compelled Production of Plaintext and Keys," *University of Chicago Legal Forum* (1996): 171–206.

8. See Peter M. Tiersma, *Parchment, Paper, Pixels: Law and the Technologies of Communication* (Chicago: University of Chicago Press, 2010). See also Bruno Latour, *The Making of Law: An Ethnography of the Conseil d'État* (Cambridge: Polity, 2010).

9. The use of writing as evidence in legal disputes was already well established in Mesopotamia—see Dominique Charpin, *Writing, Law, and Kingship in Old Babylonian Mesopotamia* (Chicago: University of Chicago Press, 2010).

10. Elizabeth A. Meyer, *Legitimacy and Law in the Roman World: Tabulae in Roman Belief and Practice* (Cambridge: Cambridge University Press, 2004), 295.

11. Ibid., 295–296.

12. Clanchy, *From Memory to Written Record, England 1066–1307*, 87–88. Photo VII shows the bottom half of a chirograph.

13. Levy-Bruhl, *La preuve judiciaire*, 120.

14. See Gabriel Marty and Pierre Raynaud, "Théorie générale des preuves," in *Droit civil* (Paris: Sirey, 1972); Laurent Aynès and Philippe Malaurie, "Formalités et preuve," in *Cours de droit civil: Les obligations* (Paris: Éditions Cujas, 1990); François Terré, *Introduction générale au droit* (Paris: Dalloz, 1994).

15. Consensualism refers to the principle that contracts between private individuals are not subjected to any forms whatsoever (including written documents); that is, contracts occur whenever there is consensual assent to obligations.

16. See Olivier Cayla, "La qualification, ou la vérité du droit," *Droits* 18 (1993): 3–18.

17. See Dennis R. Neary, Terence H. Coyle, and Don M. Avedon, "The Integration of Microfilm and the Computer," In *AFIPS '76 Proceedings of the June 7–10, 1976, National Computer Conference and Exposition* (New York: ACM Press, 1976), 627–637.

18. Michel Vion, "Les modifications apportées au droit de la preuve par la loi du 12 juillet 1980," *Desfrenois*, no. 32470 (1980): 1329–1347.

19. Marcel Rudloff, "Rapport sur la proposition de loi de M. Jacques Thyraud, tendant à actualiser les dispositions du Code Civil sur la preuve testimoniale" (Paris: Sénat, May 10, 1979).

20. "Recognizing that things happen in a certain way in the course of ordinary life, law—with varying amounts of energy—imposes the belief that things happen that way in all cases." Jean Carbonnier, *Sociologie juridique* (Paris: Presses universitaires de France, 1978), 292.

21. André Cellard, "Rapport au nom de la commission des lois constitutionelles, de la léglisation et de l'administration générale de la République sur la proposition de loi adoptée par le Sénat relative à la preuve des actes juridiques," no. 1801 (Paris: Assemblée Nationale, June 12, 1980).

22. Levy-Bruhl, *La preuve judiciaire*.

23. Jacques Larrieu, "Les nouveaux moyens de preuve: Pour ou contre l'identification des documents informatiques à des écrits sous seing privé," *Cahiers Lamy du droit de l'informatique* (1988): (H) 8–19; (I) 26–34.

24. Isabelle de Lamberterie et al., *L'écrit et les nouveaux moyens technologiques au regard du droit* (n.p., September 1997), 6.

25. Arnaud Raynouard, "Adaptation du droit de la preuve aux technologies de l'information et à la signature électronique: Observations critiques," *Répertoire Notarial Defrénois*, no. 37174 (2000): 593; Isabelle de Lamberterie, "L'écrit dans la société de l'information," in *D'ici, d'ailleurs: harmonisation et dynamique du droit—Mélanges en l'honneur de Denis Talon* (Paris: Société de législation comparée, 1999), 123.

26. Pierre Catala et al., "L'introduction de la preuve électronique dans le Code Civil," *La Semaine Juridique, Édition Générale*, no. 47 (1999): 2069–2076.

27. Ibid., 2072.

28. In particular, one important obstacle to the widespread adoption of cryptographic signatures stemmed from cryptology's historical ties to the military and to issues of national security. In the 1990s, many countries, including France and the United States, still restricted, in some form or another, the free circulation of cryptographic knowledge and technologies. In a 1996 report, the OECD affirmed the principle that "the use of cryptography to ensure integrity of data, including authentication and non-repudiation mechanisms, is distinct from its use to ensure confidentiality of data, and that each of these uses presents different issues." OECD, *Cryptography Policy: The Guidelines and the Issues* (Paris: OECD, 1997), 6.

29. UNCITRAL, *Model Law on Electronic Commerce with Guide to Enactment* (1996), 16.

30. Ibid., art. 5.

31. The Model Law also recognized the limitations of the functional equivalence approach and the highly localized, culturally specific nature of contractual agreements, recommending in article 58 of the accompanying *Guide to Enactment* the following: "In determining whether the method used [to identify the signer and to

record his consent] under paragraph one is appropriate, legal, technical and commercial factors that may be taken into account include the following: (1) the sophistication of the equipment used by each of the parties; (2) the nature of their trade activity; (3) the frequency at which commercial transactions take place between the parties; (4) the kind and size of the transaction; (5) the function of signature requirements in a given statutory and regulatory environment; (6) the capability of communication systems; (7) compliance with authentication procedures set forth by intermediaries; (8) the range of authentication procedures made available by any intermediary; (9) compliance with trade customs and practice; (10) the existence of insurance coverage mechanisms against unauthorized messages; (11) the importance and the value of the information contained in the data message; (12) the availability of alternative methods of identification and the cost of implementation; (13) the degree of acceptance or non-acceptance of the method of identification in the relevant industry or field both at the time the method was agreed upon and the time when the data message was communicated; and (14) any other relevant factor."

32. American Bar Association, "Digital Signature Guidelines: Legal Infrastructure for Certification Authorities and Secure Electronic Commerce" (Chicago: American Bar Association, August 1, 1996), 3.

33. Ibid., 105–106.

34. Ibid., 113; emphasis added.

35. C. Bradford Biddle, "Misplaced Priorities: The Utah Digital Signature Act and Liability Allocation in a Public Key Infrastructure," *San Diego Law Review* 33 (1996): 1144. See also C. Bradford Biddle, "Legislating Market Winners: Digital Signature Laws and the Electronic Commerce Marketplace," *San Diego Law Review* 34, no. 3 (1997): 1225–1246; and Winn, "The Emperor's New Clothes."

36. The bill was repealed in 2006 for lack of use—see Wendy Leibowitz, "Utah Will Repeal Its Digital Signature Law, Never Used, As Tech, National Law Diverged," *Electronic Commerce and Law Report* 10, no. 48 (December 21, 2005).

37. On the GSM directive, see Jacques Pelkmans, "The GSM Standard: Explaining a Success Story," *Journal of European Public Policy* 8, no. 3 (2001): 432–453.

38. Martin Bangemann et al., "Europe and the Global Information Society: Recommendations of the High-Level Group on the Information Society to the Corfu European Council (Bangemann group)," *Bulletin of the European Union*, Supplement No. 2/94 (1994): 17.

39. Treaty of Rome, article 249.

40. European Commission, *Proposal for a European Parliament and Council Directive on a Common Framework for Electronic Signatures*, COM(98) 297 final (May 13, 1998): 3.

41. European Commission, *Ensuring Security and Trust in Electronic Communications— Toward a European Framework for Digital Signatures and Encryption*, communication

from the Commission to the Council, the European Parliament, the Economic and Social Committee and the Committee of the Regions. COM (97) 503 final, (November 8, 1997): 10.

42. European Union, "Directive 1999/93/EC of the European Parliament and of the Council on a Community Framework for Electronic Signatures," *Official Journal of the European Union* L 13/12 (January 19, 2000): 12–20.

43. Ibid., article 2.1.

44. Ibid., article 2.2.

45. Ibid., article 5.1.

46. Ibid., article 5.2.

47. Ibid., article 21.

48. Lionel Jospin, *Préparer l'entrée de la France dans la société de l'information*, speech by the prime minister at the 18th *Université d'été de la communication*, Hourtin, August 25, 1997, http://www.admiroutes.asso.fr/action/theme/politic/lionel.htm (accessed June 25, 2011).

49. Conseil d'État, *Internet et les réseaux numériques* (Paris: La documentation française, 1998), 6.

50. Ibid., 7–8.

51. Ibid., 56.

52. Lionel Jospin, *Société de l'information*, speech by the prime minister at the 20th *Université d'été de la communication*, Hourtin, August 26, 1999, http://www.mediasinfos.com/Download/jospin260899.htm (accessed June 25, 2011).

53. Ibid.

54. République Française, "Décret n°2001-272 du 30 Mars 2001 pris pour l'application de l'article 1316-4 du Code Civil et relatif à la signature électronique," *Journal Officiel de la République Française* (March 30, 2001).

55. An industry to which I contributed—see Isabelle de Lamberterie and Jean-François Blanchette, "Le décret du 30 mars 2001 relatif à la signature électronique: Lecture critique, technique et juridique," *La Semaine Juridique, Édition Affaires et Entreprises* 30 (2001): 1269–1275.

56. Catala et al., "L'introduction de la preuve électronique dans le Code Civil," 2073.

57. Ken Alder, "Reading Characters: French Handwriting Experts From the Counter-Reformation to the Dreyfus Affair," paper presented at Berlin Summer Academy on Law, Science, and Technology, Max-Planck-Institut für Wissenschaftsgeschichte, Berlin, August 16–27, 1999.

58. Ibid.

59. Michael D. Risinger, Mark P. Denbeaux, and Michael J. Saks, "Exorcism of Ignorance as a Proxy for Rational Knowledge: The Lessons of Handwriting Identification Expertise," *University of Pennsylvania Law Review* 137, no. 3 (1989), 758–759.

60. See Ken Alder, *The Lie Detectors: The History of An American Obsession* (New York: Free Press, 2007).

61. See Lagarde, *Réflexion critique sur le droit de la preuve*, 362–365.

62. Ibid., 363; my translation.

63. "In early 2001, the number of Internet contracts that were being formed in reliance on digital signature certificates still appears to be trivially small in number, if not actually zero. Furthermore, there is no indication that the situation will suddenly change in the near future." Winn, "The Emperor's New Clothes," 355.

64. Indeed, in the fall of 2011, a major breach of a Dutch certification service provider, DigiNotar, led to the dissemination of hundreds of "rogue" certificates and the compromise of, among others, the certification authorities of the Dutch Ministry of Justice, Dutch Bar Association, and Royal Dutch Notarial Society. The incident and subsequent response by industry players and governmental authorities reveals the enormous difficulties users and courts will face when attempting to infer the specific semantics of digital signatures enacted by a given software/hardware instantiation: "In a blog, John Harris of Adobe explained that, as a result of the Dutch government's revocation, 'new digital signatures created with certificates from these certificate families will no longer show as valid in Acrobat and Reader, regardless of version. This is due to the fact that Acrobat and Reader check if certificates associated with the signing credentials are revoked at signing and at document open.' Harris cautioned that the government's move 'will not necessarily invalidate existing documents, if you are opening them with Acrobat and Reader 9.1+. This is due to the fact that these versions of the product check the validity of the signature at the signing time by default, not at the current time—assuming that the signature includes validation information from when it was signed.'" "Dutch Government Revokes DigiNotar's CA Root Certificates," *infosecurity.com*, September 26, 2011, http://www.infosecurity-magazine.com/view/20957/dutch-government-revokes-diginotars-ca-root-certificates/ (accessed October 4, 2011). A subsidiary of Vasco, an authentication service provider based in the United States, DigitNotar filed for voluntary bankruptcy on September 19, 2011, and was declared bankrupt the following day.

65. Serge Gutwirth, Paul De Hert, and Laurent De Sutter, "The Trouble with Technology Regulation: Why Lessig's 'Optimal Mix' Will Not Work," in *Regulating Technologies: Legal Futures, Regulatory Frames and Technological Fixes*, ed. Roger Brownsword and Karen Yeung (Oxford: Hart Publishing, 2008), 196.

66. Ibid., 216.

67. Ibid., 215.

6 Paper and State

1. Fraenkel, *La signature*, 27.

2. James C. Scott, *Seeing like a State: How Certain Schemes to Improve the Human Condition Have Failed* (New Haven: Yale University Press, 1998), 36.

3. Clanchy, *From Memory to Written Record, England 1066–1307*, 294.

4. Ibid., 295. Similarly, Davies notes, "Even in societies and periods in which the written record predominated it was never allowed an exclusive rôle. Procedures existed to subject documents to testing, not only in terms of the internal soundness of their drafting but also by requiring support from evidence produced orally by witnesses and/or by the invocation of spiritual sanctions through oath-taking and ordeals." Wendy Davies and Paul Fouracre, *The Settlement of Disputes in Early Medieval Europe* (Cambridge: Cambridge University Press, 1986), 213.

5. Fraenkel, *La signature*, 23.

6. See Jacques Foyer, *L'histoire du pouvoir notarial d'authentification des actes* (Paris, Institut International de l'Histoire du Notariat, December 6, 1981); Robert-Henri Bautier, "L'authentification des actes privés dans la France médiévale: Notariat public et juridiction gracieuse," in *Chartes, sceaux et chancelleries: Études de diplomatique et de sigillographie médiévales*, vol. 1 (Geneva: Librarie Droz, 1990), 269–340.

7. Fraenkel, *La signature*, 24–25.

8. Anne Lefebvre-Teillard, *Le nom: Droit et histoire* (Paris: Presses universitaires de France, 1990), 93.

9. Jean Carbonnier has argued the Code enacts in fact the "true constitution" of France, as it "recapitulated the ideas around which French society constituted itself after the Revolution," in a unique style, at once "picturesque, laconic, mnemonic." Jean Carbonnier, "The Civil Code," in *Rethinking France: Les Lieux De Mémoire. Vol. I: The State*, ed. Pierre Nora, trans. David P. Jordan (Chicago: Chicago University Press, 2002), 353.

10. Up to fifteen years of prison and up to €225,000 in fines, even when the forged documents have not led to actual prejudice.

11. Pierre Catala, "Le formalisme et les nouvelles technologies," *Rapport Defrénois* (2000): 897–910.

12. As a member of the first working group convened by the Ministry of Justice to make recommendations on a legal framework for electronic authenticity, I enjoyed

extensive access to these projects. In addition to attending the meetings of the working group itself, I was an in-house consultant/intern for six months at the *Conseil supérieur du notariat*, the head body of the profession, and twice traveled for weeklong site visits to the *Service central d'état civil* and the Alsace-Moselle land registry. In each case, I interviewed key administrative personnel, clerks, public officers, and engineers, as well as observed their ordinary interactions with the various electronic technologies deployed in their workplace.

13. Sellen and Harper, *The Myth of the Paperless Office*, 186.

14. A particularly eloquent articulation of this putative sublimity is Gordon Bell and Jim Gemmell, *Total Recall: How the E-Memory Revolution Will Change Everything* (New York: Dutton, 2009). For a critique, see Jean-François Blanchette, "The Noise in the Archive: Oblivion in the Age of Total Recall," in *Privacy and Data Protection: An Element of Choice*, ed. Serge Gutwirth et al. (Berlin: Springer, 2011), 25–38.

15. Sellen and Harper, *The Myth of the Paperless Office*, 187.

16. See Ezra N. Suleiman, *Private Power and Centralization in France: The Notaires and the State* (Princeton: Princeton University Press, 1987); see also Jean Rioufol and Françoise Rico, *Le notariat* (Paris: Presses universitaires de France, 1979).

17. The question of why English common law did not develop public notaries is often explained by arguing that customary law prevailed. Clanchy argues that the question is more complex, reflecting "the way literate modes developed." Clanchy, *From Memory to Written Record, England 1066–1307*, 307. In particular, "English legal practice was probably too accustomed to seals to replace them by notarial *signa*." Nevertheless, the 1285 Statute of Merchants "came close to the essentials of notarial practice, while avoiding the name: bonds were to be written by authorized writers, enrolled in official registers and authenticated by a *signum* (in the form of a special seal) in the writer's charge. If these rules had been enforced and extended from money bonds to all written conveyances of property, England would have had official writers and registries on a scale superior to any in Europe." Ibid., 308.

18. Sénat, "Signature Électronique," *Journal Officiel des Débats* no. 53 (Paris: Sénat, February 8, 2000): 63.

19. Ibid., 45–47.

20. Catala, "Le formalisme et les nouvelles technologies," 908.

21. See Union Internationale du Notariat Latin, *Les nouvelles technologies informatiques et l'acte authentique*, rapport de la sous-commission, sous la présidence de Me Gilles Rouzet (Amsterdam: Fondation pour la promotion de la Science Notariale, 2001).

22. Gilles Rouzet, "L'acte authentique à distance: Pour un aménagement du droit français de la preuve," in *Mélanges offerts à Roland De Valkeneer: A l'occasion du*

125ième anniversaire de la Revue du notariat belge, ed. Daniel Sterckx and Jean-Luc Ledoux (Bruxelles: Bruylant, 2000), 3.

23. Jacques Flour, "Sur une notion nouvelle d'authenticité (commentaires de la loi du 26 novembre 1971)," *Répertoire Defrénois*, no. 30159 (1972): 977; my translation.

24. Ibid., 981–982; my translation.

25. Jean-Paul Decorps, "Porte ouverte sur l'avenir," *La Lettre aux Notaires*, no. 62 (2000), 1; my translation.

26. Olivier Gard, "La carte réal: Une réalité," *Notaires Vie Professionnelle*, no. 207 (1999): 69–70; my translation.

27. See Jean-François Blanchette, "Les technologies de l'écrit électronique: Synthése et évaluation critique," in *Les actes authentiques électroniques: Réflexion juridique prospective*, ed. Isabelle de Lamberterie (Paris: La documentation française, 2002).

28. Jean-François Blanchette, "The Digital Signature Dilemma," *Annales des Télécommunications* 61, no. 7–8 (2006): 903–918.

29. Isabelle de Lamberterie, ed., *Les actes authentiques électroniques: Réflexion juridique prospective* (Paris: La documentation française, 2002), 93.

30. République Française, "Décret no. 2005-973 du 10 août 2005 modifiant le décret no. 71-941 du 26 novembre 1971 relatif aux actes établis par les notaires," *Journal officiel de la République Française* (August 11, 2005).

31. Ibid., article 28; emphasis added.

32. Bénédicte de Valicourt, "Le premier acte authentique électronique en direct," *Notaires Vie Professionelle*, no. 246 (2004): 34–36; my translation.

33. The scale of this identification apparatus cannot solely be reduced to the state's appetite for surveillance. Scott argues that "High-modernist social engineering usually came cloaked in egalitarian, emancipatory ideas: equality before the law, citizenship for all, and rights to subsistence, health, education, and shelter. The premise and great appeal of the high-modernist credo was that the state would make the benefits of technological progress available to all its citizens." Scott, *Seeing like a State*, 352. Lapierre notes that innovations like the anthroponymical system did fulfill some of these ambitions (slaves could have names) while simultaneously enabling greater control of populations. Nicole Lapierre, *Changer de nom* (Paris: Stock, 1995), 33.

34. These are fictional individuals, places, and events.

35. Vincent Denis, *Une histoire de l'identité: France, 1715–1815* (Seyssel: Éditions Champ Vallon, 2008), 19; my translation.

36. Jean Carbonnier, *Droit civil* (Paris: Presses Universitaires de France, 1955), 247.

37. Johanna Drucker refers to this process of interpretation as "probabilistic materiality." She suggests that the physical and visual properties of graphical forms determine a set of potentialities, a space defined by the totality of their relative combinations and activated by specific acts of reading, themselves grounded in specific historical conditions: "The event is the entire system of reader, aesthetic object, and interpretation—but in that set of relations, the 'text' is constituted anew each time. Like weather produced in a system around a landmass, the shape of the reading has a codependent relation to the structure from which it arises. Probability is not free play. It is constrained play, with outcomes calculable in accord with the complexity of the system and the range of variable factors, and their combinatoric and transformative relations over time." Johanna Drucker, *Speclab: Digital Aesthetics and Projects in Speculative Computing* (Chicago: University of Chicago Press, 2009), 8.

38. République Française, "Instruction générale relative à l'état civil," *Journal officiel de la République Française* (2004): 19696.

39. Scott, *Seeing like a State*, 36.

40. This section is based on information gathered during site visits and also Jean-Luc Vallens, "Le droit local d'Alsace-Moselle," *Recueil Dalloz*, 29ième cahier (1998): 275–279; Jean-Luc Vallens, "La publicité foncière en Alsace-Moselle: Une institution séculaire en cours d'informatisation," *Les Petites Affiches*, no. 248 (December 14, 1999): 13–15; Jean-Luc Vallens, "De la pierre au feuillet: Une brève histoire du livre foncier," *Les Petites Affiches*, no. 181 (September 11, 2000): 4–6.

41. IBM, *In Good Company: Annual Report* (n.p.: IBM, 2003), 27.

42. This point is also succinctly made by Luciana Duranti and the InterPARES project: "Any record preservation policy, strategy, or standard should be predicated on the understanding that it is not possible to preserve an electronic record as a stored physical object: it is only possible to preserve the ability to reproduce the record." Luciana Duranti et al., "Strategy Task Force Report," in *The Long-Term Preservation of Authentic Electronic Records* (Vancouver: InterPARES, 2002).

43. NARA, *Records Management Guidance for PKI Digital Signature Authenticated and Secured Transaction Records* (Washington, DC: National Archives and Records Administration, March 11, 2005), 5, http://www.archives.gov/records-mgmt/pdf/pki.pdf (accessed June 25, 2011). See Blanchette, "The Digital Signature Dilemma," for a detailed discussion of this issue.

44. Ibid., 28.

45. Ibid., 28.

46. Ibid., 15.

47. Michael Lynch, Ruth MacNally, and Patrick Daly, "Le tribunal, fragile espace de la preuve," *La Recherche Hors Série*, no. 8 (2002): 113; my translation.

48. Fraenkel, *La signature*, 24.

49. The visual dimension of documents is unfortunately often seen as a vestigial remain of a precomputing age. In *Being Digital*, Negroponte devotes no fewer than four pages to the fax machine, "a serious blemish on the information landscape, a step backward, whose ramifications will be felt for a long time." Negroponte, *Being Digital*, 187. He squarely lays the blame on the Japanese, who standardized and manufactured them cheaply, and whose written culture found the medium greatly advantageous. Bemoaning that "people don't understand the long-term cost, the short-term failings, and the alternatives," Negroponte ignores how Western business culture also found the technology tremendously useful for gathering handwritten signatures on forms.

50. Sellen and Harper, *The Myth of the Paperless Office*, 198.

51. Ibid., 198.

7 The Cryptographic Imagination

1. Paul Kocher, Joshua Jaffe, and Benjamin Jun, "Differential Power Analysis," in *Advances in Cryptology—CRYPTO '99*, ed. Michael Wiener (Berlin: Springer-Verlag, 1999), 388–389; emphasis added. More specifically, "EM emanations arise as a consequence of current flows within the control, I/O, data processing or other parts of a device. These flows and resulting emanations may be intentional or unintentional. Each current carrying component of the device not only produces its own emanations based on its physical and electrical characteristics but also affects the emanations from other components due to coupling and circuit geometry." Dakshi Agrawal, Bruce Archambeault, Josyula R. Rao, and Pankaj Rohatgi, "The EM Side-Channel (S)," in *Cryptographic Hardware and Embedded Systems—CHES 2002*, ed. Burton S. Kaliski (Berlin: Springer, 2003), 30.

2. Olivier Benoît and Thomas Peyrin. "Side-Channel Analysis of Six SHA-3 Candidates," in *Cryptographic Hardware and Embedded Systems—CHES 2010*, ed. Stefan Mangard and François-Xavier Standaert (Berlin: Springer, 2010), 140–157.

3. Stinson, *Cryptography: Theory and Practice*, 251. See also Landau, "Find Me a Hash," 330–332.

4. Menezes, van Oorschot, and Vanstone, *Handbook of Applied Cryptography*, 351.

5. See Rotman, *Ad Infinitum*, for an attempt to devise an arithmetic system that accounts for the physical embodiment of numbers.

6. The acrimony began with Koblitz and Menezes, "Another Look at 'Provable Security,'" followed by Oded Goldreich, "On Post-Modern Cryptography," Cryptol-

ogy ePrint Archive, Report 2006/461, available at http://eprint.iacr.org/2006/461 (accessed June 4, 2011); Neal Koblitz and Alfred J. Menezes, "Another Look at 'Provable Security' II," in *Progress in Cryptology—Indocrypt 2006*, ed. Rana Barua and Tanja Lange (Berlin: Springer, 2006), 148–175; Douglas R. Stinson, "Some Observations on the Theory of Cryptographic Hash Functions," *Designs, Codes and Cryptography* 38, no. 2 (2006): 259–277; Ivan Damgård, "A 'Proof-Reading' of Some Issues in Cryptography," in *Automata, Languages and Programming* (Berlin: Springer-Verlag, 2007), 2–11; and, most recently, Neil Koblitz and Alfred J. Menezes, "The Brave New World of Bodacious Assumptions in Cryptography," *Notices of the American Mathematical Society* 57 (2010): 357–365. A selection of unpublished letters to the editor of the *Notices of the American Mathematical Society* written in response to Koblitz and Menezes is available at Oded Goldreich's website: http://www.wisdom.weizmann.ac.il/~oded/on-pmc.html.

7. Diffie and Hellman, "New Directions in Cryptography," 653–654.

8. Mihir Bellare, "Practice-Oriented Provable-Security," in *Lectures on Data Security: Modern Cryptology in Theory and Practice*, ed. Ivan Damgård (Berlin: Springer, 1999), 4. Indeed, the title of the keynote address at CRYPTO 2010 pondered "Is Theoretical Cryptography Any Good in Practice?"

9. Mihir Bellare and Phil Rogaway, "Random Oracles Are Practical: A Paradigm for Designing Efficient Protocols," in *Proceedings of the 1st ACM Conference on Computer and Communications Security*, Fairfax, VA, November 3–5, 1993, 63.

10. RSA Laboratories, "How Fast Is the RSA Algorithm?," http://www.rsa.com/rsalabs/node.asp?id=2215 (accessed June 25, 2011).

11. Bellare, "Practice-Oriented Provable-Security," 4.

12. Menezes, van Oorschot, and Vanstone, *Handbook of Applied Cryptography*, 33.

13. As Papadimitriou notes, "By definition, cryptography involves two communicating agents, who may have different and conflicting priorities and interests. Furthermore, and more importantly, they communicate in the presence of eavesdroppers with even murkier motives. In this sense, even the simple situation . . . [with] Alice, Bob and Eve is something more complex than solving a computational problem, where the only goal is to achieve low complexity. It is a *protocol*, that is, a set of interacting computations, sharing inputs and outputs in arbitrarily complex ways. Furthermore, some of these computations are prescribed to be easy, *and for some it is desired to be hard*." Papadimitriou, *Computational Complexity*, 287–288.

14. Bellare, "Practice-Oriented Provable-Security," 4.

15. Phillip Rogaway, "On the Role of Definitions In and Beyond Cryptography," in *Advances in Computer Science—ASIAN 2004*, ed. Michael J. Maher (Berlin: Springer, 2005), 18.

Notes

16. Mihir Bellare and Phillip Rogaway, "The Exact Security of Digital Signatures: How to Sign with RSA and Rabin," in *Advances in Cryptology—EUROCRYPT '96*, ed. Ueli Maurer (Berlin: Springer, 1996), 399–416.

17. Ibid., 401.

18. Interestingly, Bellare and Rogaway claim that their model stems from the formalization of cryptographic tacit knowledge: "The idea of such a paradigm . . . incorporates viewpoints which, shared and verbally articulated by many members of our community, should be regarded as folklore. In this light, we view our contribution as follows . . . we raise the implicit philosophy behind the use of a random oracle to an explicitly articulated paradigm which we maintain brings significant benefits to practice." Bellare and Rogaway, "Random Oracles Are Practical," 63.

19. Ibid., 62.

20. Bellare, "Practice-Oriented Provable-Security," 9.

21. Ran Canetti, Oded Goldreich, and Shai Halevi, "The Random Oracle Methodology, Revisited," in *30th Annual ACM Symposium on the Theory of Computing* (New York: ACM Press, 1998), 211.

22. David Pointcheval and Jacques Stern, "Security Arguments for Digital Signatures and Blind Signatures," *Journal of Cryptology* 13, no. 3 (2000): 351–396.

23. Rogaway, "On the Role of Definitions In and Beyond Cryptography," 26.

24. Goldreich, "On Post-Modern Cryptography," 11.

25. Shoup, "Practical Threshold Signatures," 209; emphasis added.

26. Today, some researchers are content to invoke the model as simply one more assumption on which to base cryptographic schemes: "Modern cryptography is about defining security notions and then constructing schemes that provably achieve these notions. In cryptography, security proofs are often relative: a scheme is proven secure, assuming that some computational problem is hard to solve. For a given functionality, the goal is therefore to obtain an efficient scheme that is secure under a well-known computational assumption (for example, factoring is hard). However for certain functionalities, or to get a more efficient scheme, it is sometimes necessary to work in some idealized model of computation." Jean-Sébastien Coron, Jacques Patarin, and Yannick Seurin, "The Random Oracle Model and the Ideal Cipher Model Are Equivalent," in *Advances in Cryptology—CRYPTO 2008*, ed. David Wagner (Berlin: Springer-Verlag, 2008), 1.

27. See Menezes, van Oorschot, and Vanstone, *Handbook of Applied Cryptography*, chapter 3.

28. Bellare, "Practice-Oriented Provable Security," 11.

29. Rogaway, "On the Role of Definitions In and Beyond Cryptography," 27.

30. Silvio Micali and Leonid Reyzin, "Physically Observable Cryptography," in *Theory of Cryptography: Proceedings of Theory of Cryptography, TCC 2004*, ed. Moni Naor (Berlin: Springer, 2004), 278.

31. Shafi Goldwasser, Yael Tauman Kalai, and Guy N. Rothblum, "One-Time Programs," in *Advances in Cryptology—CRYPTO 2008*, ed. David Wagner (Berlin: Springer 2008), 40. The physical security model was more or less anticipated by Ross Anderson—see Ross J. Anderson and Markus Kuhn, "Tamper Resistance: A Cautionary Note," in *Second USENIX Workshop on Electronic Commerce Proceedings*, Oakland, CA, November 18–20, 1996.

32. Francois-Xavier Standaert et al., "Leakage Resilient Cryptography in Practice," in *Towards Hardware-Intrinsic Security*, ed. Ahmad-Reza Sadeghi and David Naccache (Berlin: Springer, 2010), 99.

33. François-Xavier Standaert, Tal G. Malkin, and Moti Yung, "A Unified Framework for the Analysis of Side-Channel Key Recovery Attacks," Cryptology ePrint Archive, Report 2006/139, 2, available at http://eprint.iacr.org/2006/139 (accessed June 24, 2011).

34. Like signatures, passwords straddle the frontier between secrets and biometrics, as they are often chosen in relation to some intimate aspects of one's life—stereotypically, spouses' names and birthdates.

35. Julie Thorpe and Paul C. van Oorschot, "Graphical Dictionaries and the Memorable Space of Graphical Passwords," in *Proceedings of the 13th Conference on USENIX Security Symposium* (Berkeley: USENIX Association, 2004), 10.

36. Jianxin Yan, Alan Blackwell, Ross J. Anderson, and Alasdair Grant, *The Memorability and Security of Passwords: Some Empirical Results* (University of Cambridge Computer Laboratory, September 2000).

37. Smith, *Authentication*, 157, 160–162.

38. Ian Jermyn et al., "The Design and Analysis of Graphical Passwords," in *Proceedings of the 8th Conference on USENIX Security Symposium* (Berkeley: USENIX Association, 1999), 1.

39. Fabien Monrose and Michael K Reiter, "Graphical Passwords," in *Security and Usability: Designing Secure Systems That People Can Use*, ed. Lorrie Faith Cranor and Simson Garfinkel (Sebastopol, CA: O'Reilly Media, 2005), 159.

40. Jermyn et al., "The Design and Analysis of Graphical Passwords."

41. Ibid.

42. Ibid.

43. Paul C. van Oorschot and Julie Thorpe, "On Predictive Models and User-Drawn Graphical Passwords," *ACM Transactions on Information and System Security* 10, no. 4 (2008): 5.

44. Van Oorschot and Thorpe, "On Predictive Models and User-Drawn Graphical Passwords," 7.

45. For exploratory work that suggests altogether bypassing the perceptual system using a brain-computer interface to measure the brain activity generated by password recall, see Julie Thorpe, Paul C. van Oorschot, and Anil Somayaji, "Pass-Thoughts: Authenticating with Our Minds," in *Proceedings of the 2005 Workshop on New Security Paradigms*, ed. Simon Foley (New York: ACM Press, 2005), 45–56.

46. See Ross J. Anderson, *Security Engineering*, chapter 14, and especially Christian Bessy and Francis Chateauraynaud, *Experts et faussaires: Pour une sociologie de la perception* (Paris: Métailié, 1995).

47. Ross J. Anderson et al., *The Global Internet Trust Register* (Cambridge, Mass.: MIT Press, 1999).

48. Adrian Perrig and Dawn Song, "Hash Visualization: A New Technique to Improve Real-World Security," in *International Workshop on Cryptographic Techniques and E-Commerce (CrypTEC '99)* (July 1999), 439–458; Rachna Dhamija and Adrian Perrig, "Déjà Vu: A User Study Using Images for Authentication," in *Proceedings of the 9th USENIX Security Symposium* (Berkeley: USENIX Association, 2000).

49. Michael Oehler, Dhananjay Phatak, and John Krautheim, "Visualizing Your Key for Secure Phone Calls and Language Independence," in *VizSec '10, Proceedings of the Seventh International Symposium on Visualization for Cyber Security*, ed. John Gerth (New York: ACM Press, 2010), 64–69; Patrick Juola, "Whole-Word Phonetic Distances and the PGPfone Alphabet," in *Proceedings of the Fourth International Conference on Spoken Language, ICSLP 96* (1996), 98–101.

50. PGP Corporation, *PGP Desktop for Mac OS X User's Guide, version 8.1* (June 7, 2004), 129–134.

51. Moni Naor and Adi Shamir, "Visual Cryptography," in *Advances in Cryptology—EUROCRYPT '94*, ed. Alfredo De Santis (Berlin: Springer, 1995), 1.

52. For a survey of the field, see Jonathan Weir and Wei Qi Yan, "A Comprehensive Study of Visual Cryptography," *Transactions on Data Hiding and Multimedia Security V*, ed. Yun Q. Shi (Berlin: Springer, 2010): 70–105. For a generalization of the technique in the context of the selection of candidates on voting ballots, see Jeroen van de Graaf, "Adapting Chaum's Voter-Verifiable Election Scheme to the Brazilian System," in *Annals of IV Wseg—Workshop em Segurana de Sistemas Computacionais* (2004), 187–198.

53. Moni Naor and Benny Pinkas, "Visual Authentication and Identification," in *Advances in Cryptology—CRYPTO '97*, ed. Burton S. Kaliski, Jr. (Berlin: Springer, 1997), 326.

54. Tal Moran and Moni Naor, "Polling with Physical Envelopes: A Rigorous Analysis of a Human-Centric Protocol," *Advances in Cryptology—EUROCRYPT 2006*, ed. Serge Vaudenay (Berlin: Springer, 2006), 89. See also Tal Moran and Moni Naor, "Basing Cryptographic Protocols on Tamper-Evident Seals," *Theoretical Computer Science* 411, no. 10 (2010): 1283–1310.

55. In a similar vein, Fellows and Koblitz remark that "a number of fundamental protocols, such as oblivious transfer and multi-party secure computation, can be nicely demonstrated by means of ordinary playing cards. Note that these familiar physical objects have a number of cryptographically useful properties 'built in': they have a convenient means of randomization (shuffling), are uniquely identifiable, and when face down, are indistinguishable." Michael Fellows and Neal Koblitz, "Kid Krypto," in *Advances in Cryptology—CRYPTO '92*, ed. Ernest F. Brickell (Berlin: Springer, 1993), 387.

56. Stanley L, Warner, "Randomized Response: A Survey Technique for Eliminating Evasive Answer Bias," *Journal of the American Statistical Association* 60, no. 309 (1965): 63–69.

57. Judith A. Droitcour, Eric M. Larson, and Fritz J. Scheuren, "The Three Card Method: Estimating Sensitive Survey Items—With Permanent Anonymity of Response," in *Proceedings of the American Statistical Association, Social Statistics Section* (2001). The paper describes the "three-card method" devised by the U.S. General Accounting Office for surveying the particularly sensitive issue of legal status of immigrant workers.

58. Moran and Naor, "Polling with Physical Envelopes," 89.

59. The two approaches echo Agre's analysis of the systems design literature and his identification of "two fundamental conceptions of users, or perhaps two organizing schemes for such conceptions, which I shall call the *technical* and the *managerial*. Roughly speaking, the technical conception of the user has two facets: the worldviews of designer and user are assumed to coincide, and the user is understood to be a component in a larger system. Thus the user's resistance to this arrangement is understood as something external to the system and therefore as irrational. The managerial conception, again roughly speaking, understands that the real object of design is not just the technical artifact but the whole institutional system around it; the user is understood as a human agent whose perceptions of the proposed institutional arrangements become an object of inquiry an intervention in their own right." Philip E. Agre, "Conceptions of the User in Computer Systems Design," in *Social and Interactional Dimensions of Human–Computer Interfaces*, ed. Peter J. Thomas (Cambridge: Cambridge University Press, 1995), 67–68.

Notes

60. Tim Bell et al., "Explaining Cryptographic Systems," *Computers & Education* 40, no. 3 (2003): 200.

61. Sid Stamm and Markus Jakobsson, "Privacy-Preserving Polling Using Playing Cards," Cryptology ePrint Archive, Report 2005/444, 1–2, available at http://eprint.iacr.org/2005/444 (accessed June 24, 2011).

62. Jean-Jacques Quisquater et al., "How to Explain Zero-Knowledge Protocols to Your Children," in *Advances in Cryptology—CRYPTO '89*, ed. by Gilles Brassard (Berlin: Springer, 1990), 628–631. Given that it deals with communication in the presence of adversaries, Fellows, Koblitz, and Brickell note that "implicit in any discussion of cryptography are elements of drama, of theater, of suspense." Fellows and Koblitz, "Kid Krypto," 371.

63. It may also open the door for amateurs to resume their contribution to the field. Diffie and Hellman concluded "New Directions" with a recognition of the important role of such outsiders: "The last characteristic which we note in the history of cryptography is the division between amateur and professional cryptographers. Skill in production cryptanalysis has always been heavily on the side of the professionals, but innovation, particularly in the design of new types of cryptographic systems, has come primarily from the amateurs. Thomas Jefferson, a cryptographic amateur, invented a system which was still in use in World War II, while the most noted cryptographic system of the twentieth century, the rotor machine, was invented simultaneously by four separate people, all amateurs. We hope this will inspire others to work in this fascinating area in which participation has been discouraged in the recent past by a nearly total government monopoly." Diffie and Hellman, "New Directions in Cryptography," 654. Today, one would probably talk of "a nearly total academic monopoly."

64. Fellows and Koblitz, "Kid Krypto," 372.

65. Ibid., 373.

66. Ronald Fagin, Moni Naor, and Peter Winkler, "Comparing Information Without Leaking It," *Communications of the ACM* 39, no. 5 (1996): 79.

67. First articulated by Andrew C. Yao, "Protocols for Secure Computations," in *23rd IEEE Symposium on Foundations of Computer Science* (Washington, DC: IEEE Society, 1982), 160: "Two millionaires wish to know who is richer; however, they do not want to find out inadvertently any additional information about each other's wealth. How can they carry out such a conversation?"

68. Fagin, Naor, and Winkler, "Comparing Information without Leaking It," 79.

69. For example, solution 7: "Ron and Moshe [the managers] assign a random telephone number to each candidate. Ron dials the phone number corresponding to the person (Bob) who complained to him and asks to leave a message for Moshe.

Of course, the person who answers the phone has no idea who Moshe is. A few minutes later, Moshe dials the phone number corresponding to the person who complained to him and asks if anyone has tried to leave a message for him." Ibid., 81.

70. Charles Bazerman, *The Languages of Edison's Light* (Cambridge, MA: MIT Press, 1999), 350.

71. Ruben Hersh, "Proving Is Convincing and Explaining," *Educational Studies in Mathematics* 24, no. 4 (1993): 395–396. This is echoed by MacKenzie: "The basis of a sociology of ordinary 'rigorous-argument' mathematical proof is thus that there is no abstract, context-free way of demarcating what constitutes a proof; that there is no higher criterion than the judgment of the adequacy of a putative proof by the members of the relevant specialist community; and that the judgments can both vary at any given time and change through time." Donald A. MacKenzie, *Mechanizing Proof: Computing, Risk, and Trust* (Cambridge, MA: MIT Press, 2001), 319.

72. For the discussions that probabilitic proof has generated in the mathematical community, see Don Fallis, "What Do Mathematicians Want? Probabilistic Proofs and the Epistemic Goals of Mathematicians," *Logique et Analyse* 45, no. 179–180 (2002): 373–388. Rabin's explanation of the meaning of probabilistic primality testing is itself fascinating: it "does *not* mean that an integer n asserted as prime by the use of 50 random numbers is prime with probability at least $1 - \frac{1}{2}^{100}$. Such an interpretation is nonsensical since n is either prime or not. . . . What is stated is that n was asserted to be prime by a procedure that on average will make no more than one mistake in 2^{100} applications (even when testing the same n)." Michael O. Rabin, "Probabilistic Algorithm for Testing Primality," *Journal of Number Theory* 12, no. 1 (1980): 129. In reference to zero-knowledge interactive proof systems, Jacques Stern argues: "Recent methods from the theory of computational complexity, without a doubt inspired by cryptography, relativize the concept of proof—in the traditional sense. They largely rehabilitate the algorithmic approach to the concept of demonstration that parallels the more classical logical approach. Even more, they show that, in addition to the formal and quasi biblical notion of proof, written and intended to be read, it is possible to productively introduce the notion of interactive proof, preferring dialogue to the simple verification of fixed text." Stern, *La science du secret*, 17 (my translation). For arguments relative to proof through DNA computation, see Leonard M. Adleman, "Computing with DNA," *Scientific American* 279, no. 8 (1998): 34–41; and Don Fallis, "Mathematical Proof and the Reliability of DNA Evidence," *American Mathematical Monthly* 103, no. 6 (1996): 491–497.

73. Sandra D. Mitchell, *Unsimple Truths: Science, Complexity, and Policy* (Chicago: University of Chicago Press, 2009), 117.

8 Epilogue

1. http://politicalticker.blogs.cnn.com/2010/08/04/cnnopinion-research-poll-obama-birth (accessed June 15, 2011).

2. John Crowley, "Uses and Abuses of the Secret Ballot in the American Age of Reform," in *Cultures of Voting: The Hidden History of the Secret Ballot*, ed. Romain Bertrand, Jean-Louis Briquet, and Peter Pels (London: Hurst & Co., 2007), 54.

3. Chaum, "Untraceable Electronic Mail, Return Addresses, and Digital Pseudonyms."

4. CalTech MIT Voting Technology Project, *Voting: What Is, What Could Be* (2001), 22, http://www.vote.caltech.edu/drupal/node/10 (accessed June 23, 2011).

5. David Jefferson, Aviel D. Rubin, Barbara Simons, and David Wagner, "Analyzing Internet Voting Security," *Communications of the ACM* 47, no. 10 (October 2004): 64.

6. Tadayoshi Kohno, Adam Stubblefield, Aviel D. Rubin, and Dan S. Wallach, "Analysis of An Electronic Voting System," in *2004 IEEE Symposium on Security & Privacy* (Berkeley, May 9–12, 2004), 27. Indeed, Roberta Mercuri, a computer scientist, had come to this very conclusion in her 2000 PhD thesis—see Roberta Mercuri, "A Better Ballot Box?" *IEEE Spectrum* 39, no. 10 (2002): 46–50.

7. See, for example, David Chaum et al., eds., *Towards Trustworthy Elections: New Directions in Electronic Voting* (Berlin: Springer, 2010). Specific proposals include "PunchScan," see David Chaum, "Secret-Ballot Receipts: True Voter-Verifiable Elections," *IEEE Security & Privacy* 2, no. 1 (2004): 38–47; "Prêt à Voter," see Peter Y. A. Ryan, "The Computer Ate My Vote," in *Formal Methods: State of the Art and New Directions*, ed. Paul Boca, Jonathan P. Bowen, and Jawed Siddiqi (Berlin: Springer, 2010), 147–184; "Scratch and Vote," see Ben Adida and Ron L. Rivest, "Scratch and Vote: Self-Contained Paper-Based Cryptographic Voting," in *Proceedings of the 5th ACM Workshop on Privacy in Electronic Society*, ed. Ben Adida and Ron L. Rivest (New York: ACM Press, 2006), 29–40; "ThreeBallot," see Ron L. Rivest and Warren D. Smith, "Three Voting Protocols: Threeballot, VAV, and Twin," in *Proceedings of the USENIX Workshop on Accurate Electronic Voting Technology* (Berkeley: USENIX Association, 2007), 16–16; and "Scantegrity I" and "Scantegrity II," see David Chaum et al., "Scantegrity II: End-to-End Verifiability by Voters of Optical Scan Elections through Confirmation Codes," *IEEE Transactions on Information Forensics and Security* 4, no. 4 (December 2009): 611–627.

8. Goldreich, "On Post-Modern Cryptography," 8.

9. Even defining the functionality of material artifacts is far from a simple task—see Beth Preston, "Why Is a Wing Like a Spoon? A Pluralist Theory of Function," *The*

Journal of Philosophy 95, no. 5 (1998): 215–254, and Beth Preston, "The Case of the Recalcitrant Prototype," in *Doing Things with Things: The Design and Use of Everyday Objects*, ed. Alan Costall and Ole Dreier (Farnham, UK: Ashgate, 2006), 15–27.

10. Crowley, "Uses and Abuses of the Secret Ballot in the American Age of Reform," 51. Similar debates went on in France at the turn of the century; see Alain Garrigou, Yves Déloye, and Olivier Ihl, "La construction sociale du vote: Fétichisme et raison instrumentale," *Politix* 6, no. 22 (1993): 5–42.

11. Some of these alliances have been forged in the broader field of information security. See, for example, *Security and Usability: Designing Secure Systems That People Can Use*, ed. Lorrie Faith Cranor and Simson Garfinkel (Sebastopol, CA: O'Reilly Media, 2005); Adam Shostack and Andrew Stewart, *The New School of Information Security* (Boston: Addison-Wesley Professional, 2008); and Ross Anderson's web page on economics and security resources, http://www.cl.cam.ac.uk/~rja14/econsec.html.

Bibliography

Adida, Ben, and Ronald L. Rivest. "Scratch and Vote: Self-Contained Paper-Based Cryptographic Voting." In *Proceedings of the 5th ACM Workshop on Privacy in Electronic Society*, ed. Ben Adida and Ronald L. Rivest, 29–40. New York: ACM, 2006.

Adleman, Leonard M. "Computing with DNA." *Scientific American* 279, no. 8 (August 1998): 34–41.

Agrawal, Dakshi, Bruce Archambeault, Josyula R. Rao, and Pankaj Rohatgi. "The EM Side-Channel (S)." In *Cryptographic Hardware and Embedded Systems—CHES 2002*, ed. Burton S. Kaliski, 29–45. Berlin: Springer, 2003.

Agre, Philip E. *Computation and Human Experience*. Cambridge: Cambridge University Press, 1997.

Agre, Philip E. "Toward a Critical Technical Practice: Lessons Learned in Trying to Reform AI." In *Social Science, Technical Systems, and Cooperative Work: Beyond the Great Divide*, ed. Geof Bowker, Les Gasser, Leigh Star, and Bill Turner, 131–157. Hillsdale, NJ: Lawrence Erlbaum Associates, 1997.

Agre, Philip E. "Conceptions of the User in Computer Systems Design." In *Social and Interactional Dimensions of Human-Computer Interfaces*, ed. Peter J. Thomas, 67–106. Cambridge: Cambridge University Press, 1995.

Alder, Ken. *The Lie Detectors: The History of an American Obsession*. New York: Free Press, 2007.

Alder, Ken. "Reading Characters: French Handwriting Experts from the Counter-Reformation to the Dreyfus Affair." Paper presented at the Berlin Summer Academy on Law, Science, and Technology, Max-Planck-Institut für Wissenschaftsgeschichte, Berlin, August 16–27, 1999.

American Bar Association. "Digital Signature Guidelines: Legal Infrastructure for Certification Authorities and Secure Electronic Commerce." Chicago: American Bar Association, August 1, 1996.

Anderson, Ross J., Bruno Crispo, Jong-Hyeon Lee, Charalampos Manifavas, Vaclav Matyas, and Fabien Petitcolas. *The Global Internet Trust Register*. Cambridge, MA: MIT Press, 1999.

Anderson, Ross J. *Security Engineering: A Guide to Building Dependable Distributed Systems*. 2nd ed. New York: Wiley, 2008.

Anderson, Ross J. "Why Cryptosystems Fail." *Communications of the ACM* 37, no. 11 (1994): 32–40.

Anderson, Ross J., and Markus Kuhn. "Tamper Resistance: A Cautionary Note." In *Second USENIX Workshop on Electronic Commerce Proceedings*, Oakland, CA, November 18–20, 1996.

Aronson, Jay D. *Genetic Witness: Science, Law, and Controversy in the Making of DNA Profiling*. New Brunswick: Rutgers University Press, 2007.

Atkins, Derek, Michael Graff, Arjen Lenstra, and Paul Leyland. "The Magic Words Are Squeamish Ossifrage." In *Advances in Cryptology—ASIACRYPT '94*, ed. Josef Pieprzyk and Reihanah Safavi-Naini, 261–277. Berlin: Springer, 1994.

Aynés, Laurent, and Phillipe Malaurie. "Formalités et preuve." In *Cours de droit civil: Les obligations*. Paris: Éditions Cujas, 1990.

Bailer-Jones, Daniela M. "Scientists' Thoughts on Scientific Models." *Perspectives on Science* 10, no. 3 (Fall 2002): 275–301.

Bamford, James. *Body of Secrets: Anatomy of the Ultra-Secret National Security Agency: From the Cold War through the Dawn of a New Century*. New York: Doubleday, 2001.

Bamford, James. *The Puzzle Palace. A Report on America's Most Secret Agency*. New York: Penguin Books, 1983.

Bangemann, Martin, Enrico Cabral da Fonseca, Peter Davis, Carlo de Benedetti, Pehr Gyllenhammar, Lothar Hunsel, Pierre Lescure, et al. "Europe and the Global Information Society: Recommendations of the High-Level Group on the Information Society to the Corfu European Council (Bangemann Group)." *Bulletin of the European Union*, Supplement No. 2/94 (1994): 5–39.

Banisar, David. *Cryptography and Privacy Sourcebook*. Washington, DC: Electronic Privacy Information Center, 1986.

Banisar, David, and Bruce Schneier. *The Electronic Privacy Papers: Documents on the Battle for Privacy in the Age of Surveillance*. New York: Wiley, 1997.

Barlow, John Perry. "A Declaration of the Independence of Cyberspace." *Humanist* 56, no. 3 (May/June 1996): 18–19.

Bautier, Robert-Henri. "L'authentification des actes privés dans la France médiévale: Notariat public et juridiction gracieuse." In *Chartes, sceaux et chancelleries: Études de diplomatique et de sigillographie médiévales*, vol. 1, 269–340. Geneva: Librarie Droz, 1990.

Bazerman, Charles. *The Languages of Edison's Light*. Cambridge, MA: MIT Press, 1999.

Bell, C. Gordon, and Jim Gemmell. *Total Recall: How the E-Memory Revolution Will Change Everything*. New York: Dutton, 2009.

Bell, Tim, Harold W. Thimbleby, Mike Fellows, Ian H. Witten, Neal Koblitz, and Matthew Powell. "Explaining Cryptographic Systems." *Computers & Education* 40, no. 3 (2003): 199–215.

Bellare, Mihir. "Practice-Oriented Provable Security." In *Lectures on Data Security: Modern Cryptology in Theory and Practice*, ed. Ivan Damgård, 1–15. Berlin: Springer, 1999.

Bellare, Mihir, and Sara Miner. "A Forward-Secure Digital Signature Scheme." In *Advances in Cryptology—Crypto '99*, ed. Michael Weiner, 431–448. Berlin: Springer, 1999.

Bellare, Mihir, and Phillip Rogaway. "The Exact Security of Digital Signatures: How to Sign with RSA and Rabin." In *Advances in Cryptology—EUROCRYPT '96*, ed. Ueli Maurer, 399–416. Berlin: Springer, 1996.

Bellare, Mihir, and Phillip Rogaway. "Random Oracles Are Practical: A Paradigm for Designing Efficient Protocols." In *Proceedings of the 1st ACM Conference on Computer and Communications Security*, Fairfax, VA, November 3–5, 1993, 62–73.

Bellovin, Steven M. "Frank Miller: Inventor of the One-Time Pad." *Cryptologia* 35, no. 3 (2011): 203–222.

Benedikt, Michael. *Cyberspace: First Steps*. Cambridge, MA: MIT Press, 1991.

Benoît, Olivier, and Thomas Peyrin. "Side-Channel Analysis of Six SHA-3 Candidates." In *Cryptographic Hardware and Embedded Systems—CHES 2010*, ed. Stefan Mangard and François-Xavier Standaert, 140–157. Berlin: Springer, 2010.

Bessy, Christian, and Francis Chateauraynaud. *Experts et faussaires: Pour une sociologie de la perception*. Paris: Métailié, 1995.

Biddle, C. Bradford. "Legislating Market Winners: Digital Signature Laws and the Electronic Commerce Marketplace." *San Diego Law Review* 34, no. 3 (1997): 1225–1246.

Biddle, C. Bradford. "Misplaced Priorities: The Utah Digital Signature Act and Liability Allocation in a Public Key Infrastructure." *San Diego Law Review* 33 (1996): 1143–1681.

Blanchette, Jean-François. "A Material History of Bits." *Journal of the American Association for Information Science and Technology* 62, no. 6 (2011): 1042–1057.

Blanchette, Jean-François. "The Digital Signature Dilemma." *Annales des Télécommunications* 61, no. 7–8 (2006): 903–918.

Blanchette, Jean-François. "The Noise in the Archive: Oblivion in the Age of Total Recall." In *Privacy and Data Protection: An Element of Choice*, ed. Serge Gutwirth, Yves Poullet, Paul De Hert, and Ronald Leenes, 25–38. Berlin: Springer, 2011.

Blanchette, Jean-François. "Les technologies de l'écrit électronique: Synthèse et évaluation critique." In *Les actes authentiques électroniques: Réflexion juridique prospective*, ed. Isabelle de Lamberterie, 139–204. Paris: La documentation française, 2002.

Blum, Manuel. "Coin Flipping by Telephone: A Protocol for Solving Impossible Problems." *ACM SIGACT News* 15, no. 1 (1983): 23–27.

Boczkowski, Pablo J. *Digitizing the News: Innovation in Online Newspapers*. Cambridge, MA: MIT Press, 2004.

Borgman, Christine L. *Scholarship in the Digital Age: Information, Infrastructure, and the Internet*. Cambridge, MA: MIT Press, 2007.

Boyar, Joan, David Chaum, Ivan Damgård, and Torben Pedersen. "Convertible Undeniable Signatures." In *Advances in Cryptology—CRYPTO '90*, ed. A. J. Menezes and S. A. Vanstone, 189–205. Berlin: Springer, 1991.

Brands, Stefan A. *Rethinking Public Key Infrastructures and Digital Certificates: Building in Privacy*. Cambridge, MA: MIT Press, 2000.

Brassard, Gilles. *Cryptologie contemporaine*. Paris: Masson, 1992.

Brown, John Seely, and Paul Duguid. *The Social Life of Information*. Boston: Harvard Business School Press, 2000.

CalTech MIT Voting Technology Project. *Voting: What Is, What Could Be*. 2001. http://www.vote.caltech.edu/drupal/node/10 (accessed June 23, 2011).

Canetti, Ran, Oded Goldreich, and Shai Halevi. "The Random Oracle Methodology, Revisited." In *30th Annual ACM Symposium on the Theory of Computing*, ed. Jeffrey Scott Vitter, 209–218. New York: ACM Press, 1998.

Carbonnier, Jean. "The Civil Code." In *Rethinking France: Les Lieux de Mémoire. Vol. I: The State*, ed. Pierre Nora, trans. David P. Jordan, 353–360. Chicago: Chicago University Press, 2002.

Carbonnier, Jean. *Droit civil*. Paris: Presses universitaires de France, 1955.

Carbonnier, Jean. *Sociologie juridique*. Paris: Presses universitaires de France, 1978.

Catala, Pierre. "Le formalisme et les nouvelles technologies." *Rapport Defrénois* (2000): 897–910.

Catala, Pierre, Pierre-Yves Gauthier, Jérome Huet, Isabelle de Lamberterie, and Xavier Linant de Bellefonds. "L'introduction de la preuve électronique dans le Code Civil." *La Semaine Juridique, Édition Générale*, no. 47 (1999): 2069–2076.

Cayla, Olivier. "La qualification, ou la vérité du droit." *Droits* 18 (1993): 3–18.

Cellard, André. "Rapport au nom de la commission des lois constitutionelles, de la léglisation et de l'administration générale de la République sur la proposition de loi adoptée par le Sénat relative à la preuve des actes juridiques," no. 1801. Paris: Assemblée Nationale, June 12, 1980.

Charpin, Dominique. *Writing, Law, and Kingship in Old Babylonian Mesopotamia.* Chicago: University of Chicago Press, 2010.

Chaum, David. "Achieving Electronic Privacy." *Scientific American* 267, no. 2 (1992): 96–101.

Chaum, David. "Blind Signatures for Untraceable Payments." In *Advances in Cryptology—Proceedings of CRYPTO '82*, ed. David Chaum, Ronald L. Rivest, and Alan T. Sherman, 199–203. New York: Plenum, 1983.

Chaum, David. "Designated Confirmer Signatures." In *Advances in Cryptology—EUROCRYPT '94*, ed. Alfredo De Santis, 86–91. Berlin: Springer, 1995.

Chaum, David. "Digital Money." *@Home, Doors of Perception 2*, 1994. http://www.vanriet.com/doors/doors2/content.html (accessed June 24, 2011).

Chaum, David. "FM Interviews: David Chaum." *First Monday* 4, no. 7 (1999).

Chaum, David. "Secret-Ballot Receipts: True Voter-Verifiable Elections." *IEEE Security & Privacy* 2, no. 1 (2004): 38–47.

Chaum, David. "Security without Identification: Transaction Systems to Make Big Brother Obsolete." *Communications of the ACM* 28, no. 10 (1985): 1030–1044.

Chaum, David. "Untraceable Electronic Mail, Return Addresses, and Digital Pseudonyms." *Communications of the ACM* 24, no. 2 (1981): 84–90.

Chaum, David, and Eugéne Van Heyst. "Group Signatures." In *EUROCRYPT '91*, ed. Donald W. Davies, 257–265. Berlin: Springer, 1991.

Chaum, David, and H. van Antwerpen. "Undeniable Signatures." In *Advances in Cryptology—Crypto '89 Proceedings*, ed. G. Brassard, 212–217. Berlin: Springer-Verlag, 1990.

Chaum, David L., Richard T. Carback, Jeremy Clark, Aleksander Essex, Stefan Popoveniuc, Ronald L. Rivest, Peter Y. A. Ryan, Emily Shen, Alan T. Sherman, and Poorvi Vora. "Scantegrity II: End-to-End Verifiability by Voters of Optical Scan Elections through Confirmation Codes." *IEEE Transactions on Information Forensics and Security* 4, no. 4 (December 2009): 611–627.

Chaum, David, Markus Jakobsson, Ronald L. Rivest, Peter Y. A. Ryan, and Josh Benaloh, eds., *Towards Trustworthy Elections: New Directions in Electronic Voting*. Berlin: Springer, 2010.

Ciborra, Claudio. *The Labyrinths of Information: Challenging the Wisdom of Systems*. Oxford: Oxford University Press, 2002.

Clanchy, Michael T. *From Memory to Written Record, England 1066–1307*. 2nd ed. Oxford: Blackwell, 1993.

Cole, Simon A. *Suspect Identities: A History of Fingerprinting and Criminal Identification*. Cambridge, MA: Harvard University Press, 2002.

Conseil d'État. *Internet et les réseaux numériques*. Paris: La documentation française, 1998.

Coombe, Rosemary J. *The Cultural Life of Intellectual Properties: Authorship, Appropriation, and the Law*. Durham, NC: Duke University Press, 1998.

Constance, Paul. "How Jim Bamford Probed the NSA." *Cryptologia* 21, no. 1 (1997): 71–74.

Copeland, Jack B. *Colossus: The Secrets of Bletchley Park's Code-breaking Computers*. Oxford: Oxford University Press, 2006.

Coron, Jean-Sébastien, Jacques Patarin, and Yannick Seurin. "The Random Oracle Model and the Ideal Cipher Model Are Equivalent." In *Advances in Cryptology—CRYPTO 2008*, ed. David Wagner, 1–20. Berlin: Springer-Verlag, 2008.

Cranor, Lorrie Faith, and Simson Garfinkel, eds. *Security and Usability: Designing Secure Systems That People Can Use*. Sebastopol, CA: O'Reilly Media, 2005.

Crowley, John. "Uses and Abuses of the Secret Ballot in the American Age of Reform." In *Cultures of Voting: The Hidden History of the Secret Ballot*, ed. Romain Bertrand, Jean-Louis Briquet, and Peter Pels, 43–68. London: Hurst & Co, 2007.

Curtin, Matt. *Brute Force: Cracking the Data Encryption Standard*. New York: Copernicus Books, 2005.

Dam, Kenneth W., and Herbert S. Lin, eds. *Cryptography's Role in Securing the Information Society (CRISIS)*. Washington, DC: National Academy Press, 1996.

Damgård, Ivan. "A 'Proof-Reading' of Some Issues in Cryptography." In *Automata, Languages, and Programming*, ed. Lars Arge, Christian Cachin, Tomasz Jurdzinski, and Andrzey Tarlecki, 2–11. Berlin: Springer-Verlag, 2007.

Datamonitor. *Public Key Infrastructure, 1999–2003*. n.p., 1999.

Davida, George. *Chosen Signature Cryptanalysis of the RSA (MIT) Public Key Cryptosystem*. Technical Report TR-CS-82-2, Department of Electrical and Computer Science, University of Wisconsin, 1982.

Davies, Wendy, and Paul Fouracre, eds. *The Settlement of Disputes in Early Medieval Europe*. Cambridge: Cambridge University Press, 1986.

Davis, Phillip J., and Reuben Hersh. *The Mathematical Experience*. Boston: Houghton Mifflin, 1981.

Decorps, Jean-Paul. "Porte ouverte sur l'avenir." *La Lettre aux Notaires*, no. 62 (2000), 1.

de Lamberterie, Isabelle, ed. *Les actes authentiques électroniques: Réflexion juridique prospective*. Paris: La documentation française, 2002.

de Lamberterie, Isabelle. "L'écrit dans la société de l'information." In *D'ici, d'ailleurs: Harmonisation et dynamique du droit—Mélanges en l'honneur de Denis Talon*. Paris: Société de législation comparée, 1999.

de Lamberterie, Isabelle, and Jean-François Blanchette. "Le décret du 30 mars 2001 relatif à la signature électronique: Lecture critique, technique et juridique." *La Semaine Juridique, Édition Affaires et Entreprises* 30 (2001): 1269–1275.

de Lamberterie, Isabelle, Pierre Catala, Pierre-Yves Gautier, Jérome Huet, Xavier Linant de Bellefonds, André Lucas, Lucas de Leyssac and Michel Vivant. *L'écrit et les nouveaux moyens technologiques au regard du droit*. n.p., September 1997.

Denis, Vincent. *Une histoire de l'identité: France, 1715–1815*. Seyssel: Éditions Champ Vallon, 2008.

Denning, Dorothy E. "Digital Signatures with RSA and Other Public-Key Cryptosystems." *Communications of the ACM* 27, no. 4 (1984): 388–392.

Denning, Dorothy E. "The Future of Cryptography." In *The Governance of Cyberspace: Politics, Technology and Global Restructuring*, ed. Brian Loader, 173–188. London: Routledge, 1997.

de Valicourt, Bénédicte. "Le premier acte authentique électronique en direct." *Notaires Vie Professionelle*, no. 246 (2004): 34–36.

Dhamija, Rachna, and Adrian Perrig. "Déjà Vu: A User Study Using Images for Authentication." In *Proceedings of the 9th USENIX Security Symposium*. Berkeley: USENIX Association, 2000.

Di Crescenzo, Giovanni. "Foundations of Modern Cryptography." In *Contemporary Cryptology*, ed. Dario Catalano, Ronald Cramer, Giovanni Di Crescenzo, Ivan Damgård, David Pointcheval, and Tsuyochi Takagi, 89–129. Basel: Birkhäuser Verlag, 2005.

Diffie, Whitfield, and Martin E. Hellman. "Exhaustive Cryptanalysis of the NBS Data Encryption Standard." *Computer* 10, no. 6 (1977): 74–84.

Diffie, Whitfield, and Martin E. Hellman. "New Directions in Cryptography." *IEEE Transactions on Information Theory* 22, no. 6 (1976): 644–654.

Diffie, Whitfield, and Susan E. Landau. *Privacy on the Line: The Politics of Wiretapping and Encryption*. Cambridge, MA: MIT Press, 1998.

Dourish, Paul. *Where the Action Is: The Foundations of Embodied Interaction*. Cambridge, MA: MIT Press, 2001.

Droitcour, Judith A., Eric M. Larson, and Fritz J. Scheuren. "The Three Card Method: Estimating Sensitive Survey Items—With Permanent Anonymity of Response." In *Proceedings of the American Statistical Association, Social Statistics Section* [CD-ROM], 2001.

Drucker, Johanna. *Speclab: Digital Aesthetics and Projects in Speculative Computing*. Chicago: University of Chicago Press, 2009.

Duranti, Luciana, Heather MacNeil, Terry Eastwood, Ken Thibodeau, Sharon Farb, and Jason Baron. "Strategy Task Force Report." In *The Long-Term Preservation of Authentic Electronic Records*. Vancouver: InterPARES, 2002.

Easterbrook, Frank H. "Cyberspace and the Law of the Horse." *University of Chicago Legal Forum* (1996): 207–216.

Edwards, Paul N. *A Vast Machine: Computer Models, Climate Data, and the Politics of Global Warming*. Cambridge, MA: MIT Press, 2010.

European Commission. *Ensuring Security and Trust in Electronic Communications—Towards a European Framework for Digital Signatures and Encryption*. Communication from the Commission to the Council, the European Parliament, the Economic and Social Committee and the Committee of the Regions, COM (97) 503, November 8, 1997.

European Commission. *Proposal for a European Parliament and Council Directive on a Common Framework for Electronic Signatures*. COM (98) 297, May 13, 1998.

European Union. "Directive 1999/93/EC of the European Parliament and of the Council on a Community Framework for Electronic Signatures." *Official Journal of the European Union* L 13/12, January 19, 2000: 12–20.

Fagin, Ronald, Moni Naor, and Peter Winkler. "Comparing Information without Leaking It." *Communications of the ACM* 39, no. 5 (1996): 77–85.

Fallis, Don. "Mathematical Proof and the Reliability of DNA Evidence." *American Mathematical Monthly* 103, no. 6 (1996): 491–497.

Fallis, Don. "What Do Mathematicians Want? Probabilistic Proofs and the Epistemic Goals of Mathematicians." *Logique et Analyse* 45, no. 179–180 (2002): 373–388.

Feistel, Horst. "Cryptography and Computer Privacy." *Scientific American* 228, no. 5 (1973): 15–23.

Fellows, Michael, and Neal Koblitz. "Kid Krypto." In *Advances in Cryptology—CRYPTO '92*, ed. Ernest F. Brickell, 371–389. Berlin: Springer, 1993.

Flour, Jacques. "Sur une notion nouvelle d'authenticité (commentaires de la loi du 26 novembre 1971)." *Répertoire Defrénois*, no. 30159 (1972): 977–1017.

Foyer, Jacques. *L'histoire du pouvoir notarial d'authentification des actes*. Paris: Institut International de l'Histoire du Notariat, December 6, 1981.

Fraenkel, Béatrice. *La signature: Genèse d'un signe*. Paris: Gallimard, 1992.

Frigg, Roman, and Stephan Hartmann. "Models in Science," *Stanford Encyclopedia of Philosophy* (Summer 2009 ed.), ed. Edward N. Zalta. http://plato.stanford.edu/archives/sum2009/entries/models-science/ (accessed October 10, 2011).

Froomkin, A. Michael. "The Metaphor Is the Key: Cryptography, the Clipper Chip, and the Constitution." *University of Pennsylvania Law Review* 143, no. 3 (January 1995): 709–897.

Gard, Olivier. "La carte réal: Une réalité." *Notaires Vie Professionelle*, no. 207 (1999): 69–70.

Gardey, Delphine. *Écrire, calculer, classer: Comment une révolution de papier a transformé les sociétés contemporaines (1800–1940)*. Paris: La Découverte, 2008.

Gardner, Martin. "A New Kind of Cipher That Would Take Millions of Years to Break." *Scientific American* 237, no. 8 (1977): 120–124.

Gardner, Martin. *When You Were a Tadpole and I Was a Fish: And Other Speculations about This and That*. New York: Hill and Wang, 2009.

Garrigou, Alain, Yves Déloye, and Olivier Ihl. "La construction sociale du vote: Fétichisme et raison instrumentale." *Politix* 6, no. 22 (1993): 5–42.

Giere, Ronald N. "How Models Are Used to Represent Reality." *Philosophy of Science* 71, no. 5 (2004): 742–752.

Giere, Ronald N. *Science without Laws*. Chicago: University of Chicago Press, 1999.

Gilmore, John. *Cracking DES: Secrets of Encryption Research, Wiretap Politics and Chip Design*. Sebastopol, CA: O'Reilly Media, 1998.

Global Internet Liberty Campaign. *Cryptography and Liberty: An International Survey of Encryption Policy*. 1998. http://gilc.org/crypto/crypto-survey.html (accessed June 24, 2011).

Goldreich, Oded. *Foundations of Cryptography: Basic Applications*. Cambridge: Cambridge University Press, 2004.

Goldreich, Oded. *Modern Cryptography, Probabilistic Proofs, and Pseudorandomness*. Berlin: Springer, 1999.

Goldreich, Oded. "On the Foundations of Modern Cryptography." In *Advances in Cryptology—CRYPTO '97*, ed. Burton S. Kaliski, Jr., 46–74. Berlin: Springer, 1997.

Goldreich, Oded. "On Post-Modern Cryptography." Cryptology ePrint Archive: Report 2006/461. http://eprint.iacr.org/2006/461 (accessed June 4, 2011).

Goldwasser, Shafi, Yael Tauman Kalai, and Guy N. Rothblum. "One-Time Programs." In *Advances in Cryptology—CRYPTO 2008*, ed. David Wagner, 39–56. Berlin: Springer, 2008.

Gray, Jeremy. "Modern Mathematics as a Cultural Phenomenon." In *The Architecture of Modern Mathematics*, ed. José Ferreirós and Jeremy Gray, 371–396. Oxford: Oxford University Press, 2006.

Gutwirth, Serge, Paul de Hert, and Laurent De Sutter. "The Trouble with Technology Regulation: Why Lessig's 'Optimal Mix' Will Not Work." In *Regulating Technologies: Legal Futures, Regulatory Frames and Technological Fixes*, ed. Roger Brownsword and Karen Yeung, 193–218. Oxford: Hart Publishing, 2008.

Hacking, Ian. *Representing and Intervening: Introductory Topics in the Philosophy of Natural Science*. Cambridge: Cambridge University Press, 1983.

Hacking, Ian. *The Taming of Chance*. Cambridge: Cambridge University Press, 1990.

Hardy, G. H. *A Mathematician's Apology*. Cambridge: Cambridge University Press, 1940.

Henderson, Kathryn. *On Line and on Paper: Visual Representations, Visual Culture, and Computer Graphics in Design Engineering*. Cambridge, MA: MIT Press, 1999.

Hersh, Reuben. "Proving Is Convincing and Explaining." *Educational Studies in Mathematics* 24, no. 4 (1993): 389–399.

Hesse, Mary B. *Models and Analogies in Science*. Notre Dame: University of Notre Dame Press, 1966.

Hodges, Andrew. *Alan Turing: The Enigma*. London: Vintage, 1992.

Hoffman, Lance J., ed. *Building in Big Brother: The Cryptographic Policy Debate*. New York: Springer, 1995.

Hoffman, Lance J., Faraz A. Ali, Steven L. Heckler, and Ann Huybrechts. "Cryptography Policy." *Communications of the ACM* 37, no. 9 (1994): 109–117.

IBM. *In Good Company: Annual Report*. n.p., 2003.

ISO. *Information Technology, Open Systems Interconnection, Security Frameworks for Open Systems, Part 4: Non-repudiation*. ISO/IEC 10181-4. Geneva: ISO, 1996.

ITU. *Recommendation X.509*. Geneva: International Telecommunications Union, 1997. http://www.itu.int/rec/T-REC-X.509 (accessed June 24, 2011).

Jakobsson, Markus, and Moti Yung. "Revokable and Versatile Electronic Money." In *Proceedings of 3rd ACM Conference on Computer and Communications Security (CCS '96)*, 76–87. New York: ACM Press, 1996.

Jasanoff, Sheila. *Science at the Bar: Law, Science, and Technology in America.* Cambridge, MA: Harvard University Press, 1995.

Jefferson, David, Aviel D. Rubin, Barbara Simons, and David Wagner. "Analyzing Internet Voting Security." *Communications of the ACM* 47, no. 10 (2004): 59–64.

Jermyn, Ian, Alain Mayer, Fabien Monrose, Michael K. Reiter, and Aviel Rubin. "The Design and Analysis of Graphical Passwords." In *Proceedings of the 8th Conference on USENIX Security Symposium*, 1–14. Berkeley: USENIX Association, 1999.

Jospin, Lionel. *Préparer l'entrée de la France dans la société de l'information.* Speech by the prime minister at the 18th Université d'été de la communication, Hourtin, August 25, 1997. http://www.admiroutes.asso.fr/action/theme/politic/lionel.htm (accessed June 25, 2011).

Jospin, Lionel. *Société de l'information.* Speech by the prime minister at the 20th Université d'été de la communication, Hourtin, August 26, 1999. http://www.mediasinfos.com/Download/jospin260899.htm (accessed June 25, 2011).

Juola, Patrick. "Whole-Word Phonetic Distances and the PGPfone Alphabet." In *Proceedings of the Fourth International Conference on Spoken Language, ICSLP 96* (1996), 98–101.

Kahn, David. *The Codebreakers: The Story of Secret Writing.* New York: Macmillan, 1967.

Kahn, David. "The CRYPTO '82 Conference, Santa Barbara. A Report on a Conference." *Cryptologia* 7, no. 1 (1983): 1–5.

Kahn, David. "EUROCRYPT 83: A Report." *Cryptologia* 7, no. 3 (1983): 254–256.

Kahn, David. *The Reader of Gentlemen's Mail: Herbert O. Yardley and the Birth of American Codebreaking.* New Haven: Yale University Press, 2004.

Kaliski, Burton S., Jr. "Emerging Standards for Public-Key Cryptography." In *Lectures on Data Security: Modern Cryptology in Theory and Practice*, ed. Ivan Damgård, 87–104. Berlin: Springer, 1999.

Kaliski, Burton, and Jessica Staddon. "Public-Key Cryptography Standards (PKCS) #1: RSA Cryptography Specifications Version 2.0." RSA Laboratories, 1998.

Kelly, Kevin. *Out of Control: The New Biology of Machines, Social Systems, and the Economic World.* Reading, MA: Addison-Wesley, 1994.

Kerckhoffs, Auguste. "La cryptographie militaire." *Journal des Sciences Militaires* 9 (1883): 5–38.

Kessler, Jack. "Networked Information in France, 1993: The Internet's Future." *Internet Research* 4, no. 1 (1994): 18–30.

Koblitz, Neal, and Alfred J. Menezes. "Another Look at 'Provable Security.'" *Journal of Cryptology* 20, no. 1 (2007): 3–37.

Koblitz, Neal, and Alfred J. Menezes. "Another Look at 'Provable Security' II." In *Progress in Cryptology—Indocrypt 2006*, ed. Rana Barua and Tanja Lange, 148–175. Berlin: Springer, 2006.

Koblitz, Neil, and Alfred J. Menezes. "The Brave New World of Bodacious Assumptions in Cryptography." *Notices of the American Mathematical Society* 57 (2010): 357–365.

Kocher, Paul, Joshua Jaffe, and Benjamin Jun. "Differential Power Analysis." In *Advances in Cryptology—CRYPTO '99*, ed. Michael Wiener, 388–397. Berlin: Springer, 1999.

Kohnfelder, Loren M. "Towards a Practical Public-Key Cryptosystem." B.S. thesis, Massachusetts Institute of Technology, Electrical Engineering, 1978.

Kohno, Tadayoshi, Adam Stubblefield, Aviel D. Rubin, and Dan S. Wallach. "Analysis of an Electronic Voting System." In *IEEE Symposium on Security & Privacy*, Berkeley, California, May 9–12, 2004.

Kolata, Gina. "Cryptography: On the Brink of a Revolution?" *Science* 197, no. 4305 (1977): 747.

Lagarde, Xavier. *Réflexion critique sur le droit de la preuve*. Paris: Librairie générale de droit et de jurisprudence, 1994.

Lamport, Leslie. "Constructing Digital Signatures from One-Way Function." Technical Report SRI-CSL-98, SRI International, October 1979.

Landau, Susan. "Find Me a Hash." *Notices of the American Mathematical Society* 53, no. 3 (2006): 330–332.

Landau, Susan. "Primes, Codes and the National Security Agency." *Notices of the American Mathematical Society* 30, no. 1 (1983): 7–10.

Landau, Susan. "Zero Knowledge and the Department of Defense." *Notices of the American Mathematical Society* 35, no. 1 (1988): 5–12.

Landau, Susan, Stephen Kent, Clinton C. Brooks, Scott Charney, Dorothy E. Denning, Whitfield Diffie, Anthony Lauck, Douglas Miller, Peter G. Neumann, and David L. Sobel. "Crypto Policy Perspectives." *Communications of the ACM* 37, no. 8 (1994): 115–121.

Lapierre, Nicole. *Changer de nom*. Paris: Stock, 1995.

Larrieu, Jacques. "Les nouveaux moyens de preuve: Pour ou contre l'identification des documents informatiques à des écrits sous seing privé," *Cahiers Lamy du droit de l'informatique* (1988): (H) 8–19; (I) 26–34.

Latour, Bruno. "Drawing Things Together." In *Representation in Scientific Practice*, ed. Michael Lynch and Steve Woolgar, 19–68. Cambridge, MA: MIT Press, 1990.

Latour, Bruno. *The Making of Law: An Ethnography of the Conseil d'État*. Cambridge: Polity, 2010.

Lefebvre-Teillard, Anne. *Le nom: Droit et histoire*. Paris: Presses universitaires de France, 1990.

Leibowitz, Wendy. "Utah Will Repeal Its Digital Signature Law, Never Used, As Tech, National Law Diverged." *Electronic Commerce and Law Report* 10, no. 48 (December 21, 2005).

Lessig, Lawrence. *Code and Other Laws of Cyberspace*. New York: Basic Books, 1999.

Lessig, Lawrence. *Code: Version 2.0*. New York: Basic Books, 2006.

Lessig, Lawrence. "The Law of the Horse: What Cyberlaw Might Teach." *Harvard Law Review* 113, no. 2 (1999): 501–549.

Levy, Steven. "The Cypherpunks vs. Uncle Sam." In *Building in Big Brother: The Cryptographic Policy Debate*, ed. Lance J. Hoffman, 266–283. New York: Springer, 1995.

Levy, Steven. "Clipper Chick." *Wired*, September 1996: 162.

Levy, Steven. *Crypto: How the Code Rebels Beat the Government, Saving Privacy in the Digital Age*. New York: Viking, 2001.

Levy, Steven. "Crypto: The Story of How a Group of Code Rebels Saved Your Privacy on the Internet." Newsweek, January 15, 2001: 42–52.

Levy-Bruhl, Henri. *La preuve judiciaire*. Paris: Librairie Marcel Rivière et Cie, 1964.

Ludlow, Peter. *High Noon on the Electronic Frontier: Conceptual Issues in Cyberspace*. Cambridge, MA: MIT Press, 1996.

Lynch, Michael, Simon A. Cole, Ruth McNally, and Kathleen Jordan. *Truth Machine: The Contentious History of DNA Fingerprinting*. Chicago: University of Chicago Press, 2008.

Lynch, Michael, Ruth MacNally, and Patrick Daly. "Le tribunal, fragile espace de la preuve." *La Recherche Hors Série*, no. 8 (2002): 108–113.

MacKenzie, Donald A. *An Engine, Not a Camera: How Financial Models Shape Markets*. Cambridge, MA: MIT Press, 2006.

MacKenzie, Donald A. "An Equation and Its Worlds." *Social Studies of Science* 33, no. 6 (2003): 831–868.

MacKenzie, Donald A. *Material Markets: How Economic Agents Are Constructed*. Oxford: Oxford University Press, 2009.

MacKenzie, Donald A. *Mechanizing Proof: Computing, Risk, and Trust*. Cambridge, MA: MIT Press, 2001.

Marty, Gabriel, and Pierre Raynaud. "Théorie générale des preuves." In *Droit civil*. Paris: Sirey, 1972.

Massey, James L. "An Introduction to Contemporary Cryptography." *Proceedings of the IEEE* 76, no. 5 (1988): 533–549.

May, Timothy C. "The Crypto Anarchist Manifesto." 1992. http://www.activism.net/cypherpunk/crypto-anarchy.html (accessed June 24, 2011).

Mehrtens, Herbert. "Mathematical Models." In *Models: The Third Dimension of Science*, ed. Soraya De Chadarevian and Nick Hopwood, 276–306. Stanford: Stanford University Press, 2004.

Menezes, Alfred J., Paul C. van Oorschot, and Scott A. Vanstone. *Handbook of Applied Cryptography*. Boca Raton, FL: CRC Press, 1997.

Mercuri, Roberta. "A Better Ballot Box?" *IEEE Spectrum* 39, no. 10 (2002): 46–50.

Merkle, Ralph C. "Secure Communications over Insecure Channels." *Communications of the ACM* 21, no. 4 (1978): 294–299.

Meyer, Elizabeth A. *Legitimacy and Law in the Roman World: Tabulae in Roman Belief and Practice*. Cambridge: Cambridge University Press, 2004.

Micali, Silvio. "Fair Public-Key Cryptosystems." In *Advances in Cryptology—CRYPTO '92*, ed. Ernest F. Brickell, 113–138. London: Springer, 1992.

Micali, Silvio, and Leonid Reyzin. "Physically Observable Cryptography." In *Theory of Cryptography: Proceedings of Theory of Cryptography*, TCC 2004, ed. Moni Naor, 278–296. Berlin: Springer, 2004.

Mitchell, Chris J., Fred Piper, and Peter R. Wild. "Digital Signatures." In *Contemporary Cryptology: The Science of Information Integrity*, ed. Gustavus J. Simmons, 325–378. Piscataway, NJ: IEEE Press, 1992.

Mitchell, Sandra D. *Unsimple Truths: Science, Complexity, and Policy*. Chicago: University of Chicago Press, 2009.

Mitchell, William J. *The Reconfigured Eye: Visual Truth in the Post-Photographic Era*. Cambridge, MA: MIT Press, 1994.

Monrose, Fabien, and Michael K. Reiter. "Graphical Passwords." In *Security and Usability: Designing Secure Systems That People Can Use*, ed. Lorrie Faith Cranor and Simson Garfinkel, 157–174. Sebastopol, CA: O'Reilly Media. 2005.

Moran, Tal, and Moni Naor. "Basing Cryptographic Protocols on Tamper-Evident Seals." *Theoretical Computer Science* 411, no. 10 (2010): 1283–1310.

Moran, Tal, and Moni Naor. "Polling with Physical Envelopes: A Rigorous Analysis of a Human-Centric Protocol." In *Advances in Cryptology—EUROCRYPT 2006*, ed. Serge Vaudenay, 88–108. Berlin: Springer, 2006.

Morgan, Mary S. "Models, Stories and the Economic World." *Journal of Economic Methodology* 8, no. 3 (2001): 361–384.

Morgan, Mary S, and Margaret Morrison, eds. *Models as Mediators: Perspectives on Natural and Social Sciences*. Cambridge: Cambridge University Press, 1999.

NARA. *Records Management Guidance for PKI Digital Signature Authenticated and Secured Transaction Records*. Washington, DC: National Archives and Records Administration, March 11, 2005. http://www.archives.gov/records-mgmt/pdf/pki.pdf (accessed June 25, 2011).

Naor, Moni, and Benny Pinkas. "Visual Authentication and Identification." In *Advances in Cryptology—CRYPTO '97*, ed. Burton S. Kaliski, Jr., 322–336. Berlin: Springer, 1997.

Naor, Moni, and Adi Shamir. "Visual Cryptography." In *Advances in Cryptology—EUROCRYPT '94*, ed. Alfredo De Santis, 1–12. Berlin: Springer, 1995.

Neary, Dennis R., Terrence H. Coyle, and Don M. Avedon. "The Integration of Microfilm and the Computer." In *AFIPS '76: Proceedings of the June 7–10, 1976, National Computer Conference and Exposition*, 627–637. New York: ACM Press, 1976.

Negroponte, Nicholas. *Being Digital*. New York: Vintage Books, 1996.

OECD. *Cryptography Policy: The Guidelines and the Issues*. Paris: OECD, 1997.

Oehler, Michael, Dhananjay Phatak, and John Krautheim. "Visualizing Your Key for Secure Phone Calls and Language Independence." In *VizSec '10, Proceedings of the Seventh International Symposium on Visualization for Cyber Security*, ed. John Gerth, 64–69. New York: ACM Press, 2010.

Otis, Laura. *Networking: Communicating with Bodies and Machines in the Nineteenth Century*. Ann Arbor: University of Michigan Press, 2001.

Papadimitriou, Christos H. *Computational Complexity*. Reading, MA: Addison-Wesley, 1994.

Paul, George L. *Foundations of Digital Evidence*. Chicago: American Bar Association, 2008.

Pelkmans, Jacques. "The GSM Standard: Explaining a Success Story." *Journal of European Public Policy* 8, no. 3 (2001): 432–453.

Perrig, Adrian, and Dawn Song. "Hash Visualization: A New Technique to Improve Real-World Security." In *International Workshop on Cryptographic Techniques and E-Commerce (CrypTEC '99)* (1999), 439–458.

Petitcolas, Fabien A. P., Ross J. Anderson, and Markus G. Kuhn. "Information Hiding—A Survey." *Proceedings of the IEEE* 87, no. 7 (1999): 1062–1078.

Pfitzmann, Birgit. "Fail-Stop Signatures: Principles and Applications." In *Proceedings of Compsec '91, Eighth World Conference on Computer Security, Audit, and Control*, 125–134. New York: Elsevier Science Publishers, 1991.

PGP Corporation. *PGP Desktop for Mac OS X User's Guide, Version 8.1*. June 7, 2004.

Pointcheval, David, and Jacques Stern. "Security Arguments for Digital Signatures and Blind Signatures." *Journal of Cryptology* 13, no. 3 (2000): 351–396.

Pomerance, Carl. "Prime Numbers and the Search for Extraterrestrial Intelligence." In *Mathematical Adventures for Students and Amateurs*, ed. David F. Hayes and Tatiana Shubin, 3–50. Washington, DC: The Mathematical Association of America, 2004.

Porter, Theodore M. *Trust in Numbers: The Pursuit of Objectivity in Science and Public Life*. Princeton: Princeton University Press, 1995.

Preston, Beth. "The Case of the Recalcitrant Prototype." In *Doing Things with Things: The Design and Use of Everyday Objects*, ed. Alan Costall and Ole Dreier, 15–27. Farnham, UK: Ashgate, 2006.

Preston, Beth. "Why Is a Wing Like a Spoon? A Pluralist Theory of Function." *Journal of Philosophy* 95, no. 5 (1998): 215–254.

Quisquater, Jean-Jacques, Myriam Quisquater, Muriel Quisquater, Michaël Quisquater, Louis Guillou, Marie Annick Guillou, Gaïd Guillou, Anna Guillou, and Gwenolé Guillou. "How to Explain Zero-Knowledge Protocols to Your Children." In *Advances in Cryptology—CRYPTO '89*, ed. Gilles Brassard, 628–631. Berlin: Springer, 1990.

Rabin, Michael O. "Probabilistic Algorithm for Testing Primality." *Journal of Number Theory* 12, no. 1 (1980): 128–138.

Ratcliff, Rebecca A. *Delusions of Intelligence: Enigma, Ultra and the End of Secure Ciphers*. New York: Cambridge University Press, 2006.

Raynouard, Arnaud. "Adaptation du droit de la preuve aux technologies de l'information et à la signature électronique: Observations critiques." *Répertoire Notarial Defrénois*, no. 37174 (2000): 593.

Reidenberg, Joel R. "Lex Informatica: The Formulation of Information Policy Rules through Technology." *Texas Law Review* 76, no. 3 (1998): 553–593.

Reitinger, Phillip R. "Compelled Production of Plaintext and Keys." *University of Chicago Legal Forum* (1996): 171–206.

Relyea, Harold C., ed. *Silencing Science: National Security Controls and Scientific Communication*. Norwood, NJ: Ablex Publishing Corporation, 1994.

République Française. "Décret n°2001-272 du 30 mars 2001 pris pour l'application de l'article 1316-4 du Code Civil et relatif à la signature électronique." *Journal officiel de la République Française*, March 30, 2001.

République Française. "Décret no. 2005-973 du 10 août 2005 modifiant le décret no. 71-941 du 26 novembre 1971 relatif aux actes établis par les notaires." *Journal officiel de la République Française*, August 11, 2005.

République Française. "Instruction générale relative à l'état civil." *Journal officiel de la République Française*, November 23, 2004.

Rioufol, Jean, and Françoise Rico. *Le notariat*. Paris: Presses universitaires de France, 1979.

Risinger, D. Michael, Mark P. Denbeaux, and Michael J. Saks. "Exorcism of Ignorance as a Proxy for Rational Knowledge: The Lessons of Handwriting Identification Expertise." *University of Pennsylvania Law Review* 137, no. 3 (1989): 731–792.

Rivest, Ronald L. "The Case against Regulating Encryption Technology." *Scientific American* 279, no. 4 (October 1998): 88–89.

Rivest, Ronald L. "Chaffing and Winnowing: Confidentiality without Encryption." *CryptoBytes* 4, no. 1 (1998): 12–17.

Rivest, Ronald L. "Cryptology." In *Handbook of Theoretical Computer Science*, ed. Jan van Leeuwen, 617–755. New York: Elsevier, 1990.

Rivest, Ronald L., Adi Shamir, and Leonard Max Adleman. *Cryptographic Communications System and Method*. Patent, September 1983.

Rivest, Ronald L., Adi Shamir, and Yael Tauman. "How to Leak a Secret." In *Advances in Cryptology—ASIACRYPT 2001*, ed. Colin Boyd, 552–565. Berlin: Springer, 2001.

Rivest, Ronald L., Adi Shamir, and Leonard Max Adleman. "A Method for Obtaining Digital Signatures and Public-Key Cryptosystems." *Communications of the ACM* 21, no. 2 (1978): 120–126.

Rivest, Ronald L., and Warren D. Smith. "Three Voting Protocols: ThreeBallot, VAV, and Twin." In *Proceedings of the USENIX Workshop on Accurate Electronic Voting Technology*, 16. Berkeley: USENIX Association, 2007.

Roe, Michael. "Cryptography and Evidence." Ph.D. dissertation, University of Cambridge, 1997.

Roe, Michael. "Non-repudiation and the Metaphysics of Presence." In *Proceedings of the 13th International Conference on Security Protocols*, ed. Bruce Christianson, Bruno Crispo, James A. Malcolm, and Michael Roe, 204–206. Berlin: Springer, 2007.

Rogaway, Phillip. "On the Role of Definitions In and Beyond Cryptography." In *Advances in Computer Science—ASIAN 2004*, ed. Michael J. Maher, 13–32. Berlin: Springer, 2005.

Rosenheim, Shawn J. *The Cryptographic Imagination: Secret Writing from Poe to the Internet*. Baltimore: Johns Hopkins University Press, 1995.

Rotman, Brian. *Ad Infinitum . . . The Ghost in Turing's Machine: Taking God Out of Mathematics and Putting the Body Back In. An Essay in Corporeal Semiotics*. Stanford: Stanford University Press, 1993.

Rotman, Brian. *Mathematics as Sign: Writing, Imagining, Counting*. Stanford: Stanford University Press, 2000.

Rotman, Brian. "Thinking Dia-Grams: Mathematics, Writing, and Virtual Reality." *South Atlantic Quarterly* 94, no. 2 (1995): 389–416.

Rouzet, Gilles. "L'acte authentique à distance: Pour un aménagement du droit français de la preuve." In *Mélanges offerts à Roland De Valkeneer: À l'occasion du 125ième anniversaire de la Revue du notariat belge*, ed. Daniel Sterckx and Jean-Luc Ledoux. Bruxelles: Bruylant, 2000.

RSA Laboratories. "How Fast Is the RSA Algorithm?," n.d. http://www.rsa.com/rsalabs/node.asp?id=2215 (accessed June 25, 2011).

Rudloff, Marcel. "Rapport sur la proposition de loi de M. Jacques Thyraud, tendant à actualiser les Dispositions du Code Civil sur la preuve testimoniale" (no. 324). Paris: Sénat, May 10, 1979.

Ryan, Peter Y. A. "The Computer Ate My Vote." In *Formal Methods: State of the Art and New Directions*, ed. Paul Boca, Jonathan P. Bowen, and Jawed Siddiqi, 147–184. Berlin: Springer, 2010.

Schneier, Bruce. *Secrets and Lies: Digital Security in a Networked World*. New York: Wiley, 2000.

Scott, James C. *Seeing like a State: How Certain Schemes to Improve the Human Condition Have Failed*. New Haven: Yale University Press, 1998.

Sellen, Abigail J., and Richard H. R. Harper. *The Myth of the Paperless Office*. Cambridge, MA: MIT Press, 2002.

Sénat, "Signature électronique." *Journal Officiel des Débats*, no. 53 (February 8, 2000): 39–79.

Shannon, Claude E. "Communication Theory of Secrecy Systems." *Bell System Technical Journal* 28, no. 4 (1949): 656–715.

Shoup, Victor. "Practical Threshold Signatures." In *Advances in Cryptology—EUROCRYPT 2000*, ed. Bart Preneel, 207–220. Berlin: Springer, 2000.

Shostack, Adam, and Andrew Stewart. *The New School of Information Security*. Boston: Addison-Wesley Professional, 2008.

Shparlinski, Igor E. "Numbers at Work and Play." *Notices of the American Mathematical Society* 57, no. 3 (March 2010): 334–342.

Simmons, Gustavus J. "Contemporary Cryptology: A Foreword." In *Contemporary Cryptology: The Science of Information Integrity*, ed. Gustavus J. Simmons, vii–xv. Piscataway, NJ: IEEE Press, 1992.

Simmons, Gustavus J. "The History of Subliminal Channels." *IEEE Journal on Selected Areas in Communications* 16, no. 4 (2002): 452–462.

Simmons, Gustavus J. "How to Insure That Data Acquired to Verify Treaty Compliance Are Trustworthy." In *Contemporary Cryptology: The Science of Information Integrity*, ed. Gustavus J. Simmons, 615–630. Piscataway, NJ: IEEE Press, 1992.

Simmons, Gustavus J. "The Prisoners' Problem and the Subliminal Channel." In *Advances in Cryptology, Proceedings of CRYPTO '83*, ed. David Chaum, 51–67. New York: Plenum Press, 1984.

Simmons, Gustavus J. "The Subliminal Channel and Digital Signatures." In *Advances in Cryptology, Proceedings of EUROCRYPT '84*, ed. Thomas Beth, Norbert Cot, and Ingemar Ingemarsson, 364–378. Berlin: Springer, 1985.

Singh, Simon. *The Code Book: The Science of Secrecy from Ancient Egypt to Quantum Cryptography*. New York: Anchor Books, 2000.

Sismondo, Sergio. "Models, Simulations, and Their Objects." *Science in Context* 12, no. 2 (1999): 247–260.

Smid, Miles E., and Dennis K. Branstad. "The Data Encryption Standard: Past and Future." *Proceedings of the IEEE* 76, no. 5 (1988): 550–599.

Smith, Richard E. *Authentication: From Passwords to Public Keys*. Boston: Addison-Wesley, 2002.

Spalding, Helen. "Let Us Now Praise Prime Numbers." In *Strange Attractors: Poems of Love and Mathematics*, ed. Sarah Glaz and JoAnne Growney, 190. Wellesley, MA: A. K. Peters, Ltd., 2008.

Stadler, Markus, Jean-Marc Piveteau, and Jan Camenisch. "Fair Blind Signatures." In *Proceedings of the 14th Annual International Conference on Theory and Application of Cryptographic Techniques*, ed. Louis C. Guillou and Jean-Jacques Quisquater, 209–219. Berlin: Springer, 1995.

Stamm, Sid, and Markus Jakobsson. "Privacy-Preserving Polling Using Playing Cards." Cryptology ePrint Archive: Report 2005/444. http://eprint.iacr.org/2005/444 (accessed June 24, 2011).

Standaert, François-Xavier, Tal G. Malkin, and Moti Yung. "A Unified Framework for the Analysis of Side-Channel Key Recovery Attacks." Cryptology ePrint Archive: Report 2006/139. http://eprint.iacr.org/2006/139 (accessed June 24, 2011).

Standaert, Francois-Xavier, Olivier Pereira, Yu Yu, Jean-Jacques Quisquater, Moti Yung, and Elisabeth Oswald. "Leakage Resilient Cryptography in Practice." In *Towards Hardware-Intrinsic Security*, ed. Ahmad-Reza Sadeghi and David Naccache, 99–134. Berlin: Springer, 2010.

Standage, Tom. *The Victorian Internet: The Remarkable Story of the Telegraph and the Nineteenth Century's On-Line Pioneers*. New York: Walker and Co., 1998.

Stengers, Isabelle. *La vierge et le neutrino: Les scientifiques dans la tourmente*. Paris: Les empêcheurs de penser en rond, 2006.

Stern, Jacques. *La science du secret*. Paris: Editions Odile Jacob, 1998.

Stinson, Douglas R. *Cryptography: Theory and Practice*. Boca Raton, FL: CRC Press, 1995.

Stinson, Douglas R. "Some Observations on the Theory of Cryptographic Hash Functions." *Designs, Codes and Cryptography* 38, no. 2 (2006): 259–277.

Suchman, Lucille Alice. *Human-Machine Reconfigurations: Plans and Situated Actions*. Cambridge: Cambridge University Press, 2007.

Suleiman, Ezra N. *Private Power and Centralization in France: The Notaires and the State*. Princeton: Princeton University Press, 1987.

Terré, François. *Introduction générale au droit*. Paris: Dalloz, 1994.

Thorpe, Julie, and Paul C. van Oorschot. "Graphical Dictionaries and the Memorable Space of Graphical Passwords." In *Proceedings of the 13th Conference on USENIX Security Symposium*, 10. Berkeley: USENIX Association, 2004.

Thorpe, Julie, Paul C. van Oorschot, and Anil Somayaji. "Pass-Thoughts: Authenticating with Our Minds." In *Proceedings of the 2005 Workshop on New Security Paradigm*, ed. Simon Foley, 45–56. New York: ACM Press, 2005.

Tiersma, Peter M. *Parchment, Paper, Pixels: Law and the Technologies of Communication*. Chicago: University of Chicago Press, 2010.

Tikhonov, A. N. "Mathematical Model." In *Encyclopaedia of Mathematics*, ed. Michiel Hazewinkel. Berlin: Springer, 2002. http://eom.springer.de/m/m062670.htm (accessed June 24, 2011).

UNCITRAL. *Model Law on Electronic Commerce with Guide to Enactment*. 1996. http://www.uncitral.org/pdf/english/texts/electcom/05-89450_Ebook.pdf (accessed June 24, 2011).

Union Internationale du Notariat Latin. *Les nouvelles technologies informatiques et l'acte authentique*. Rapport de la sous-commission, sous la présidence de Me Gilles Rouzet. Amsterdam: Fondation pour la promotion de la science notariale, 2001.

Bibliography

Vallens, Jean-Luc. "De la pierre au feuillet: Une brève histoire du livre foncier." *Les Petites Affiches*, no. 181 (September 11, 2000): 4–6.

Vallens, Jean-Luc. "Le droit local d'Alsace-Moselle." *Recueil Dalloz*, 29ième cahier (1998): 275–279.

Vallens, Jean-Luc. "Le publicité foncière en Alsace-Moselle: Une institution séculaire en cours d'informatisation." *Les Petites Affiches*, no. 248 (December 14, 1999): 13–15.

van De Graaf, Jeroen. "Adapting Chaum's Voter-Verifiable Election Scheme to the Brazilian System." In *Annals of IV Wseg—Workshop em Segurana de Sistemas Computacionais* (2004), 187–198.

van Fraassen, Bas C. *Scientific Representation: Paradoxes of Perspective*. Oxford: Clarendon Press, 2008.

van Oorschot, P. C., and Julie Thorpe. "On Predictive Models and User-Drawn Graphical Passwords." *ACM Transactions on Information and System Security* 10, no. 4 (2007): 17:1–17:33.

Vion, Michel. "Les modifications apportées au droit de la preuve par la loi du 12 juillet 1980." *Repertoire Defrénois*, no. 32470 (1980): 1329–1347.

Warner, Stanley L. "Randomized Response: A Survey Technique for Eliminating Evasive Answer Bias." *Journal of the American Statistical Association* 60, no. 309 (1965): 63–69.

Weir, Jonathan, and Wei Qi Yan. "A Comprehensive Study of Visual Cryptography." In *Transactions on Data Hiding and Multimedia Security V*, ed. Yun Q. Shi, 70–105. Berlin: Springer, 2010.

Winkler, Peter. "The Advent of Cryptology in the Game of Bridge." *Cryptologia* 7, no. 4 (1983): 327–332.

Winn, Jane K. "The Emperor's New Clothes: The Shocking Truth about Digital Signatures and Internet Commerce." *Idaho Law Review* 37 (2001): 353–388.

Yan, Jianxin, Alan Blackwell, Ross J. Anderson, and Alasdair Grant. *The Memorability and Security of Password: Some Empirical Results*. Cambridge: University of Cambridge Computer Laboratory, September 2000.

Yao, Andrew C. "Protocols for Secure Computations." In *23rd IEEE Symposium on Foundations of Computer Science*, 160–164. Washington, DC: IEEE Society, 1982.

Yates, JoAnne. "From Press Book and Pigeonhole to Vertical Filing: Revolution in Storage and Access Systems for Correspondence." *Journal of Business Communication* 19, no. 3 (1982): 6–26.

Young, Adam, and Moti Yung. "The Dark Side of 'Black-Box' Cryptography, or: Should We Trust Capstone?" In *Advances in Cryptology—CRYPTO '96*, ed. Neal Koblitz, 89–103. Berlin: Springer, 1996.

Young, Adam, and Moti Yung. "Kleptography: Using Cryptography against Cryptography." In *Advances in Cryptology—EUROCRYPT '97*, ed. David Chaum, Christoph G. Günther, and Franz Picher, 62–74. Berlin: Springer, 1997.

Young, Adam, and Moti Yung. *Malicious Cryptography. Exposing Cryptovirology*. New York: Wiley, 2004.

Zagier, Don. "The First 50 Million Prime Numbers." *Mathematical Intelligencer* 1, no. 0 (1977): 7–19.

Zhou, Jianying, and Dieter Gollmann. "Evidence and Non-repudiation." *Journal of Network and Computer Applications* 20, no. 3 (1997): 267–281.

Zimmermann, Phil. *PGP: Source Code and Internals*. Cambridge, MA: MIT Press, 1995.

Žižek, Slavoj. *Iraq: The Borrowed Kettle*. London: Verso Books, 2005.

Index

Adleman, Leonard
 digital signatures and, 75–76, 80
 public-key cryptography and, 41, 45, 47
Adversaries, 10, 12–13
 access levels of, 168
 attacks and, 74–80
 digital signatures and, 68, 74–84, 92
 forgery and, 27, 66, 68, 78–79, 82–83, 126, 143, 150
 historical perspective on cryptography and, 17–38
 mutations and, 80–84
 public-key cryptography and, 17, 57
 repudiation and, 79–80
 resources of, 9, 32
 Shannon paper and, 32
 substitution threats and, 75–78
Agre, Philip E., 228n59
Alder, Ken, 118–119, 121
Algeria, 140
Algorithms, 15
 computational complexity and, 8–9, 13, 162–164, 166, 167, 178, 182–183
 digital signatures and, 9, 67–71, 79–80
 El-Gamal, 58
 Enigma machines and, 27–30, 32, 69, 159
 hash functions and, 8, 57, 59, 68, 71–72, 161, 164–167, 174–176, 183
 knapsack, 47
 Lucifer, 34–35, 47, 71
 monoalphabetic substitution and, 19–21, 28
 polyalphabetic substitution and, 19–21, 34
 probabilistic, 184
 public-key cryptography and, 39, 44, 46–51, 58–59, 161
 Random Oracle Model (ROM) and, 162–169, 183
 RSA encryption and, 45–51, 58, 67–68, 72, 75, 79–80, 161, 163–164, 167
Alsace-Moselle land registers, 127, 148–154
American Bar Association, 10, 14, 96, 106, 108–109
American Civil War, 24
Anderson, Ross J., 174, 195n22
Anonymity, 184, 189
 authentication and, 59–60
 blind signatures and, 59, 81
 cash and, 5, 81, 163
 digital signatures and, 81, 83–84, 95
 historical perspective on cryptography and, 24
 public-key cryptography and, 41, 53–54, 59–60
Archivists, 11, 99, 134, 154–155
Arecibo radio telescope, 46
ASCII files, 145
ATM machines, 35

Attacks, 8
  adversaries and, 74–80
  Bellare-Rogaway program and, 163–168
  brute-force, 20, 22, 28, 173
  chosen-message, 78
  dictionary, 170–173
  digital signatures and, 68–69, 74–80
  direct, 18
  Draw-A-Secret (DAS) scheme and, 172–173
  historical perspective on cryptography and, 18–25, 28, 35, 37
  key-only, 78
  known-plaintext, 21–22
  known signature, 78
  Random Oracle Model (ROM) and, 162–169, 183
  side-channel, 15, 159–161
  substitution and, 75–78
  sustained, 25, 162
  unbreakable codes and, 17, 25, 32
  unforeseen, 24
Authentication, 1–2, 11, 14
  anonymity and, 59–60
  behavioral, 69
  blind signatures and, 59, 81
  certificates and, 76–77
  challenge-response protocols and, 69
  Conseil supérieur du notariat (CSN) and, 127–131, 136, 139–141
  cryptographic imagination and, 172, 174–179
  defined, 69
  digital preservation and, 91, 137, 139
  digital signatures and, 64–65, 69–77, 83, 91
  electronic authentic acts and, 116, 123, 126–127, 132–140, 147, 150, 156
  entity, 69–70, 91
  fingerprinting and, 10, 68–69, 72, 91, 155, 174–176
  formalism and, 133–137
  government and, 123–150, 153–157
  historical perspective on cryptography and, 23, 27, 36
  legal issues and, 95–98, 101, 106, 108–111, 116
  message, 69–70, 78
  Napoleonic code and, 126
  notaries and, 124 (*see also* Notaries)
  PINs and, 69–70
  presumptions of authenticity and, 123–124, 157
  public-key cryptography and, 39, 41, 51, 54–60
  registers and, 127, 148–154
  retinal patterns and, 69, 91
  security services and, 69–70
  Service central d'état civil (SCEC) and, 127, 140–148
  typing patterns and, 70
  verification and, 69 (*see also* Verification)
  voting and, 4–9, 15, 56–57, 59, 178–181, 185, 187–190

Baltimore Technologies, 5
Bangemann, Martin, 110
Barlow, John Perry, 6
Baudot code, 30
Bazerman, Charles, 183–184
Being Digital (Negroponte), 6, 223n49
Bellare, Mihir, 163–165, 167, 225n18
Benedikt, Michael, 194n5
Big Brother, 17, 48
Binary code
  biometric word lists and, 176
  cryptographic imagination and, 176, 182
  digital signatures and, 71, 90
  historical perspective on cryptography and, 30–31, 34–35, 41, 46
  Lucifer cipher and, 34–35, 47, 71
  Vernam cipher and, 27, 30–34

Biometrics, 27, 70, 91, 153, 176, 226n34
Birth certificates, 1–4, 7, 14, 143, 187
Birthers, 1, 12
Bishop of Nantes, 125
Bit shaking, 161
Black chambers, 19, 205n22
Black-Scholes-Merton model, 87–88
Bletchley Park, 29–30, 32
Blind signatures, 59, 81
Bloatware, 116
Block ciphers, 8, 67, 163
Blum, Manuel, 57–58
Bombes, 29
Bona fides, 17, 97, 99, 187
Born-digital materials, 96, 101
Brute-force attacks, 20, 22, 28, 173
Bush, George W., 187

CalTech/MIT Voting Technology Project, 188, 231n4
Capstone, 59
Cash
  anonymity and, 5, 81, 163
  ATM machines and, 35
  digital signatures and, 81
  dispensers and, 39
  electronic, 5, 53, 59, 189
  public-key cryptography and, 39, 53, 57, 59
Catala, Pierre, 126
Censorship
  crypto wars and, 40–41
  historical perspective on, 33, 38
  legal issues and, 94
  public-key cryptography and, 47, 58
Challenge-and-response protocols, 169
Chaum, David, 24, 40–41, 47, 59–60, 81, 188–189
Cheating, 56–57, 188
China, 51, 131
Chinese remainder theorem, 195n21
Chirographs, 97, 119, 124

Chosen-message attacks, 78
Ciphers. *See also* Encryption
  block, 8, 67, 163
  cryptographic imagination and, 163, 176–178
  digital signatures and, 66–67, 71
  historical perspective on, 18–37
  legal issues and, 116
  Lorenz, 32
  Lucifer, 34–35, 47, 71
  MIT, 46
  public-key cryptography and, 43, 46, 51, 57
  scrambling and, 23
  Vernam, 27, 30–34, 162, 176
  Vigenère, 20, 24–25
Cipher secretaries, 19
Civil code, 93, 97, 99, 103–105, 116, 120, 131, 134, 148, 154
Civilist approach, 98, 134
Clanchy, Michael T., 123–124
Clipper chip, 48
CNN, 187
Code and Other Laws of Cyberspace (Lessig), 11
Code Book, The (Singh), 17, 202n1
Codebooks
  historical perspective on, 19, 21–22, 24, 28–29, 32
  inverted, 21
  nomenclators and, 21–24, 37
Codebreakers, The (Kahn), 18–19, 47
Cognition, 15
  cryptographic imagination and, 169–170, 180–183
  cryptographic literacy and, 180–181
  digital signatures and, 64
  models and, 14
  number theory and, 204n1
  operators and, 37
Collision resistance, 175–176
Commercial codes, 31
Common law, 118, 131, 220n17

"Communication Theory of Secrecy Systems" (Shannon), 32, 34
"Comparing Information Without Leaking It" (Fagin, Naor, and Winkler), 181–182
Computational assumptions, 46, 79, 82–83, 164, 178–179
Computational complexity, 8–9, 224n13
  certification and, 13, 162–169
  cryptographic imagination and, 162–169, 178, 182–183
  Random Oracle Model (ROM) and, 162–169, 183
Computer Output Microfilm (COM), 99
Confusion, 34–35, 132, 161, 180
Conseil supérieur du notariat (CSN), 127–131, 136, 139–141
Consensualism, 97–98, 214n15
Contact (Sagan), 46
Contemporary Cryptology: The Science of Information Integrity (Simmons), 55
Contracts
  burden of proof and, 97
  civilist approach and, 98
  consensualism and, 98
  digital signatures and, 14 (*see also* Digital signatures)
  formal requirements and, 98
  government and, 124–127, 131–138, 145, 148–152, 156–157
  legal issues and, 93, 96–99, 119, 124–127, 131–138, 145, 148–152, 156–157
  non-repudiation and, 10 (*see also* Non-repudiation)
  notaries and, 131 (*see also* Notaries)
  oral, 124
  power of performance and, 97
  public-key cryptography and, 39, 55
  real estate, 4, 7, 14, 127, 131, 134, 149–150, 152
  Roman law and, 96–97
Contradictory evidence, 65, 98

Coombe, Rosemary, 11
Copyright, 5, 24, 94
Cover signal, 23
Cover text, 23
Credit cards, 9, 103, 109, 210n31
Cryptanalysis
  bit shaking and, 161
  Bletchley Park and, 29–30, 32
  bombes and, 29
  cryptographic imagination and, 159–187
  Discrete Log problem and, 161
  Enigma machines and, 27–32, 69, 159
  frequency analysis and, 20–22, 28, 34
  historical perspective on, 20–22, 26–29, 32, 37
  Random Oracle Model (ROM) and, 162–169, 183
  S-boxes and, 35–36
  side-channel attacks and, 15, 159–161
  Turing and, 27, 161, 200n34
CRYPTO conferences, 47
Cryptographic imagination
  authentication and, 172, 174–179
  binary code and, 176, 182
  cognition and, 169–170, 180–183
  cryptographic literacy and, 180–181
  dictionary attacks and, 170–173
  Draw-A-Secret (DAS) scheme and, 172–173
  heuristic arguments and, 165–166
  material objects and, 179–180
  memory and, 168–171, 169–173, 183
  passwords and, 169–173
  perception and, 169, 173–178
  picture effect and, 171
  plausibility arguments and, 173, 179
  randomness and, 162–169, 176–180, 183
  secret function evaluation and, 182
  side-channel attacks and, 15, 159–161
  verification and, 174, 178, 180, 182, 184
  visual cryptography and, 171–173, 176–180

Index

Cryptographic literacy, 180–181
Cryptographie militaire (Kerckhoff), 25
Cryptography
  academic community and, 5
  Adleman and, 41, 45, 47, 75–76, 80
  authority of proof and, 9
  black chambers and, 19
  block ciphers and, 8, 67, 163
  centralized systems and, 42–43
  codebooks and, 19, 21–22, 24, 28–29, 32
  computational assumptions and, 46, 79, 82–83, 164, 178–179
  computational complexity and, 8–9, 162–164, 167, 178, 182–183
  contradictory evidence and, 65–66, 98
  decentralized, 41–47
  Diffie-Hellman paradigm and, 8, 13, 38–47, 51, 53–56, 60
  digital signatures and, 5, 9 (*see also* Digital signatures)
  dot-com crash and, 5
  electromagnetic leakage and, 159–161, 168, 183
  elusive certainty and, 37–38
  embodiment and, 37
  Enigma machines and, 27–30, 32, 69, 159
  false information and, 30
  free strong, 49–52
  hash functions and, 8, 57, 59, 68, 71–72, 161, 164–167, 174–176, 183
  historical perspective on, 12–13, 17–38
  materiality and, 18, 33
  mathematics and, 4, 8 (*see also* Mathematics)
  military and, 5, 9–10 (*see also* Military)
  models and, 7–9, 13–15, 61, 64 (*see also* Models)
  monoalphabetic substitution and, 19–21, 28
  Morse code and, 18, 24, 27, 37
  multibillion-dollar market for, 5
  national security and, 5, 35–36, 38, 47–52, 54, 92
  non-repudiation and, 10, 13, 64, 69, 72–74, 81, 91–92, 96, 109–112, 118, 164
  number theory and, 45–46, 70, 79–83, 164, 178–179
  paper and, 19–24
  plaintext and, 19–22, 27–28, 32–35, 163, 176–178
  polyalphabetic substitution and, 19–21, 34
  prime numbers and, 45–46, 70, 79–83, 164, 178–179
  provable security and, 8–9, 12–13, 15, 68, 161–168, 180
  public-key, 4–5, 10, 13 (*see also* Public-key cryptography)
  radio and, 12, 18, 26–27, 33, 37, 126
  Random Oracle Model (ROM) and, 162–169, 183
  research agenda for, 5, 40–41, 54–60
  Rivest and, 41, 45, 51–52, 57, 72, 75–76, 80, 83
  secret function evaluation and, 182
  Shamir and, 41, 45, 47, 75–76, 80, 83, 176
  simplicity and, 182
  steganography and, 23, 32–33, 37, 41, 51, 57, 61
  telegraphs and, 12, 18, 24–27, 30, 126
  three stages of, 17–18
  traffic analysis and, 18, 26, 29, 37, 53, 59
  unbreakable codes and, 17, 25, 32
  underlying functionality and, 189
  unplugged, 181–182, 228n55
  visual, 171–173, 176–180
  voting and, 4–9, 15, 56–57, 59, 178–181, 185, 187–190

Cryptography: Theory and Practice (Stinson), 57
Crypto (Levy), 17, 202n1
Crypto wars
  Clipper chip and, 48
  collaborators and, 52–54
  criminal investigations and, 49
  Cypherpunk and, 48
  Denning and, 52, 68
  digital anarchy and, 48–49
  Electronic Frontier Foundation (EFF) and, 51
  Electronic Privacy Information Center and, 51–52
  export regulations and, 48–49, 51, 95
  fair cryptosystems and, 52–53
  key escrow and, 48, 52
  Micali and, 52–53, 168
  MIT Press and, 49
  privacy and, 40–41, 47–54, 60
  public-key cryptography and, 40–41, 47–54
  T-shirts and, 49
CSI (TV show), 10
Cyberlibertarian movement, 5, 9, 13, 40, 48, 56
Cypherpunk, 48

Data Encryption Standard (DES), 35–36, 47, 51, 161–163, 201n52
Dati, Rachida, 139–140
Davida, Georges, 68
Decrees
  government issues and, 123, 126–127, 133, 135, 138–139, 148, 154, 157
  legal issues and, 100, 114–116, 123, 126–127, 133, 135, 138–139, 148, 154, 157

Decryption
  Bellare-Rogaway program and, 163–168, 225n18
  bit shaking and, 161
  Discrete Log problem and, 161
  electromagnetic leakage and, 159–161, 168, 183
  frequency analysis and, 20–22, 28, 34
  Random Oracle Model (ROM) and, 162–169, 183
  side-channel attacks and, 15, 159–161
  unbreakable codes and, 17, 25, 32
De Hert, Paul, 120–121
Denning, Dorothy, 52, 68
DES Challenges, 51
DES Cracker machine, 51
Designated verifier signatures, 82
Di Crescenzo, Giovanni, 89
Dictionary attacks, 170–173
Diffie, Whitfield, 8, 13, 15, 229n63
  contradictory evidence and, 65–66, 98
  crypto wars and, 53–54, 60
  decentralization and, 41–42
  digital signatures and, 63–69, 72, 75–76, 81, 85
  historical perspective on cryptography and, 35, 38
  information integrity and, 54–55
  mathematics and, 162–163, 167, 183
  public-key cryptography and, 39–47, 51, 53–56, 60
  Random Oracle Model (ROM) and, 162–163, 167, 183
  substitution threats and, 75–77
Diffusion, 34–35, 161
DigiCash, 59–60, 189
Digital anarchy, 48–49, 52, 60
Digital preservation, 91, 137, 139
"Digital Signature Guidelines" (American Bar Association), 108, 112

Digital signatures, 13
 Adleman and, 75–76, 80
 adversaries and, 68, 74–84, 92
 algorithms and, 9, 67–71, 79–80
 American Bar Association (ABA) and, 108–109
 attacks and, 68–69, 74–80
 authentication and, 64–65, 69–77, 83, 91
 Bellare-Rogaway program and, 163–168
 binary code and, 71, 90
 blind signatures and, 59, 81
 cash and, 81
 certificates and, 76–77
 ciphers and, 66–67, 71
 contradictory evidence and, 65–66
 cryptographic imagination and, 161, 163–164, 167
 designated verifier and, 82
 Diffie and, 63–69, 72, 75–76, 81, 85
 dispute protection and, 66–69, 81
 document dependency and, 72
 electronic authentic acts and, 116, 123, 126–127, 132–140, 147, 150, 156
 electronic signature bill and, 115, 131
 electronic writing and, 103–106
 essential design of, 66
 European Union and, 109–112
 evidence law reform and, 4
 fail-stop, 82–83
 forensic properties of, 10
 forgery and, 66, 68, 78–79, 82–83
 forward-signature, 82
 global recognition of, 106–112
 group signatures and, 81
 handwritten signatures and, 63–64, 69–70, 80, 83, 90–91, 132, 139–140, 144–148, 155–157
 hash functions and, 68, 71–72
 Hellman and, 63–69, 72, 75–76, 81, 85

 historical perspective on, 65–69
 immateriality and, 63
 integrity and, 60, 63–64, 71–75, 78, 90–91
 legal issues and, 63–64, 74, 92, 95–98, 105–121, 123, 127–128, 131–133, 136–140, 146–149, 153–157
 mathematics and, 8, 10, 14, 63–64, 67–68, 73, 78, 80–90
 message-dependency and, 66–67
 Model Law on E-Commerce and, 107–108
 models and, 64, 74, 78–79, 81, 84–92
 mutations and, 80–84
 networks and, 63, 65, 74, 76–77
 non-repudiation and, 64, 72–74, 82, 91–92, 164
 notaries and, 91, 98, 121, 123–143, 148–150, 154, 156–157
 number theory and, 68, 70, 79–80
 one-time signatures and, 81
 passwords and, 69–70, 91
 prime numbers and, 70, 79–80
 proof and, 14, 64, 67–68, 72, 79–81, 90, 92
 protocols and, 63–64, 68–69, 81, 84–85
 randomness and, 65, 78, 80
 Random Oracle Model (ROM) and, 162–169
 real world and, 85–90
 receipts and, 65
 Rivest and, 72, 75–76, 80, 83
 RSA encryption and, 67–68, 72, 79–80
 security and, 64, 68–77, 80–85, 89–92
 Service central d'état civil and, 127, 140–148, 156–157
 Shamir and, 75–76, 80, 83
 UNCITRAL and, 106–108
 undeniable, 82–83
 verification and, 15, 57, 59, 66–69, 72–77, 80–84, 90–91, 108, 111–112, 116, 137, 174
 VeriSign and, 108, 114, 174

Direct-recording electronic (DRE) voting machines, 188
Discrete Log problem, 161
Distance acts, 139
DNA, 10, 86, 155, 184
Documents
  Alsace-Moselle land registers and, 148–154
  birth certificates, 1–4, 187
  born-digital, 96, 101
  colonial rule and, 143
  defining writing and, 102–104
  dependency and, 72
  digital-immaterial narrative and, 5–6
  digital preservation and, 91, 137, 139
  digital signatures and, 72 (*see also* Digital signatures)
  electronic authentic act and, 137–140
  evolution of, 123–124
  feuillets and, 149–153
  good science and, 10
  Groupement pour l'Informatisation du Livre Foncier d'Alsace-Moselle and, 152–154, 157
  inscriptions and, 125–126, 148–153, 157
  Instruction générale à l'état civil (IGREC) and, 144–148
  long-term legibility and, 137
  notaries and, 91, 98, 123–143, 148–150, 154, 156–157
  official copies and, 1, 96–102, 106, 124, 126, 139–147, 150, 153
  ordonnances and, 148–154
  PDF, 137
  perception and, 173–178
  physical, 4, 7, 12, 14, 70, 93–126, 154
  registers and, 124–127, 143, 148–155, 157
  Service central d'état civil and, 127, 140–148, 156–157
  trust and, 123–124
  Word, 137
  written evidence and, 4, 7, 12, 14, 93–126, 154
  XML, 153
Dot-com crash, 5
Draw-A-Secret (DAS) scheme, 172–173
Drucker, Johanna, 222n37
DSA federal standard, 58

Easterbrook, Frank, 14, 94, 121
E-commerce, 13, 95, 106–107, 120
Edmond, Jack, 203n12
Edwards, Paul, 87
Electromagnetic radiation, 159–161, 168, 183, 223n1
Electromechanical devices
  bombes and, 29
  Enigma machines and, 27–30, 32, 69, 159
  Hagelin machines and, 27–30
  period length and, 28
  rotors and, 27–30
  Vernam and, 27, 30–34, 162, 176
Electronic authentic acts
  Dati and, 139–140
  digital preservation and, 91, 137, 139
  formalism and, 133–137
  legal issues and, 116, 123, 126–127, 132–140, 147, 150, 156
  toward the first, 137–140
  unlimited preservation of, 133
Electronic evidence, 7, 10–11, 103, 106–107
Electronic Frontier Foundation (EFF), 51
Electronic Fund Transfer Act, 109
Electronic Privacy Information Center, 51–52
Electronic signature bill, 115, 131
Electronic writing, 103–106
El-Gamal algorithm, 58
Elliptic Curve Method, 79, 167

Index

Encryption, 5
  codebooks and, 19, 21–22, 24, 28–29, 32
  confusion and, 34–35, 161, 180
  context and, 36–37
  cover text and, 23
  Data Encryption Standard (DES) and, 35–36, 47, 51, 161–163
  diffusion and, 34–35, 161
  digital signatures and, 66–69 (*see also* Digital signatures)
  electromechanical devices and, 27–33
  El-Gamal and, 58
  Enigma machines and, 27–30, 32, 69, 159
  false information and, 27, 30
  Hagelin machines and, 27–30
  modulo arithmetic and, 20
  monoalphabetic substitution and, 19–21, 28
  Morse code and, 18, 24, 27, 37
  networked computers and, 34–36
  nomenclators and, 21–24, 37
  on-line, 31
  plaintext and, 19–22, 27–28, 32–35, 163, 176–178
  polyalphabetic substitution and, 19–21, 34
  RSA, 45–51, 58, 67–68, 72, 75, 79–80, 161, 163–164, 167
  scrambling and, 23
  silent alarms and, 27
  unbreakable codes and, 17, 25, 32
  Vigenère cipher and, 20, 24–25
  visual cryptography and, 171–173, 176–180
Encyclopedia of Mathematics, 85
End-to-end voting (E2E), 188–189
Enigma machines, 27–30, 32, 69, 159, 199n30, 200n37
Espionage, 26, 33
European Information Society, 110
European Union, 10, 96, 106, 109–112

Exclusive-or (XOR) operator, 31
Export regulations, 48–49, 51, 95

Factorization, 45–46, 79, 167, 210n37
Fagin, Ronald, 181–182
Fail-stop signatures, 82–83
Fair cryptosystems, 52–53
False information, 30, 65
Federal Bureau of Investigation, 51
Federal Information Processing Standard (FIPS), 36
Federal Register, 35
Feistel, Horst, 34, 71
Fellows, Michael, 181, 228n55
Feuillets, 149–153
Fingerprints, 10, 68–69, 72, 91, 155, 174–176
Fists, 27
Flour, Jacques, 135
Forgery, 27
  digital signatures and, 66, 68, 78–79, 82–83
  existential, 78–79
  government and, 126, 143, 150
  rogue certification and, 218n64
  selective, 78
  total break, 78–79
  universal, 78
Formalism
  authentication and, 133–137
  electronic authentic acts and, 133–137
  legal, 97, 104, 132–137
  long-term legibility and, 137
  mathematical, 17
  notaries and, 133–137
  symbolic, 89
Forward-secure signatures, 82
Fraenkel, Béatrice, 63, 156
France
  bureaucracy and, 93
  dirigisme and, 94
  Grande écoles and, 93

France (cont.)
  information age and, 113–118
  Jospin and, 113–115
  Louis XIV and, 125
  Minitel and, 94, 113, 146, 213n1
  monopolies and, 131
  Napoleonic code and, 97–98, 126
  Roman law and, 96–97, 123–124
  scribes and, 123–124
  true constitution of, 219n9
Free speech, 5
Funkspiel, 27, 30, 36, 61

Gardner, Martin, 46
Geometry of the line, 7
Germany, 27, 31, 131
Giere, Ronald N., 86–87
Gilmore, John, 51
Global Trust Register (Anderson), 174
Goldreich, Oded, 41, 56–57, 60, 89, 166, 189, 213n76
Good science, 10
Google, 8
Government, 15
  black chambers and, 19
  burden of proof and, 97, 100, 103–105, 109, 115, 119–120
  Capstone proposal and, 59
  cipher secretaries and, 19
  crypto wars and, 40–41, 47–54, 60
  Data Encryption Standard (DES) and, 35–36, 47, 51, 161–163
  decrees and, 100, 114–116, 123, 126–127, 133, 135, 138–139, 148, 154, 157
  digital anarchy and, 48–49, 52, 60
  emergence of modern state and, 123
  export regulations and, 48–49, 51, 95
  Federal Information Processing Standard (FIPS) and, 36
  inscriptions and, 125–126, 148–153, 157
  national security and, 47–54 (*see also* National security)
  real estate and, 14, 127, 131, 134, 136, 148–153
  records of civil status and, 140–148
  reform and, 126, 131–132, 136, 143
  subliminal channels and, 57–59
Graham-Shamir knapsack public-key algorithm, 47
Graphical dictionaries, 173
Graphical passwords, 171–173
Gray, Jeremy, 212n74
Greeks, 33
Groupement pour l'Informatisation du Livre Foncier d'Alsace-Moselle (GILFAM), 152–154, 157
Group signatures, 81
GSM directive, 109–110
Guigou, Élisabeth, 132–133
Gutwirth, Serge, 120–121

Hagelin, Boris, 27
Hagelin machines, 27–30
Handbook of Applied Cryptography, 6, 56–57, 74, 82, 197n3, 198n14, 206n47
Handbook of Theoretical Computer Science, 57
Handwritten signatures, 1, 8, 13
  developing digital equivalent of, 63–64, 69–70, 80, 90–91 (*see also* Digital signatures)
  fists and, 27
  government standards and, 132, 139–140, 144–148, 155–157
  legal issues and, 83, 93, 105, 112, 118–121, 132, 139–140, 144–148, 155–157
  perception and, 173
Harper, Richard, 7, 128, 157
Hash functions, 8
  Bellare-Rogaway program and, 163–168

Index

bit shaking and, 161
collision resistance and, 175–176
compression and, 175
digital signatures and, 68, 71–72
Discrete Log problem and, 161
efficiency and, 175–176
finite number of strings and, 68
image generation and, 176
MD4, 161
MD5, 164
nearness and, 175
perception and, 174–176
perceptual indistinguishability and, 175
public-key cryptograpny and, 57, 59
Random Oracle Model (ROM) and, 162–169, 183
RIPEMD-160, 165
SHA-1, 164–165
side channel attacks and, 15, 159–161
visualization, 174–176
Hellman, Martin, 8, 13, 15, 229n63
  public-key cryptography and, 39–47, 51, 54–56
Henri II, 124–125
Henri III, 93
Heuristic arguments, 8, 15, 56, 165–166
Hodges, Alan, 30, 200n34
"How to Leak a Secret" (Rivest, Shamir, and Tauman), 83–84

IBM, 35, 152
Imann, Bobby, 47
Imputability, 104, 114
Indicator, 28–29
Indochina, 140
Information, 7, 14
  hiding, 18, 23–24, 41
  random, 28–29, 176, 178 (*see also* Randomness)
  redundancy and, 34–35, 58

Information Society, 4, 17, 95, 109–110, 113, 115, 121
Input orderings, 170–171
Instruction générale relative à l'état civil (IGREC), 144–148
Instrumentum, 135
Integrity
  defined, 71
  digital signatures and, 60, 63–64, 71–75, 78, 90–91
  electronic writing and, 104
  government and, 139, 144, 154–156
  information and, 4–5, 12–13, 41, 54–57, 60, 63–64, 69, 71–75, 78, 90–91, 104, 107, 109, 111, 114–115, 139, 144, 154–156, 188
  legal issues and, 104, 107, 109, 111, 114–115
  non-repudiation and, 10, 13, 64, 72–74, 82, 91–92, 96, 109–112, 118, 164
  public-key cryptography and, 41, 54–57, 60
  science of, 54–56
  security services and, 71–72
Intellectual property, 11, 58, 94, 113
  copyright and, 5, 24, 94
  patents and, 48, 51, 53, 59, 72, 84, 106
International Association for Cryptologic Research (IACR), 47
International Union of Latin Law Notaries UINL), 131
Internet, 5, 13, 24, 188, 193n4, 218n63
  as cyberspace, 6
  government and, 132, 146
  legal issues and, 93–95, 107, 109, 113–114
  public-key cryptography and, 40, 49, 54
Inverse function, 43, 45–46
ISO/IEC 1388 standard series, 73–74
Italy, 131

Jasanoff, Sheila, 10, 195n23
Jefferson, Thomas, 229n63
Jermyn, Ian, 173
Jospin, Lionel, 113–115
Judges
  computerized *ordonnances* and, 153
  government and, 124–125, 134, 137, 148–157
  legal issues and, 94, 98–101, 104–105, 118–121, 124–125, 134, 137, 148–157
Junk science, 10, 119

Kahn, David, 18–19, 27, 47, 199n27
Keeper of the seals, 123, 139
Kerckhoff, Auguste, 23–25, 37
Key escrow, 48, 52, 95
Key-only attack, 78
Keys. *See also* Public-key cryptography
  algorithms and, 20 (*see also* Algorithms)
  Clipper chip and, 48
  confidentiality of, 25
  Data Encryption Standard (DES) and, 35–36, 47, 51, 161–163
  Diffie-Hellman paradigm and, 39–47, 51, 53–56, 60
  digital signatures and, 80–84 (*see also* Digital signatures)
  distribution and, 13, 17, 37
  factorization and, 45–46, 79, 167
  false information and, 27
  forgery and, 78–79
  frequency analysis and, 20–22, 28, 34
  historical perspective on cryptography and, 17, 20–37
  inverse function and, 43, 45–46
  length of, 20–21, 35–36
  one-way functions and, 44–45, 67
  quadratic residuosity and, 41, 45, 167
  random sequences and, 31
  refreshing, 22, 29
  remembering, 25
  renewal of, 25
  revocation of, 77
  space of, 20
  splitting of, 43
  substitution threats and, 75–78
  trapdoors and, 36, 44–45, 61, 67
Key space, 20–22, 28
Kid Krypto, 181
Kleptography, 59
Knapsack algorithms, 47
Known knowns, 38
Known-plaintext attact, 21–22
Known signature attacks, 78
Known unknowns, 38
Koblitz, Neal, 181, 228n55
Kocher, Paul, 159
Kohnfelder, Loren M., 76–77
Kolata, Gina, 46

Lambert, Alain, 131–132, 135
Landau, Susan, 53–54
Land titles, 7, 14, 127, 148–154
Languages of Edison's Light, The (Bazerman), 183–184
Larrieu, Jacques, 102
Latour, Bruno, 4, 63
Legal issues
  algorithms and, 111
  American Bar Association and, 10, 14, 96, 106, 108–109
  authentication and, 95–98, 101, 106, 108–111, 116
  behavior regulation and, 94–95, 113
  bona fides and, 97, 99, 187
  born-digital materials and, 96, 101
  burden of proof and, 97, 100, 103–105, 109, 115, 119–120
  Bush v. Gore and, 187
  certification and, 108–109, 112, 114, 116
  chirographs and, 97, 119, 124
  ciphers and, 116

Index

civil code and, 93, 97, 99, 103–105, 116, 120, 131, 134, 148, 154, 219n9
civilist approach and, 98, 134
common law and, 118, 131, 220n17
consensualism and, 98
contracts and, 93, 96–99, 119, 124–127, 131–138, 145, 148–152, 156–157
crypto wars and, 40–41, 47–54
cyberlaw and, 94–95, 128
decrees and, 100, 114–116, 123, 126–127, 133, 135, 138–139, 148, 154, 157
defining writing and, 102–104
digital signatures and, 63–64, 74, 92, 95–98, 105–121, 123, 127–128, 131–133, 136–140, 146–149, 153–157
digital vs. material space and, 5–6
distance acts and, 139
DNA profiling and, 10, 155
electronic authentic acts and, 116, 123, 126–127, 132–140, 147, 150, 156
electronic evidence and, 7, 10–11, 103, 106–107
Electronic Privacy Information Center and, 51–52
electronic signature bill and, 115, 131
electronic writing and, 103–106
European Union and, 10, 96, 106, 109–112
evidence law reform and, 4
evidentiary presumptions and, 96, 100–101, 105, 108–120, 123–124, 157
export regulations and, 48–49, 51, 95
fair cryptosystems and, 52–53
formalism and, 97–98, 104, 132–137
France and, 93–103, 106, 113–121
good science and, 10
Groupement pour l'Informatisation du Livre Foncier d'Alsace-Moselle and, 152–154, 157

GSM directive and, 109–110
handwritten signatures and, 83, 93, 105, 112, 118–121, 132, 139–140, 144–148, 155–157
imputability and, 104, 114
information and, 95, 107–115, 121
inscriptions and, 125–126, 148–153, 157
instrumentum/negotium and, 135
integrity and, 104, 107, 109, 111, 114–115
intellectual property and, 11, 58, 94, 113
judges and, 94, 98–101, 104–105, 118–121, 124–125, 134, 137, 148–157
junk science and, 10, 119
Lessig and, 11, 14, 94–95, 120–121
loopholes and, 98
mathematics and, 106, 116
Micali and, 52–53, 168
microfilm and, 96, 99–100, 143–144
Middle Ages and, 97
Ministry of Justice and, 7, 102, 133–134, 137–138, 146–147, 156, 219n12
Model Law on E-Commerce and, 107–108
models and, 93, 96, 106–111, 114
Napoleonic code and, 97–98, 126
National Assembly and, 101
networks and, 94–95, 110, 113–114
New Code of Civil Procedure and, 116, 118
non-repudiation and, 96, 109–112, 118
notaries and, 91, 98, 121, 123–143, 148–150, 154–157
official copies and, 1, 96–102, 106, 124, 126, 139–147, 150, 153
ordonnances and, 93, 97, 125–126, 149–154, 157

Legal issues (cont.)
  patents and, 48, 51, 53, 59, 72, 84, 106
  power of performance and, 97
  prima facie evidence and, 98–99, 102
  proof and, 93, 97–105, 109, 114–115, 118–121
  property concepts and, 6
  protocols and, 94–97
  public-key cryptography and, 36, 52, 55–56, 61, 95, 108–111, 116, 121
  records of civil status and, 140–148
  reform and, 93–96, 99–106, 114, 116, 120–121, 126, 131–132, 136, 143
  registers and, 124–127, 143, 148–155, 157
  Roman law and, 96–97, 123–124
  security and, 95, 108–112, 115–116, 120–121
  Service central d'état civil and, 127, 140–148, 156–157
  Simpson trial and, 155–156
  technological mediation and, 100
  testimony and, 93, 98–101, 124–126
  tribunals and, 23, 124, 155
  United Nations Commission on International Trade Law and, 10, 96, 106–108
  verification and, 108, 111–112, 116
  written evidence and, 4, 7, 12, 14, 93–126, 154
Legitimacy, 4, 12, 81, 100, 118–121, 187
Lessig, Lawrence, 11, 14, 94–95, 120–121
Levy, Steven, 17, 202n1
Levy-Bruhl, Henri, 102
Lorenz cipher, 32
Louis XIV, 125
Lucifer cipher, 34–35, 47, 71

Mackenzie, Donald, 87–88, 212n69
Malkin, Tal G., 168

Massey, James L., 17
Materiality, 158, 231n9
  digital information and, 6, 56, 63
  freedom from, 18
  historical perspective on cryptography and, 18, 33
  mathematics and, 169, 183
  media and, 33
  paper shuffling and, 4
  probabilistic, 222n37
  public-key cryptography and, 56
Material objects, 179–180
Mathematics, 190
  algorithms and, 15, 67–71, 79–80 (*see also* Algorithms)
  bloatware and, 116
  block ciphers and, 8, 67, 163
  Chinese remainder theorem and, 195n21
  cognition and, 170, 180–182
  complexity theory and, 13, 164, 166
  computational assumptions and, 46, 79, 82–83, 164, 178–179
  computational complexity and, 8–9, 162–164, 167, 178, 182–183
  development of public-key cryptography and, 4, 39–48, 55–56, 59, 61
  Diffie-Hellman paradigm and, 8, 13, 38–39, 47, 60, 162–163, 167, 183
  digital signatures and, 8, 10, 14, 63–64, 67–68, 73, 78, 80–90
  Enigma machines and, 27–30, 32, 69, 159
  factorization and, 45–46, 79, 167, 210n37
  government and, 9
  hash functions and, 8, 57, 59, 68, 71–72, 161, 164–167, 174–176, 183
  historical perspective on cryptography and, 17, 19, 25, 27, 29, 32–33, 37–38
  human behavior and, 178
  immateriality and, 169, 183

intuition and, 89
inverse function and, 43, 45–46
legal issues and, 106, 116
materiality and, 6, 184
models and, 161–170 (*see also* Models)
modulo arithmetic and, 20
number theory and, 45–46 (*see also* Number theory)
one-way functions and, 44–45, 67
peer-review and, 40
prime numbers and, 45–46, 70, 79–83, 164, 178–179
proof and, 4, 9, 162–169, 173–174, 178, 180, 184
provable security and, 8–9, 12–13, 15, 68, 161–168, 180
purism and, 89
quadratic residuosity and, 41, 45, 167
Random Oracle Model (ROM) and, 162–169, 183
real world and, 85–90, 162
relationship with computing, 161
Shannon and, 27, 32–34, 162
side-channel attacks and, 15, 159–161
statistics and, 8, 20–22, 34, 159, 197n7
surveillance and, 5
voting security and, 188–189
May, Timothy, 48, 60
McCarthy, John, 65
MD4, 161
MD5, 164
Media, 1, 33, 60, 93, 120
Mehrtens, Herbert, 89
Memory, 4, 15, 25
  challenge-and-response protocols and, 169
  cryptographic imagination and, 168–173, 183
  dictionary attacks and, 170–173
  government and, 124
  human capacity and, 169, 183
  input orderings and, 170–171

location access and, 168
passwords and, 169–171
picture effect and, 171
Mesopotamia, 19
Message dependency, 66–67
Metadata, 139, 156
"Method for Obtaining Digital Signatures and Public-Key Cryptosystems, A" (RSA), 67
Micali, Silvio, 52–53, 168
Microfilm, 96, 99–100, 143–144
Military, 5, 10, 13, 190, 215n28
  biometric word lists and, 176
  Enigma machines and, 27–30, 32, 69, 159
  historical perspective on, 17–19, 22, 24, 26–30, 33, 37
  Kerckhoff and, 25
  military-grade technology and, 9, 17, 92
  paperwork explosion and, 99
  public-key cryptography and, 39, 49, 55, 61
  telegraph and, 24
Mill, John Stuart, 189
Minitel, 94, 113, 146, 213n1
Mitchell, Sandra, 184
MIT cipher, 46
MIT Press, 49
Mobile phones, 91, 109
Model Law on E-Commerce, 107–108, 215n31
Models, 8–9, 13–15, 189
  Black-Scholes-Merton, 87–88
  cryptographic imagination and, 161–170, 173, 178–180, 183–185
  digital signatures and, 64, 74, 78–79, 81, 84–92
  fitness of, 85–91
  government and, 127–128, 133, 136–137, 149, 152–154, 157
  legal issues and, 93, 96, 106–111, 114
  physical security and, 168–169

Models (cont.)
  practice-oriented, 168–169
  public-key cryptography and, 61
  Random Oracle Model (ROM) and, 162–169, 183
  real world and, 85–90
  Velcro, 7
Modulo arithmetic, 20
Monoalphabetic substitution, 19–21, 28
Moran, Tal, 179–180
Morgan, Mary, 85
Morocco, 140
Morrison, Margaret, 85
Morse code, 18, 24, 27, 37
Multi-party secure computation, 228n55
Munitions Control Act, 47
Mutations, 80–84
Myth of the Paperless Office, The (Sellen and Harper), 7, 128

Naor, Moni, 176–182
Napoleonic code, 97–98, 126
National Assembly, 101
National Bureau of Standards (NBS), 35–36
National security, 5
  crypto wars and, 40–41, 47–54
  digital signatures and, 92
  Electronic Frontier Foundation (EFF) and, 51
  export regulations and, 48–49, 51, 95
  historical perspective on, 35–36, 38
  military and, 215n28 (*see also* Military)
  Munitions Control Act and, 47
  nuclear weapons and, 58
  public-key cryptography and, 47–54
  Sandia National Laboratories and, 58
National Security Agency (NSA), 35, 51, 201n51
Nearness, 175

Negotium, 135
Negroponte, Nicolas, 6, 223n49
Networks, 5–6, 11–12, 188
  cryptographic imagination and, 163, 174, 180, 182, 185
  decentralized cryptography and, 41–47
  digital signatures and, 63, 65, 74, 76–77
  e-commerce and, 13, 41, 95, 106–107, 120
  Feistel and, 34
  government and, 123, 127–128, 134, 136
  historical perspective on cryptography and, 18, 26, 30, 34–39
  legal issues and, 94–95, 110, 113–114
  public-key cryptography and, 39–43, 48, 52–55, 59–60
"New Directions in Cryptography" (Diffie and Hellman)
  cryptographic imagination and, 162
  digital signatures and, 65, 85
  public-key cryptography and, 8, 13, 38–41, 43, 47, 54, 60, 65, 85, 162, 189–190, 229n63
Newspapers, 4, 33
New York Times Magazine, 48
Nomenclators, 21–24, 37
Non-repudiation, 10, 13
  concept of, 72–74
  digital signatures and, 64, 72–74, 82, 91–92, 164
  ISO/IEC 1388 standard series and, 73–74
  legal issues and, 96, 109–112, 118
  Rivest and, 72–73
  third parties and, 72
Notaires Vie Professionelle newsletter, 139

Index

Notaries, 14
  Conseil supérieur du notariat and, 128–131, 136, 139–141
  dematerialized, 128–140
  digital signatures and, 91, 98, 121, 123–143, 148–150, 154–157
  distance acts and, 139
  electronic authentic acts and, 116, 123, 126–127, 132–140, 147, 150, 156
  Flour and, 135
  formalism and, 133–137
  government and, 123–143, 148–150, 154, 156–157
  Guigou and, 132–133
  Henri II and, 124–125
  instrumentum/negotium and, 135
  International Union of Latin Law Notaries (UINL) and, 131
  Lambert and, 131–132, 135
  legal issues and, 91, 98, 121, 123–143, 148–150, 154, 156–157
  as monopoly, 131
  public-key cryptography and, 55–56
  Réseau Electronique NotariAL (REAL) and, 128, 136
  wills and, 131
  written evidence and, 124–125
Nuclear weapons, 58
Number theory
  beauty of, 204n1
  Chinese remainder theorem and, 195n21
  cognition and, 204n1
  computational assumptions and, 46, 79, 82–83, 164, 178–179
  cryptographic imagination and, 161, 163–164, 167, 178–179, 182–184
  digital signatures and, 68
  factorization and, 45–46, 79, 167, 210n37
  inverse function and, 43, 45–46
  prime numbers and, 45–46, 70, 79–83, 164, 178–179

  public-key cryptography and, 45–46, 56
  Random Oracle Model (ROM) and, 163–164, 167, 183
  RSA encryption and, 45

Obama, Barack, 1–4, 187
Oblivious transfer, 228n55
Obscurity, 12, 25, 54, 196n29
One-time pads, 27, 30–34, 162, 176, 200n38
One-time signatures, 81
One-way functions, 44–45, 67
On-line encipherment, 31
Ordonnances
  French government and, 93, 97, 125–126, 148–154, 157
  Henri III and, 93
  judge's signature and, 150–154
  Louis XIV and, 125
  Napoleonic code and, 97
  paper documents and, 125–126, 148–154, 157
  registers and, 125–126, 149

Paper. *See also* Documents
  codebooks and, 19, 21–22, 24, 28–29, 32
  digital-immaterial narrative and, 5–6
  feuillets and, 149–153
  historical perspective on cryptography and, 19–24
  information hiding and, 18, 23–24, 41
  liberation from, 6
  monoalphabetic substitution and, 19–21, 28
  ordonnances and, 148–154
  perception and, 173–174
  polyalphabetic substitution and, 19–21, 34
  red tape and, 4
  Vernam one-time pad and, 27, 30–34, 162, 176

Paperless office, 7, 128
Passwords, 226n34
  challenge-and-response protocols and, 169
  cryptographic imagination and, 169–173
  dictionary attacks and, 170–173
  digital signatures and, 69–70, 91
  Draw-A-Secret (DAS) scheme and, 172–173
  government and, 153
  graphical, 171–173
  input orderings and, 170–171
  memory and, 169–171
  plausibility arguments and, 173
  public-key cryptography and, 44
  weak, 173
Patents, 48, 51, 53, 59, 72, 84, 106
PDF files, 137
Pearl Harbor, 33
Peer-review, 40, 59
Perception, 15, 183, 227n45
  cryptographic imagination and, 169, 173–178
  hash functions and, 174–176
  indistinguishability and, 175
  legal issues and, 120
  pixels and, 176–178
  visual cryptography and, 171–173, 176–180
Perl programming language, 49
Pfitzmann, Birgit, 166
PGP (Pretty Good Privacy), 49, 176
Photocopiers, 94, 96, 99, 101, 143–144, 178
Photography, 4, 101
Physical security, 55, 70, 168–169, 184
Picture effect, 171
Pinkas, Benny, 178
PINs, 69–70
Plausible deniability, 179
Pointcheval, David, 166
Polyalphabetic substitution, 19–21, 34

"Practice-Oriented Provable Security" (Bellare and Rogaway), 164
Presumptions
  of authenticity, 123–124, 157
  legal issues and, 96, 100–101, 105, 108–120, 123–124, 157
  of trustiworthiness, 114–120, 149, 153
Prima facie evidence, 98–99, 102
Prime numbers, 70
  computational assumptions and, 46, 79, 82–83, 164, 178–179
  factorization and, 45–46, 79, 167, 210n37
  weak, 79–80
Privacy, 183
  anonymity and, 5, 24, 41, 53–54, 59–60, 81, 83–84, 95, 163, 184, 189
  cryptographic literacy and, 180–181
  crypto wars and, 40–41, 47–54, 60
  digital signatures and, 81, 83–84
  historical perspective on, 17, 24, 32–37
  passwords and, 44, 69–70, 91, 153, 169–173
  public-key cryptography and, 41, 43, 48–56, 59–60
  surveillance and, 5, 60, 221n33
  unplugged cryptography and, 181–182
  wiretapping and, 40, 48, 53
Privacy on the Line (Diffie and Landau), 53
Proof
  authority of, 9
  burden of, 97, 100, 103–105, 109, 115, 119–120
  digital signatures and, 14, 64, 67–68, 72, 79–81, 90, 92
  electronic writing and, 103–106
  government and, 124–125, 128, 132, 152, 155
  historical perspective on cryptography and, 17, 31–32

Index

legal issues and, 93, 97–105, 109, 114–115, 118–121
mathematics and, 4, 9, 162–169, 173–174, 178, 180, 184
probabilistic, 230n72
public-key cryptography and, 45, 55–56, 225n26
voting and, 188
Protocols, 5, 188–190
  challenge-and-response, 169
  cryptographic imagination and, 161, 163–169, 178–185
  cryptographic literacy and, 180–181
  digital signatures and, 63–64, 68–69, 81, 84–85
  government and, 157
  human-centric, 180
  legal issues and, 94–97
  material objects and, 179–180
  multi-party secure computation and, 228n55
  oblivious transfer and, 228n55
  public-key cryptography and, 53–61
  simplicity and, 182
  unplugged cryptography and, 181–182
  zero-knowledge, 181
Proxy signatures, 81
Psychology, 9, 33, 89, 170, 173
Public-key cryptography, 5, 10
  Adleman and, 41, 45, 47, 75–76, 80
  adversaries and, 17, 57
  algorithms and, 39, 44, 46–51, 58–59, 161
  authentication and, 39, 41, 51, 54–60
  birth of, 17
  bloatware and, 116
  cash and, 39, 53, 57, 59
  certification and, 55–56
  ciphers and, 43, 46, 51, 57
  Clipper chip and, 48
  computational assumptions and, 46, 79, 82–83, 164, 178–179

contracts and, 39, 55
contradictory evidence and, 65–66, 98
cryptographic imagination and, 161, 174–176
crypto wars and, 40–41, 47–54, 60
decentralization and, 41–47
Diffie-Hellman paradigm and, 8, 13, 38–47, 51, 53–56, 60
digital anarchy and, 48–49, 52, 60
government and, 40–41, 47–54, 60, 127, 132, 136, 138, 153, 156
immateriality and, 56
information and, 39–44, 49–60
integrity and, 41, 54–57, 60
inverse function and, 43, 45–46
legal issues and, 36, 52, 55–56, 61, 95, 108–111, 116, 121
mathematics and, 4, 39–48, 55–56, 59, 61
methodology of, 43–47
military and, 39, 49, 55, 61
models and, 61
Munitions Control Act and, 47
national security and, 47–54
networks and, 39–43, 48, 52–55, 59–60
notaries and, 55–56
number theory and, 45–46, 56, 70, 79–83, 163–164, 178–179, 182, 184
one-way functions and, 44–45, 67
passwords and, 44
patents and, 48, 51, 53, 59, 72, 84, 106
prime numbers and, 45–46, 70, 79–83, 164, 178–179
proof and, 45, 55–56, 225n26
protocols and, 53–61
quadratic residuosity and, 41, 45, 167
Random Oracle Model (ROM) and, 162–169, 183
Rivest and, 41, 45, 51–52, 57
RSA encryption and, 45–51, 58, 67–68, 72, 75, 79–80, 161, 163–164, 167

Public-key cryptography (cont.)
  security and, 39–44, 47–61
  Shamir and, 41, 45, 47
  splitting keys and, 43
  subliminal channels and, 57–59
  trapdoors and, 36, 44–45, 61, 67
Public-key infrastructures (PKI), 5, 64, 78, 108, 131, 155

Quadratic residuosity, 41, 45, 167
Quisquater, Jean-Jacques, 181

Radio, 12, 18, 26–27, 33, 37, 46, 126
Randomness, 229n69
  cryptographic imagination and, 162–169, 176–180, 183
  digital signatures and, 65, 78, 80
  Enigma machines and, 28–29
  hash function and, 165
  historical perspective on cryptography and, 28–33, 37
  perfect secrecy and, 30–33
  randomized response technique and, 179–180
  random noise and, 176
  tamper-evident seals and, 179
  visual cryptography and, 176–178
Random Oracle Model (ROM)
  Bellare-Rogaway program and, 163–168, 225n18
  cryptographic imagination and, 162–169, 183
  Diffie-Hellman paradigm and, 162–163, 167, 183
  epistemological validity and, 166–167
  heuristic arguments and, 165–166
  number theory and, 163–164, 167, 183
  RSA and, 7, 163–164
Reagan, Ronald, 58
Real estate
  contracts and, 4, 7, 14, 127, 131, 134, 149–150, 152

deeds and, 4
government and, 14, 127, 131, 134, 136, 148–153
notaries and, 131 (*see also* Notaries)
Red tape, 4, 114
Redundancy, 34–35, 58
Referendaries, 123
Reform
  government and, 126, 131–132, 136, 143
  legal issues and, 93–96, 99–106, 114, 116, 120–121, 126, 131–132, 136, 143
Registers
  Alsace-Moselle, 148–154
  computerized, 152–154
  evidential value of, 125
  feuillets and, 149–153
  Groupement pour l'Informatisation du Livre Foncier d'Alsace-Moselle and, 152–154, 157
  legal issues and, 124–127, 143, 148–155, 157
  ordonnances and, 149–154
Research agendas, 5, 40–41
  anonymity and, 59–60
  authentication and, 59–60
  information integrity and, 54–56
  mathematical foundations and, 56–57
  public-key cryptography and, 54–60
  subliminal channels and, 57–59
Réseau Electronique NotariAL (REAL), 128, 136
Retention, 14, 137, 154
Retinal patterns, 69, 91
Reyzin, Leonid, 168
RFID tags, 168
RIPEMD-160, 165
Rivest, Ronald
  digital signatures and, 72–76, 80, 83
  information revolution and, 205n26
  non-repudiation and, 72–73
  public-key cryptography and, 41, 45, 51–52, 57

Index

Roe, Michael, 209n27
Rogaway, Philip, 163–168, 225n18
Roman Empire, 19, 96–97, 123–124
Rosenheim, Shawn, 198n15
Rotman, Brian, 195n19
RSA encryption
 digital signatures and, 67–68, 72, 79–80
 public-key cryptography and, 45–51, 58, 67–68, 72, 75, 79–80, 161, 163–164, 167
 Random Oracle Model (ROM) and, 7, 163–164
Rumsfeld, Donald, 37–38
Russia, 51, 58, 131

SAGA, 145
Sagan, Carl, 46
Sandia National laboratories, 58
S-boxes, 35–36
Scherbius, Arthur, 27
Science du Secret, La (Stern), 17–18
Science journal, 46
Scientific American journal, 34, 46–48, 205n26
Scott, James C., 123
Scrambling, 23
Scribes, 123–124
Secret function evaluation, 182
Secret writing, 23
Secure Socket Layer (SSL), 193n4
Security
 centralized systems and, 42–43
 different meanings of, 185
 literature on, 10
 Munitions Control Act and, 47
 national, 5, 35–36, 38, 47–52, 54, 92
 natural concerns and, 57, 60, 189
 by obscurity, 12, 25, 54, 196n29
 physical, 55, 70, 168–169, 184
 provable, 8–9, 12–13, 15, 68, 161–168, 180
Seeing Like a State (Scott), 123

Sellen, Abigail J., 7, 128
Service central d'état civil (SCEC)
 authentication and, 140–148
 digital signatures and, 127, 140–148, 156–157
 Instruction générale à l'état civil (IGREC) and, 144–148
 purpose of, 140–141
 records of civil service and, 140–148
 SAGA and, 145
SHA-1, 164–165
Shamir, Adi
 digital signatures and, 75–76, 80, 83
 public-key cryptography and, 41, 45, 47
 visual cryptography and, 176
Shannon, Claude, E., 27, 32–34, 162, 201n43
Side-channel attacks, 15, 159–161
Silent alarms, 27
Simmons, Gustavus, 55–59, 63, 85, 190, 207n51
Simpson, O. J., 155–156
Singh, Simon, 17, 202n1
Six Books of Polygraphy (Trithemius), 28
Standaert, François-Xavier, 168
Statistics, 8, 20–22, 34, 159, 197n7
Steganography, 23, 32–33, 37, 41, 51, 57, 61
Stern, Jacques, 17–18, 166
Stinson, Doug, 57, 164
Strong assumption, 22
Subliminal channels, 57–59
Substitution threats, 75–78
Surveillance, 5, 60, 221n33
Sutter, Laurent De, 120–121

Tabulae ceratae, 97
Tabulae signatae, 97
Tampering, 36, 58, 76, 99, 168, 179
Tape-feeding mechanisms, 31
Tauman, Yael, 83–84
Telegraphs, 12, 18, 24–27, 30, 126

Telephones, 99, 126, 176
Teleprinters, 30–32
Telex, 99, 126
Testimony, 93, 98–101, 124–126
Thorpe, Julie, 173
Threshold-type signatures, 81
TIFF files, 152
Traffic analysis, 18, 26, 29, 37, 53, 59
Trapdoors, 36, 44–45, 61, 67, 203n9
Tribunals, 23, 124, 155
Trithemius, 28
Truth in Lending Act, 109
Turing, Alan, 27, 161, 200n34

U-boats, 29, 30
Unbreakable codes, 17, 25, 32
Undeniable signatures, 82, 82–83, 211n49
United Nations Commission on International Trade Law (UNCITRAL), 10, 96, 106–108, 131
University of California, Santa Barbara, 47
Unplugged cryptography, 181–182
U.S. National Archives and Records Administration (NARA), 154–155
U.S. Supreme Court, 187

Van Oorschot, Paul C., 173
Velcro model, 7
Venetian state, 19
Venture capital, 5
VeriSign, 108, 114, 174
Vernam, Gilbert, 30–32, 34
Vernam one-time pad, 27, 30–34, 162, 176, 200n38
Vigenère cipher, 20, 24–25
Visual cryptography, 171–173, 176–180
Voting, 4–9, 15, 185, 232n10
 CalTech/MIT Voting Technology Project and, 188
 cryptographic imagination and, 178–181

 direct-recording electronic (DRE) machines and, 188
 end-to-end, 188–189
 mathematics and, 188–189
 public-key cryptography and, 56–57, 59
 U.S. election of 2000 and, 187–188
 verification of, 4–9, 15, 56–57, 59, 178–181, 185, 187–190

Warner, Stanley L., 179
Watson, James D., 86
Wills, 131
Winkler, Peter, 181–182
Wired magazine, 48
Wiretapping, 40, 48, 53
Word files, 137
World War I, 26
World War II, 27–32, 69, 159

XML documents, 153

Young, Adam, 58–59
Yung, Moti, 58–59, 168

Zimmerman, Phil, 49, 176
Žižek, Slavoj, 38